The Danish Cinema
Before Dreyer

by
RON MOTTRAM

The Scarecrow Press, Inc.
Metuchen, N.J., & London
1988

Library of Congress Cataloging-in-Publication Data

Mottram, Ron
    The Danish cinema before Dreyer / by Ron Mottram.
        p. cm.
    Bibliography: p.
    Includes index. T
    ISBN 0-8108-2035-8
    1. Moving-pictures--Denmark--History. I. Title.
PN1993.5.D4M68   1988   87-16125
791.43'09489--dc19

100 1363735

CONTENTS

ACKNOWLEDGMENTS

The research for this study would not have been possible without the cooperation of the Danish Film Museum and the Museum of Modern Art. I would particularly like to thank Ib Monty, Karen Jones, Per Calum, Louisa Roos, Janus Barfoed, and Eileen Bowser for their generous assistance. Special thanks should also go to Marguerite Engberg, whose willingness to share with me the results of her own research in early Danish cinema has been invaluable. Support for this project from the American-Scandinavian Foundation and the George C. Marshall Memorial Fund in Denmark is also much appreciated. Finally, I would like to express the deepest appreciation for the support and patience of my wife during the research and writing of this study.

INTRODUCTION

The history of the Danish cinema properly begins long before the invention of the motion picture camera or the making of the first Danish film. As in other countries, literature, the theater, and still photography played significant roles in shaping the new medium. More important, however, was the role played by foreign trade. From its earliest history Denmark's cultural development, as well as its actual survival as a nation, has been intimately associated with its policies of trade and colonial expansion.[1] Although geographically a small nation today, Denmark, at the beginning of the nineteenth century, consisted not only of its present territory, but also of Norway, Iceland, Greenland, Schleswig-Holstein, West Pomerania, and the Faroe Islands. Farther back in its history, during the Viking Age, Danish hegemony extended as far as Byzantium. Along with this political control went economic power, based on an extensive trade network and the give and take of intercultural influences.[2]

By the end of the nineteenth century Danish territorial ambitions, along with the territories themselves, with the exception of Greenland, were a matter of history. Danish dependence on foreign trade, however, was as strong as ever. Denmark's economy depended on its ability both to sell goods abroad and to import raw materials. To facilitate trade and to encourage other nations to trade in and with Denmark, the Frihavnen (Free Port) was established in Copenhagen in 1894, allowing certain trade to take place without the paying of import duties. Among the businesses to benefit from the Free Port was Denmark's leading film producer, Nordisk Films Kompagni, which located its technical plant there in 1906. Since all raw film had to be imported because none was manufactured in Denmark, Nordisk was able to avoid the 10 percent duty on both negative and copy film. This exemption from the tariff was important to Nordisk Films Kompagni's

1

film export business, which became the foundation on which
the growth and influence of the Danish motion picture industry were founded.[3]

"In the days of the silent films when speech raised no
barriers to the distribution of a film," writes Ebbe Neergaard,
"the Danish film industry was not only one of the world's big
suppliers of the new form of entertainment, but it also had,
at essential stages, a decisive influence on the development
of the film art."[4] Illustrative of the influence of this "valuable item of export"[5] is the story of its effect on a young
Hungarian theater actor named Mihaley Kertész, later known
in cinema as Michael Curtiz. In the summer of 1913 Kertész
arrived in Copenhagen where he hoped to get work at Nordisk Films Kompagni whose productions he had seen and admired in Budapest. He succeeded and, according to István
Nemeskürty, during six months at Nordisk worked as an
actor, a cutter, and a director, experiences which helped
make Kertész, on his return home, "the most popular director"
in Hungary.[6]

Kertész was not the only Hungarian to be impressed by
Danish films in that period and to make the journey to Copenhagen as a result. Mór Ungerleider, owner of the Apollo
Theater in Budapest, saw Asta Nielsen's first film, Afgrunden,
during the spring of 1911. Keeping in mind his role as an
exhibitor, he is reported to have written "a scathing review,
lest somebody else should conceive the idea of purchasing this
treasure...." A short time later, he was in Copenhagen ne-
gotiating for the rights "on all Nordisk films for years to
come."[7]

A number of prominent film historians have testified to
the wide-ranging influence of early Danish cinema. In their
book The German Cinema, Roger Manvell and Heinrich Frankel
claim that Scandinavian films, by which they mean primarily
Danish films, were more popular and important in Germany
than French, British, Italian, or American films.[8] When UFA
was formed in 1917 Nordisk had considerable German holdings
which were incorporated into the new company.[9] Pierre
Leprohon cites a vogue for Danish films in Italy that helped
foster an interest in bourgeois dramas with modern subjects,
a type of film that developed alongside the costume film.[10]
Bardeche and Brassillach mention the high esteem in which
Danish films were held in the prewar period.

Nordisk flooded the French market with pictures
which were admired for their dramatic intensity and
their artistic qualities.
  Germany was Nordisk's best market, and several
films were made by the firm specifically for German
distributors. The German firms--Messter, Union,
Biograph, Bioscop--were of quite secondary importance in comparison with Nordisk, for at that time
Germany was, as regards the cinema, simply a trib-
utary of Copenhagen.[11]

  In Kino Jay Leyda mentions the influence in Russia of
specific Danish films, notably Afgrunden (The Abyss) and
De fire Djaevle (The Four Devils), claiming also that "Afgrunden was universally admired, influencing films of every country" and that Danish dramas were "the only models that it was
profitable for the unsure Russian producers to follow."[12] In
the United States Moving Picture World and Motion Picture
News frequently commented on the quality of the Nordisk
films, comparing them favorably to the best American films,
while Robert Grau in The Theater of Science cited Nordisk
Films' "enviable high standard of quality," giving Nordisk
the credit for introducing the multiple-reel feature into America.[13]

  Historically, Danish trade has depended on the sea.
Viggo Starcke has described how the Danish exploitation of
the sea both united the country and established communication with the rest of the world. "In this element," writes
Starcke, "lies most of Denmark's external history...." When
the sea routes were open, the culture of the country flour-
ished; when these were closed "the level of culture dropped."[14]
As we shall see later in this study, Denmark's film culture
also dropped when the sea routes were severely restricted
during World War I, cutting Denmark off from its foreign
markets and its most important sources of income.

  The outward-looking quality of Danish culture and the
influence it exerted in the world has had many manifestations.
Even during certain periods of political isolation, as after its
disastrous war with Germany in 1864, Denmark remained culturally oriented toward the rest of Europe. In that period
the aristocracy, though it retreated into "an extreme conservatism" and an attachment to tradition, continued to look abroad
for its cultural values. Culturally, they were "Europeans

first and Danes after," maintaining these shared values by
means of extensive communication with other European nations
and making fluency in other languages, especially German,
French, and English, a necessary part of aristocratic education. Letter writing, foreign travel, entertaining of foreign
visitors, and reading widely in foreign literature helped establish a network of connections with the Danish aristocrats'
counterparts in other European nations.[15]

   The international character of the Danish aristocracy
was nowhere better illustrated than in Danish court life.
Around the turn of the century the royal residence at Fred-
ensborg Palace became the meeting ground for much of Europe's
royalty. The monarchs of England, Russia, and Greece were
related to the Danish king Christian IX, and the various
royal families took turns being Christian's guests.[16] These
impressive gatherings of European royalty also became the
subjects for some of Denmark's earliest films when they were
recorded by Peter Elfelt, the court photographer and Denmark's first filmmaker.

   More significant to European culture than these aristocratic connections, however, have been the artistic, scientific,
philosophic, and industrial contributions that Denmark has
made. These stand as monuments to a more modern tradition
that emerged at the same time that conservatism and tradi-
tionalism marked most of Danish culture.

   Of special importance is the role played by literature
in leading Denmark into the mainstream of late nineteenth-
century thought. Spearheaded by a young, French-trained
critic named Georg Brandes, a new generation of writers
emerged that stressed materialism and the social function of
literature. Prior to their work the great Danish writer had
been Hans Christian Andersen, whose fairy tales had been
widely read and translated, and, in the early days of cinema,
also provided source material for numerous films. With the
movement away from romanticism toward realism, known as
the "Modern Breakthrough," new names of international significance emerged, the most important of which was J. P.
Jacobsen, whose psychologically based novels dealing with
modern problems made him a distinctive and influential Danish
writer.[17] His novel Niels Lyhne, a naturalistic study of a
man who searches for meaning to his life but fails to find it,

helped Jacobsen "hold an international audience for dec-
ades...."[18] The novel was also used by Frederick Delius as
the basis for his opera Fennimore and Gerda. Previous to
this period in his career Jacobsen had been a lyric poet whose
work included a cycle of poems which later were used as a
text for Schönberg's Gurrelieder.[19]

Many other notable Danish writers emerged in the same
period, among them two other social novelists, Henrik Pontoppidan and Johannes V. Jensen, both of whom won the Nobel
Prize for literature.[20] The popularity of Pontoppidan's most
famous novel, Lykke-Per, is attested to by its numerous
translations, eventually appearing in German, Swedish, Russian, Dutch, Hungarian, Polish, and French.[21] Even more
widely read was a 1910 novel by Karen Michaëlis called The
Dangerous Age, a psychological work inspired by Sigmund
Freud, which won readers in twenty languages.[22]

Of all writers in Danish, however, none has received
more attention or been more significant than Henrik Ibsen.
Although a Norwegian by birth, Ibsen's plays were originally
published by Gyldendal in Copenhagen during a period in
which the Danish and Norwegian languages were essentially
the same and in which publication in Denmark meant success
for the Norwegian writer. Copenhagen's Royal Theater also
presented the premiere productions of all Ibsen's plays.[23]
Although Ibsen often outraged conventional Danish society,
he was also hailed by a new generation engendered by the
literary upheaval of the 1870s and 1880s. The times tended
to see Ibsen as "an arbiter of social problems," writes P. M.
Mitchell,[24] on the one hand influencing the Danish literary
Left, and on the other helping to prepare more general audiences for the treatment of social problems both on stage and
in the cinema. The freedom of subject matter found in the
social dramas of the great period in Danish cinema owes something to the theatrical changes initiated by Ibsen and other
Norwegian dramatists, including Björnstjerne Björnson, whose
play Newly Married Couple was produced by the Danish Royal
Theater in 1865. Among the leaders of a realistic Danish
theater movement were Einar Christiansen, Otto Benzon, and
Edward Brandes, brother of the radical literary critic Georg
Brandes.[25]

The catalog of important Danes continues beyond the

bounds of art and includes the work of Valdemar Poulsen in
early radio communication, Niels Bohr in physics (Nobel prize
1922), Wilhelm Johannsen in plant physiology, August Krogh
in biology (Nobel prize 1920), Niels Finsen (Nobel prize 1903)
and Johannes Fibiger (Nobel prize 1927) in medicine, Vilhelm
Thomsen and Otto Jespersen in linguistics, and Søren Kirkegaard in theology. This list, of course, is only partial, but
it indicates the energetic intellectual and artistic life and the
wide-ranging influence that Denmark has had.

No less influential was the Danish cinema which reached
its zenith of artistic accomplishment and industrial significance
in the period prior to the end of World War I. The years
1910-14 were especially significant and have been called the
Danish cinema's "golden age." Marguerite Engberg, the leading authority on the early Danish cinema, ends her two-volume
history of the Danish silent film, Dansk Stumfilm, with the
year 1914. Before her, Ebbe Neergaard, author of The Story
of Danish Film, cited 1911-16 as "the great period of Nordisk
film."[26] That Neergaard shifted the period slightly does not
alter the main point, though it suggests the necessity of a
more expansive treatment of the subject. Accordingly, the
early history of the Danish film can be divided into three
periods: 1896 to 1909, years dominated at first by the film
of fact but which progressively saw the development of the
fiction film; 1910 to 1914, the golden age in which the most
important and characteristic film forms developed; and 1915 to
1917, a time of decline both artistically and economically.
Within the parameters of these three periods, this present
study gives a description and analysis of the early Danish
cinema and examines the distribution, exhibition, and critical
reception of Danish films in the United States.

The most important sources used in this book are the
films themselves, although reviews, plot synopses, memoirs,
trade notices, business documents, and other original materials have also proved invaluable. Of the secondary sources
consulted, Marguerite Engberg and Ebbe Neergaard deserve
special mention. Neergaard's The Story of Danish Film is
the only book on Danish film in English and, despite its limitations, is often referred to in the following pages. Especially important has been Engberg's Registrant over danske
film, 1896-1914, a collection of factual information compiled
largely from the records of the early Danish film companies.

Engberg's painstaking work brings together in three volumes
much valuable and previously scattered material.

   This work is also meant to be a documentation of the
early Danish cinema and, as such, includes extensive plot
descriptions, the titles of many films that have not survived
and for which there is little available information, biographical material on certain important filmmakers, and technical
and credit data. Also, in order to give the fullest attention
to the surviving films, I have included some information and
discussion on every surviving fiction film no matter how minor
it may be. Commentary on the minor films is in the body of
the text, while plot descriptions are in Appendix A. Plot
descriptions of more important films are integrated with the
commentary on those films. Since much of the technical and
credit information comes from Registrant over danske film,
1896-1914, readers interested in more complete technical information than is provided here should consult that book.

   The principal goal of this book is the critical restoration
of the early Danish cinema, including an affirmation of the
prominent position it occupied in the world market during
the years immediately preceding World War I. By describing
this period in Danish film history, especially through a documentation and analysis of the surviving films and the individuals who made them, I hope to add to the general body of
knowledge concerning the early cinema and its international
character. The usefulness of this work, then, is partly based
on its relation to studies of other early national cinemas. As
such, it is offered as foundational work which can help inform
the work of other researchers. The critical judgments made
as to the importance of certain films and filmmakers are to be
taken as tentative, open to revision and reconsideration, and
suggestive of subjects for further study.

   Although I have tried to make generalizations about my
subject, the early Danish cinema was diverse in its artistic
accomplishments. Even within Nordisk Films Kompagni, where
a certain stylistic coherence pervaded production, there arose
distinct directoral personalities. When Nordisk is compared to
other companies, to Det Skandinavisk-russike Handelshus for
example, the artistic differences are sometimes very great.
Often these differences and the idiosyncratic nature of certain
films can only be described, since not enough information is
available to explain them or to place them in context. Since

it is always possible, however, that additional information
may come to light or that other researchers may have different use for this material, I have included much information
that is only fragmentary and which may have greater future,
rather than present, use.

One final comment should be made in this brief introduction, and it pertains to the repeated reference to Nordisk
Films Kompagni, founded by Ole Olsen. This history of Danish cinema is largely the history of this one production company because it dominated Danish production in the period
under consideration. That is not to say that other Danish
producers were unimportant, only that their work, and their
actual existence, must be understood in relation to the films
and business practices of Nordisk. In the area of foreign
distribution the history of Danish film in America is almost
solely that of Nordisk Films Kompagni as it operated through
its branch the Great Northern Film Company. It was the
only Danish film company that distributed films here in any
significant number and, with few exceptions, all the films they
distributed were their own.

NOTES

1. Viggo Starcke, Denmark in World History, trans.
Commander Frank Noel Stagg and Dr. Ingeborg Nixon (Philadelphia: University of Pennsylvania Press, 1962), p. 17.
2. W. Glynn Jones, Denmark (New York and Washington: Praeger Publishers, 1970), pp. 17-19, 44-45.
3. Marguerite Engberg, Dansk Stumfilm, 2 vols. (Copenhagen: Rhodos Internationalt Forlag for Videnskab, Kunst
og Debat, 1977), pp. 64-65.
4. Ebbe Neergaard, The Story of the Danish Film,
trans. Elsa Gress (Copenhagen: Det Danske Selskab, 1963),
p. 7.
5. Steward Oakley, A Short History of Denmark (New
York and Washington: Praeger Publishers, 1972), p. 218.
6. István Nemeskürty, Word and Image, trans. Zšuz-
šanna Horn (Budapest: Corvina Press, 1968), p. 25. Some
of the claims made about Kertész in this book appear to be
exaggerated. For example, Nemeskürty says that Kertész
played a leading role in August Blom's 1913 feature Atlantis,
whereas he played only a minor role. Both Nordisk Film Company records (he is not listed among the credits) and a viewing

of the film itself (all the major actors can be identified by sight) refute Nemeskürty's claim. That he did appear in the film is known by a reference in the Danish periodical Folkets avis of August 2, 1913, where Kertész was talked about as an actor from the Royal Theater in Budapest (cited by Marguerite Engberg in Dansk Stumfilm, p. 485). Also questionable is the claim that Kertész was an assistant director on Atlantis since, according to Marguerite Engberg, no documentation has been found to support this claim, even though other authorities, including Bjorn Rasmussen in "Verdens bedsti film" (Politikens forlag, 1970) have also given Kertész this credit.

7. Nemeskürty, p. 14. The author incorrectly identifies Afgrunden as a Nordisk film; it was produced by Kosmorama. Whether Ungerleider purchased the rights to Afgrunden from Kosmorama or whether Nordisk had acquired some of the foreign rights to the film is not clear. Hjalmar Davidsen, the producer of Afgrunden, did sell the general rights to another Danish company, Skandinavisk-russike Handelshus, while retaining the rights to exhibit the film himself in Copenhagen. See Engberg, Dansk Stumfilm, p. 260.

8. Roger Manvell and Heinrich Frankel, The German Cinema (New York: Praeger Publishers, 1971), p. 6.

9. Neergaard, p. 48.

10. Pierre Leprohon, The Italian Cinema, trans. Robert Greaves and Oliver Stallybrass (New York: Praeger Publishers, 1972), p. 34.

11. Maurice Bardeche and Robert Brasillach, The History of Motion Pictures, English ed. (New York: W. W. Norton and Co., 1938), pp. 56-57.

12. Jay Leyda, Kino: A History of the Russian and Soviet Film (London: George Allen and Unwin Ltd., 1960), pp. 47-48, 52, 59.

13. Robert Grau, The Theater of Science (New York: Broadway Publishing Co., 1914), pp. 76-77.

14. Starcke, p. 17.

15. Robert T. Anderson, Denmark: Success of a Developing Nation (Cambridge, Mass.: Schenkman Publishing Co., 1975), pp. 21-29.

16. Palle Lauring, A History of the Kingdom of Denmark, trans. David Hohnen, 2d ed. (Copenhagen: Host and Son, 1963), pp. 234-35.

17. Jones, pp. 102-3.

18. P. M. Mitchell, A History of Danish Literature (New York: The American Scandinavian Foundation, 1958), p. 184.

19.   Jones, p. 102.

20.   John Danstrup, A History of Denmark, 2d ed.
(Copenhagen: Wivels Forlag, 1949), pp. 139-50.

21.   Mitchell, p. 195.

22.   Mitchell, p. 230.

23.   Eric Johns, "The Theatre in Copenhagen,"
Theatre World (October 1934):   157.

24.   Mitchell, pp. 175-76.

25.   William Archer, "The Royal Danish Theater, "
Harper's New Monthly Magazine (February 1892).

26.   Neergaard, pp. 23-38.

CHAPTER ONE:

1896-1909

As Ebbe Neergaard has pointed out, Denmark "belongs
to the relatively few countries that do not claim to have in-
vented the film."[1] Nevertheless, film production in Denmark
began shortly after it did in France, England, and the United
States, and it was begun by a Dane rather than by representatives of the Lumière interests as was the case in other European countries.[2] In December 1896 Peter Elfelt, the court
photographer, made the first Danish film, Kørsel med grønlandske Hunde (Driving with Greenland Dogs), a 10-m. fake
reportage film made in a Copenhagen park.[3] During the next
fifteen years Elfelt made over 200 films, including his only
dramatic narrative, Henrettelsen (The Execution) (1903).[4]
These short actualities, newsreels, and reportage films are
similar to those produced by Edison, Billy Bitzer, Albert
Smith, the Lumières, and others. Elfelt showed the same
wide-ranging concern with recording the variety of contemporary life as he turned his cameras not only on royalty,
but on the people and events prominent in the business and
cultural life of the country. The catalog of Elfelt films compiled by Denmark Radio gives a good indication of the extent
of Elfelt's interests. The catalog headings include geography,
travel, philosophy, psychology, science, business, religion,
pedagogy, folk life, nature, mathematics, art, theater, music,
literature, and history.[5] Among the personalities he photographed were actors and actresses (Ellen Aggerholm, Augusta
Blad, Peter Fjeldstrup, Dagmar Hansen, Jacob Jacobsen, Sophus Neuman, Asta Nielsen, Clara Pontoppidan, Johs. Poulsen,
Charlotte Wiehe); dancers (Hans Beck, Valborg Borchsenius,
Richard Jensen, Ellen Price de Plane, Wania Tartakoff, Uhlen-
dorf); royalty (Queen Alexandra of England, Princess Alex-
andrine of Denmark, Prince Carl of Sweden, King Christian
IX of Denmark, Prince Christian of Denmark, Empress Dagmar

11

of Russia, King Gustav V of Sweden, King Håkon of Norway,
Czar Nicholas II of Russia, King Oscar II of Sweden, Kaiser
Wilhelm of Germany); politicians (P.A.A. Alberti, Frederik
Borgbjerg, I. C. Christensen, J. H. Deuntzer, Viggo Hørup,
Theodore Stauning, Wiiblad, C. Th. Zahle); journalists (Ber-
til Bing, Hjorth Clausen, Herbert Drucker, Jens Locker,
A. C. Meyer, Poul Sarauw); businessmen (H. N. Andersen,
Benny Dessau, Høffner, Francis James Zachariæ); composers
(J.P.E. Hartmann, Charles Kjerulff); and sportsmen (Elle-
gaard, Orla Nord).[6] To this variety of material Elfelt brought
an attention to composition that he developed as a still photographer and a feeling for movement, both within the frame
and of the camera itself, that make these films exemplary of
the best in early cinematography.[7]

Most important to this study, however, is Peter Elfelt's
one dramatic narrative, Henrettelsen (1903), only a fragment
of which has survived.[8] The film was based on the true incident of a mother who murdered her two children, a crime
for which she was executed. The script was written by
Christian Lundsgaard and Scheel Vandel, the cast included
Francesca Nathansen and Victor Betzonich, and the photography and direction were by Elfelt. Its exact release date
is unknown.[9]

The fragment begins as a bearded man in uniform enters from a door in the background of the frame. The setting
is real, the arcades of the Palace of Christiansborg in Copenhagen. The man is seen in full length and walks into medium
shot as he motions off-screen left. He then walks back to
the door. Turned away from the camera, he waves to people
out of sight behind the doorway. A minister and a woman
enter and, accompanied by the bearded man, walk into medium
shot. All exit screen left while the camera remains on the
vacated space. The bearded man reenters screen left, crosses
the frame, and exits screen right. The space again remains
vacated until a man in an overcoat and a bowler hat enters
screen right and crosses the frame. Before the man exits
frame there is a cut to a new scene showing a long vaulted
corridor occupying the right half of the frame and receding
on a slight diagonal toward the right frame line. A man in
a top hat stands at the left in the foreground, creating a
carefully balanced composition in relationship to the vaulted
corridor. The woman, minister, and bearded man (apparently
a guard) from the first scene are walking along the corridor

toward the camera.   The man standing at the left removes
his top hat as they reach him.   He helps the minister with
the woman, who is now hesitant in her movements, and, along
with the bearded man and the woman, exits screen left.   The
minister, now alone in the space, bows his head, wipes away
a tear, then looks off to the left after those who have just
exited.

Although incomplete in the form in which it has come
down to us, Henrettelsen shows a sophisticated use of space
that makes it worthy of note.   Of particular interest is the
way off-screen space is brought into play.   Three times
characters indicate the existence of space beyond the frame.
In the first of the two scenes, the uniformed man gestures
twice to people whom the viewer cannot see.   The first time
he gestures off-screen left to characters, whom in the present
version of the film, we never see.   After that he gestures to
the woman and the minister who are behind a portion of the
set and who soon enter camera range.   In the second scene
the minister, after being left alone in the frame, glances to
the left, the direction in which the guard and the woman
have exited.   In addition to these gestures and glances, the
film contains a number of exits and entrances of the characters, that, combined with the camera's immobility in relation
to the given space, also create a strong sense of a world
existing beyond the frame.

This promising beginning for the fiction film in Denmark
proved abortive, since it appears to have been the only one
made prior to Ole Olsen's entry into the market early in 1906.
A period, therefore, that was important in the development
of other national cinemas, that saw the birth of many of the
major early film companies and the rise and dominance of the
fiction film, including such important works as Edwin S.
Porter's The Life of an American Fireman and The Great Train
Robbery, Ferdinand Zecca's Au Bagne (Scenes of Convict Life),
George Méliès's many fantasy films, and Cecil Hepworth's
Rescued by Rover, remains dark in the case of Denmark.
That no foreign producers moved to fill this vacuum (Pathé,
for example, which was very active in establishing production
companies in other countries) may be due to the small market
Denmark offered.   As later became evident, the Danish cinema
itself survived and grew largely because of its success in
foreign markets.10

Although the first ten years of Danish film history are
dominated by Peter Elfelt, one other producer can be mentioned in passing. In the years 1904 to 1906 Thomas S. Hermansen is known to have produced four short films for a company called Dansk Kino-Foto-Film Industri. The films were
made in and around the city of Aarhus in Jutland; the titles
explain their content: Indvielse af Aarhus Elektriske Sporveje
(Opening of the Aarhus Electric Tram Line), 90 m.; Kongebesøg
i Aarhus 1906 (The King's Visit to Aarhus 1906); Fra Marsel-
isborg (From Marselis Castle); Aarhusianerne paa Glatis
(Aarhus Residents on Thin Ice). Hermansen had learned
about filmmaking during a stay in America in 1900, and in
1906 had opened a motion picture theater in Aarhus, the
Frederiksbjerg Biografteater. In January 1908, with local
business partners, he expanded his activities and formed a
production company, called at first "A/S Th. S. Hermansen"
but soon changed to Fotorama.[11] Under this name Hermansen
produced several notable films, including Den lille Hornblaeser
(The Little Bugler), 1909, the first film by director Eduard
Schnedler-Sørensen, later to become one of the major directors at Nordisk Films Kompagni, and Den hvide Slavehandel
(The White Slave Trade), 1910, which because of its success
moved Ole Olsen to make his own version the same year.[12]

Although the Danish cinema continued to produce nonfiction subjects throughout the early period, the principal
production, as in all countries, was in the narrative film.
In this regard, Henrettelsen is the most significant film made
prior to 1906. That is not to say that Peter Elfelt's other
films are not worthy of serious consideration, but simply that
they lie outside the major concern of this study--the films that
made Denmark a leading producing country of the prewar silent cinema. The important period of early Danish cinema
began ten years after Peter Elfelt's first film.

Despite the Danish cinema's late start in the production
of fiction films, it quickly became an important force in the
world market. This is largely due to the efforts of Ole Olsen,
the founder of Nordisk Films Kompagni of Copenhagen. Like
many of the American movie moguls, he was a businessman
who saw the possibilities in the new medium and rapidly made
a fortune from it. Before Laemmle, Fox, or Zukor he built
an international organization in which he controlled all aspects
of production, distribution, and exhibition. Only Théophile
Pathé seems to have preceded Olsen as this kind of movie

figure.   Like his American counterparts and the members of
the Motion Picture Patents Company, he shared a desire to
monopolize the film industry, although he succeeded more
completely than any of them.   The Trust never managed to
halt independent production, and the successful independents,
Laemmle, Fox, and Zukor, had to share power with each
other.   Olsen managed to create a film company that was not
only bigger than any of his competitors, but which also managed to stifle the competition that arose.   It was common for
Nordisk to buy out other Danish companies or control the
films they made, to make its own versions of other companies'
subjects, and to hire the competitor's actors, directors, and
technicians.[13]   Through his energetic direction of Nordisk,
he dominated the limited home market and moved into foreign
distribution.   He established branch offices in all the major
European countries and in the United States and, through
these, gained worldwide recognition for Nordisk films.

By the time Olsen founded Nordisk, the film industries
in the United States, France, and England had reached some
degree of significance.   In America, for example, the cinema
had already become an important economic force and entertainment medium.   It had passed through the first years of
excitement based on novelty and had seen the rise of the nickelodeon and the exchange system.[14]   Although the three leading American producers, Edison, Vitagraph, and Biograph,
had already opened European offices, the main thrust of the
American industrial achievement was in developing and expand-
ing a domestic market.   The size of the American market per-
mitted this kind of expansion, and the fierce struggles among
the competing companies, especially between the Trust and
the independents after 1909, kept American energies turned
inward.   Of course, this did not keep American companies
from exploiting foreign markets, but it seems to have inhibited
the process, an inhibition that with the success of the independents and the closing down of European production during
World War I was completely dissipated.[15]   The multiplicity of
competing interests in a potentially vast market helped cause
rapid domestic expansion in the United States, while in Denmark, a stifling of competition and a consolidation by one company in a small market helped cause a rapid expansion in foreign markets.   In both cases dynamic film industries arose
that contributed significantly to the art of film and to the
development of industrial forms that affected the future growth
of the industry.

Comparable to many of his counterparts in other countries Ole Olsen came from a poor background. He grew up
in a rural environment where as a boy he tended sheep, cows,
and geese, where a part of his life was so "wretched and mis-
erable and so full of adversity and harshness that it only deserves to be forgotten."[16] At age eighteen he went to Copenhagen and for a time worked as a waiter in the Café Tissø on
on Vesterbrogade; later, being out of work, he went to sea
as a coal trimmer aboard the Christian IX bound for England.
He stayed in England for a time, but finances again caused
him to go to sea. On his return to Copenhagen he became
a shopkeeper at the corner of Købmagergade and Strøget
where he enticed his customers by hawking his wares in a
loud voice in front of his shop. Shortly after, Olsen rented
a peephole motion picture machine for five kroner per day.
By evening of the first day he had taken in 260 kroner at
ten ore per head. From this modest beginning Olsen expanded
his operations, arranging numerous attractions, including a
traveling African show that played upon contemporary interest
in the recently published book by Stanley, In Darkest Africa.
Olsen himself says that he was becoming known as Denmark's
P. T. Barnum, a role in which he excelled.[17]

This entertainment success brought an offer from the
Swedish city of Malmö to establish an amusement park modeled
on the famous Tivoli in Copenhagen. Olsen managed the
Malmö enterprise from 1898 to 1901. During this time he became interested in projected motion pictures, and after selling
the Malmö enterprise, returned to Denmark opening a film
theater in Copenhagen in 1905 at 47 Vimmelskaftet. An earlier motion picture theater, called the Kosmorama, had been
opened by Constantin Philipsen in September 1904 on Øster-
gade. Olsen's theater was called the Biograf Theartret and
seated about one hundred people. Admission prices were 25
ore for adults, 35 for reserved seats, and ten ore for children.
His first program included a travelogue on Switzerland, an
Indian drama based on a Cooper novel, and a comedy about
Joan of Arc.[18]

In January 1906 Olsen obtained his own motion picture
camera, in time to make a reportage film on the death of King
Christian IX and the crowning of the new king, Frederick
VIII.[19] For film historian Ebbe Neergaard this event marks
the beginning of "the golden days of the Danish silent film."[20]
Although Neegaard overstates the significance of this filming,

it does mark the entry of Ole Olsen into film production, an
event which helped bring on a golden age in the short space
of three or four years.[21]

Olsen continued production with other reportage and
actuality films, the titles of which indicate the range of his
subject matter: Pigeons and Gulls, Copenhagen Participants
in the Olympic Games, Zoological Garden, Women Gymnasts,
Shrovetide Celebrations on Amager, The Chinese Commission
in Copenhagen, Sports Rally in Copenhagen, Fire in the Free
Port, Coronation in Trondhjem, A Trip Through Norway, A
Trip Through Sweden, Grand-Prix Racing on Ordrup Track,
The King and the Crown Prince Inspect the Training Squadron,
August 20, and others. Some of these films were photographed
by Olsen himself, while others were done with the assistance
of Viggo Larsen, Axel Sørensen, and Rasmus Bjerregaard.
In most cases, however, the exact credits are not known.[22]

Soon after his first actuality and reportage films, Olsen
began production of short fictional films. Among the earliest
were two that featured Jean Hersholt, who was later to achieve
prominence in America, perhaps most notably in Erich von
Stroheim's Greed. Both Hersholt films were directed by Louis
Halberstadt, who appears to have been the first director for
Olsen.[23] Other early films featured Robert Storm Petersen
who was later to become famous as a cartoonist. The Petersen films and most other Olsen productions made between 1906
and 1909 were directed by Viggo Larsen, a former army sergeant turned actor. Toward the end of his first year as a
film producer, on November 1, 1906, Olsen formed Nordisk
Films Kompagni, giving his growing business a name that
would soon gain both national and international prominence.[24]

As Ebbe Neergaard points out, this rapid rise to prominence was due largely to the personal characteristics of
Nordisk's founder.

> He was, in the first place, a brilliant organizer, who
> through many years invariably predicted the devel-
> opments and stood ready to meet them with a thor-
> oughly worked out organization that could answer
> the constantly increasing demands.
>   In the second place, he was a daring and imagina-
> tive business man with a sense for the major trends,
> but at the same time with a sober eye out for the
> facts and the dangers....

His third characteristic, which is seldom pointed
out, was his obstinate and severe demand for quality
in N.F.'s production. Its technical quality was, in
any case in the beginning, one of the two characteristics of N.F.'s production that acquired for it a
world market....
He personally supervised the photographers, ...
he engaged the best artists available, he educated
his directors and nursed them and held on to them,
he emphasized few and valuable manuscripts and
tried to be on this work too.
This is connected with a fourth quality of his,
one that was of great importance, ... his spontane-
ous joy in story-telling.... It is not completely un-
justified to say of Ole Olsen that he was related to
the great primitive narrators....
... a fifth quality of his, which should be under-
lined, ... he believed that he performed an educational task with regard to the masses.[25]

It is difficult, of course, to weigh these personal at-
tributes in a scale that must include the specific historical,
social, and economic circumstances in which Olsen entered
motion picture work and which formed the context for the development of Nordisk Films Kompagni. But like his counterparts in the United States, men such as Carl Laemmle, Adolph
Zukor, and William Fox, he made great personal efforts in the
direction of success which imprinted his personality on a large
and talent-filled organization.

Of the thirty-seven fiction films known to have been
made by Nordisk in 1906 and listed by Marguerite Engberg
in volume I of Registrant over danske film, 1896-1914, only
three are known to have survived: En ny Hat til Madammen
(A New Hat for Madame) and Anarkistens Svigermoder (The
Anarchist's Mother-in-Law), both comedies, and Den hvide
Slavinde (The White Slave Girl), a drama. Some of the basic
stories of the thirty-four missing films are known and illustrate
the type of subjects that Olsen was using. They include: a
smuggling drama (Den sorte Maske--The Black Mask); a fisherman sea drama (Fiskerliv i Norden--Fishing Life in the North);
a domestic comedy about a drunk husband's breaking of a
gift for his wife (En Foraering til Min Kone--A Present for
My Wife); a love story (Gaardmandssøn og Husmandsdotter--
Farmer's Son and Crofter's Daughter); a suicide drama

(Datteren Solgt--The Daughter Sold); a crime of passion drama
in which a jilted woman kills her lover (Stenhuggeren--The
Stone Cutter); a bank robbery adventure (Røverhøvdingens
Flugt og Død--The Robber Chief's Flight and Death); a sentimental drama in which a little girl intercedes in behalf of
a crippled man arrested for burglary (Krøblingen--The Cripple); a convict story involving the escape of a galley slave
and his eventual capture and execution (Galejslaven--The Galley Slave); a costume drama of the love of a poor nobleman
for a young girl and her father's objections to their alliance
(Rosenborg Have--Rosenborg Garden); a story of the love of
a poacher's son for a forester's daughter (Krybskytten--The
Poacher); a comedy about a man who loses his patience when
his lunch is constantly interrupted by tradesmen (Forstyrret
Middag--A Disturbed Lunch); and a drama of the seduction
of a flowergirl by a squire (Blomsterpigen--The Flower Girl).
In many cases only the titles indicate the subjects of the
missing films:

> Caros Død (Bob's Death)
>
> Lars Hovedstadsrejse (Lar's Trip to the Capital)
>
> Violinistindens Roman (The Violinist's Romance)
>
> Journalisten som Sjover (The Journalist as Cad)
>
> Vitrioldrama (Vitriolic Drama)
>
> To Forældreløse (Two Orphans)
>
> Rivalinder (The Rivals)
>
> Feriedrengen (The Holiday Boy)
>
> Triste Skabner (Sad Destinies)
>
> Uskyldig Dømt (Wrongfully Convicted)
>
> Gavtyve (Rogues)
>
> Ivrige Kortspillere (Ardent Card Players)
>
> Falliten (Bankruptcy)
>
> Tandpinens Kvaler (The Painful Toothache)[26]

These titles and descriptions are given not only to illustrate the first fictional subjects of Nordisk films, but, as will
become evident in this study, to indicate that the subjects
typical of Danish production even during the so-called golden

age were already present at the beginning of the Danish film
industry. The underlying sensationalism of most of the films
in this list, clearly illustrated in the surviving Den hvide
Slavinde, developed into the sophisticated and internationally
acclaimed erotic and social melodramas of the period 1910-14.

Den hvide Slavinde was the first of a number of white
slavery films made in Denmark in the prewar period. It was
directed by Viggo Larsen, who made thirty-five of the thirty-
seven 1906 Nordisk films. Although it is not one of the significant white slave films, either artistically or in influence,
its plot is a pattern for those which followed. A girl sees a
newspaper advertisement for a job far from home. Much to
the dismay of her fiancé, she takes it. He gives her a carrier pigeon, apparently to use for messages should she need
help. Arriving at her new job, the girl finds herself impressed into white slavery. She sends the pigeon to her
fiancé with a message telling of her plight. The fiancé goes
to the slave house with the police and rescues the girl.

The film is noteworthy as an early example of the white
slave genre and for several interesting shots that are characteristic of Nordisk films in this period. As the girl is getting
off the train at her destination, there is a cut within the
scene from long shot to medium long shot, a scene-structur-
ing idea that was still quite rare in 1906.[27] When she releases
the pigeon, the action is covered in two shots, an interior
showing her opening the window and reaching out, followed
by an exterior of the building showing the girl at the window
releasing the pigeon. The next shot shows the fiancé visiting
the girl's father and mother, bringing the pigeon and note
with him. The temporal and spatial ellipsis involved in this
shot change may have been covered by an intertitle in the
original prints; currently available prints have no intertitles.
The film contains mostly exterior shots, which are composi-
tionally more interesting than the interiors. In addition, the
interiors were photographed in bright sunlight and show heavy
shadows, indicating that they were done on an outdoor stage.
Olsen built a glass studio in Valby, a suburb of Copenhagen,
toward the end of 1907.[28]

Better than Den hvide Slavinde is Anarkistens Svigermoder, made shortly before the white slave film. It is a fast-
paced chase farce, rather broadly played. The film opens on
a realistically rendered, though not very solid-looking, interior

photographed at an angle, rather than head-on as is customary
in films of this period. The actors are always seen in full
length and, except for the change from shot one to shot two,
direction of movement during the chases is maintained. If
the characters exit left in one shot, they enter right in the
next and vice versa. As in Den hvide Slavinde there is a
three-shot sequence in which the location changes from interior to exterior and back to interior during a single action.
The anarchist leaps out a window as he is being chased by
his mother-in-law for flirting with the maid. There is a cut
to an exterior of the building with the man falling to the
ground, followed by a return to the interior position showing
the mother-in-law's upset reaction to the anarchist's leap.
Also similarly to Den hvide Slavinde, the camera is placed on
a diagonal to the rear wall of the set, though the harsh sunlight of Den hvide Slavinde is not evident in Anarkistens
Svigermoder. This angled treatment of some interiors is seen
again in En ny Hat til Madammen and two later Viggo Larsen
films, Røverens Brud (The Robber's Bride) and Et Drama fra
Riddertiden (A Drama from the Age of Chivalry), both from
1907. In addition, Et Drama fra Riddertiden takes the three-
shot sequence and develops it into a more complex spatial
structuring in eight shots, a sequence that will be described
in detail later in this chapter. Since all five films were directed by Viggo Larsen, these traits may constitute internal
evidence as to his style. Any conclusions in this direction
must be guarded, however, since all five films had Axel
Sørensen as cameraman and all were done under the general
supervision of Ole Olsen. Whatever the cause of these stylistic traits, of course, the traits themselves remain and make
these films of special interest.

The third of the surviving 1906 films, En ny Hat til
Madammen, exhibits an unusually absurd humor. The story
involves a woman who buys a new hat that has such a large
brim that the boy delivering the hat box cannot get it through
the door of the woman's house. Instead, they hoist the box
to the second floor where the husband breaks out the window
frame to get it through. Later, the woman causes havoc with
the brim while walking along the street. To contain the damage, her husband buys a little wagon in which he pulls his
wife. Another man sees this, likes the idea, and buys a
wagon for his wife. The two men get into a race with the
wagons, and the wives fall out. Finally, the husband is injured in a duel over the hat, which is then used as a stretcher

to carry him away. In its absurdist humor En ny Hat til
Madammen is like the American Biograph Company films, The
Curtain Pole and Those Awful Hats, some of the Mack Sennett-
directed Biographs, especially When Fire Bells Rang, the later
Sennett Keystone films, and the Italian Cretinetti films, such
as A Duel Under Difficulties.

Another trait of this film, found in many chase films of
the period, is the entrance and exit of the characters past
the camera rather than laterally left and right, a quality that
gives a dynamic aspect to the characters and their movement.
What this film lacks in montage ideas, the strongest points of
Anarkistens Svigermoder and to a lesser extent Den hvide
Slavinde, it makes up in the mise-en-scène.

In 1907 Nordisk Films Kompagni almost doubled its production of fictional films while continuing to produce actualities,
scenics, and documentaries. Peter Elfelt also continued to be
active in the factual film, but there appear to have been no
other film producers on the scene. Viggo Larsen and Axel
Sørensen were still the only director and cameraman given
credit for Nordisk Films' output.[29] About thirty-eight of the
1907 fiction films and seven of the factual films were distributed in the United States in 1907 and 1908, evidence that Ole
Olsen sought to establish an international business almost from
the beginning.[30]

As part of this overall expansion Olsen began the production of series films, a practice which continued to grow in
importance throughout the next ten years. Two series were
produced in 1907, one featuring a character named Happy
Bob, played by Robert Storm Petersen, and the other going
under the general title of Ripp og Rapp. The format of the
Happy Bob films gave the title character some occupation or
task which could be exploited for its comic possibilities. Six
Happy Bob films were made in all: Happy Bob paa Rottejagt
(Happy Bob Rat-Catching), Happy Bob paa Keglebanen (Happy
Bob at the Bowling Alley), ... som Bokser (... as Boxer),
... som Tjener (... as Waiter), ... som Frier (... as Suitor),
and ... som Cyklist (... as Cyclist). They ranged in length
from 77 m. to 137 m., and a few were moderately successful.
Happy Bob paa Rottejagt sold eighty copies and Happy Bob
som Cyklist fifty-three, while Happy Bob paa Keglebanen
sold only ten copies. The Ripp og Rapp films, also six comedies, have extra titles defining their subject matters:

Akrobater (Acrobats), Fotografen (The Photographer), Mekanisk
Statue (Mechanical Statue), Aftensmaden (The Supper), Kun-
stykket (A Trick), and Gabestokken (The Pillory). They
ranged in length from 50 m. to 114 m. and sold as few as
twenty-six copies (Gabestokken) and as many as seventy-five.
(Aftensmaden).[31] No copies of either the Happy Bob or the
Ripp and Rapp films are known to have survived. At least
three of the Happy Bob films, ... paa Rottejagt (three copies),
... som Frier (four copies), ... som Tjener (six copies), and
two of the Ripp and Rapp films, Fotografen (three copies)
and Gabestokken (sixteen copies) were sent to the United
States in May 1908 and distributed by the American Mutoscope
and Biograph Company.[32] One copy of Happy Bob som Bokser
was sent to the Nordisk Films Kompagni office in New York in
August 1908.[33] In addition to the twelve series films just
named, there were at least five, or as many as eight, other
comedies produced in 1907.[34]

   In Sjælebytning (Changing of Souls) a professor,
through hypnotism, changes souls with a student recovering
from a drunken spree. The student goes to the professor's
house, but the professor's wife has him thrown in jail. The
professor meanwhile is arrested for drunken rioting. Ending
up in the same jail they exchange souls again.[35]

   Den Forfaldne Husleje (U.S. title, When the House Rent
Was Due) is the story of a poor artist in love with his rich
model. To fend off the landlord, the artist lies and says he
is about to marry a wealthy woman. The landlord spies on
the proposal, but the model refuses the artist. However,
when the landlord makes himself known, the girl changes her
mind, pays the debts, and, for good measure, boxes the landlord's ears.

   Kejser Nero paa Krigsstren (U.S. title, Emperor Nero
on the Warpath) is a trick comedy in which an artist's bust
of Nero comes to life and goes on a rampage through the
city, ending in a fight in the artist's studio, at which point
the artist wakes up.

   From the plot description, Lykkens Galoscher (U.S.
title, The Magic Rubbers) appears to be a comedy with a
serious moral. An old professor of history receives a pair of
magic rubbers, provided by the Fairy of Fortune and the
Fairy of Sorrow, which enable him to travel back in time.

A night watchman then comes into possession of the rubbers.
He wishes himself to be a lieutenant and then changes his
mind and becomes a watchman again. Then he wishes for
money, but soon tires of that. Finally, he wishes himself
returned to his family.

Although no descriptions exist for Rheumatisme or
Russik Bad (Rheumatism or Russian Bath) and Madkaeresten
(The Cupboard Lover), their titles indicate that they were
comedies. In addition, there were several parody films, Bry-
der Parodi (Wrestler Parody) and Bokserparodi (Boxer Parody),
both with two clowns named Ihles and Antonio, and Danserin-
den or Balletparodi (The Dancer or Ballet Parody), that would
most likely fall into the comic category.[36]

None of the 1907 comedies described so far is known
to have survived. In fact, only one Danish comedy from
1907 can be seen today, a vaudeville act called Tryllesækken
(U.S. title, The Magic Bag). It was originally 75 m. in
length[37] and was quite successful, selling 144 copies.[38] The
action is seen in long shot from one camera position. The
space functions essentially as a stage on which the act is
performed. Two clowns enter and do comic tricks. Behind
them is a painted backdrop that includes palm trees. Their
act includes acrobatics in which they push each other around
while frequently gesturing toward the camera. One of them
gets into a large bag, and trick photography is used to make
the bag move from place to place, as it repeatedly becomes
empty and full. Finally, both clowns get in the bag and
fight. The film ends with them becoming friends again. Except for the extra dimension of trick photography, the film
is a straight recreation of a vaudeville act.

More numerous and more important to the future of
Danish films were the costume dramas produced by Nordisk
Films in 1907. At least eleven films seem to belong in this
category. Eight of these films are now lost, although five
have surviving plot descriptions.

Vikingeblod (U.S. title, The Hot Temper) is a Viking
story centering on an argument between two families that
leads to the arrest of one of the family leaders and the killing
of his men. The leader's son tries to rescue his father but
is himself caught. Just as a fight is about to break out, the
leader of the other family intervenes and peace is brought

about based on the marriage of his daughter to the son of
the rival leader.

Angelo, Tyran fra Padua (U.S. title, Angelo, Tyrant
of Padua) is a drama of adultery, jealousy, and murder based
on a Victor Hugo play. Angelo has both a wife and a mistress, Thisbe, a servant once saved by Angelo's wife. The
wife also has a lover, Rudolph. Thisbe informs Angelo's
servant, Homoder, about the affair between Rudolph and
Angelo's wife. When Angelo finds out about his wife's infidelity, he sentences her to death. Meanwhile, Thisbe repents
of her deed and to save Angelo's wife, she substitutes a sleeping potion for the poison that was to be the instrument of
death. Thinking his lover dead, Rudolph kills Thisbe, only
to discover his error when Angelo's wife awakens.

Rosen (U.S. title, From the Rococo Times) tells of an
old nobleman who wants his daughter to marry a rich old
man. She refuses because she is in love with a younger man.
The girl's father sets a contest for his daughter's hand which
the young man wins.

In Texas Tex (U.S. title, Texas Tex) the hero (whose
name gives the film its title) loves a girl whom another cowboy, aided by an Indian, kidnaps. The Indian loves her, too,
and kills his cowboy accomplice, after which he dances wildly
around the girl. Tex arrives, kills the Indian, and rescues
the girl.

That Nordisk made Texas Tex at this early date testi-
fies to the international popularity that the Western had already achieved. The film was then exported to the United
States were the genre had been born. A critic for The New
York Dramatic Mirror (August 1, 1908, p. 7) declared the
film to be a "hit" in which the "acting is good, the story
plainly told and the photography perfect." Only the locations
were criticized for not looking Western enough. Other Western films that Nordisk produced were Røverens Brud (1907)
and De to Guldgravere (1909) (see Engberg, Dansk Stumfilm,
pp. 196-97).

Den sorte Hertug (The Black Duke) is set during war
against a callous count and involves the saving of a man's
daughter by a character named Svend Trøst. Among the
costume dramas for which no descriptions are available are

three based on well-known writers: Den glade Enke (The
Merry Widow) after Franz Lehar; Opstandelse (Resurection)
after Leo Tolstoy; and Dansen paa Koldingshus (U.S. title,
The Viking's Love) after Holger Drachmann, principally a
Danish lyric poet, but also a writer of novels, stories, and
operettas. Presumably, the films followed, to some extent,
the story lines of the original sources.

Three of the 1907 costume dramas have survived: Der
Var Engang (Once upon a Time), based on a play by Holger
Drachmann, Et Drama fra Riddertiden (A Drama from the Age
of Chivalry), and Kameliadamen (U.S. title, The Lady with
the Camellias), after Alexander Dumas.[39] In 1923 Holger
Drachmann's play was again adapted to the screen, this time
by Denmark's most distinguished director, Carl Dreyer. Only
a fragment of the second version has survived, however.

The main plot complication of Der Var Engang is a
familiar one. A prince is in love with the king's daughter
and, although the king likes him, the princess treats her
suitor in a haughty manner. The prince concocts a plot to
disgrace the princess by dressing up as an entertainer and
sneaking into her bed chamber. The couple is discovered,
and the princess is cast out along with her supposed lover.
The prince, maintaining his disguise, takes the princess to a
forest cottage and humbles her by making her work hard.
Finally, he reveals himself as a nobleman, and they take the
throne together.

The film has a fairy-tale quality and, in keeping with
its origins and much of the film work of the period, a definite theatrical look. It is shot entirely on a stage with artificial sets, although it is lighted with sunlight which casts
heavy shadows, much like Den hvide Slavinde. The camera
always shows the actors in full length as they perform in
broad-gestured style. The opening shot has the camera at
an angle to the set, as in other Viggo Larsen films, but has
no interesting uses of montage like those found in Anarkistens Svigermoder, Den hvide Slavinde, Et Drama fra Riddertiden, and another surviving 1907 film, Løvejagten (U.S. title,
Lion Hunting).

In Et Drama fra Riddertiden, also known as For en
Kvindes Skyld (For a Woman's Sake), a young knight named
Kuno rides into the palace yard and is met by the lord of the

manor and another young knight, Knud, who is also on a
visit. Both knights have come as suitors to the lord of the
manor's daughter, Inger. From the moment they meet, the
two knights become bitter rivals. Inger's preference for Kuno
moves Knud to vengeance. That night, Inger lets a thick silk
cord down from her window to the garden below where Kuno
is waiting. As Kuno is climbing, Knud cuts the cords and
Kuno falls to his death. The lord of the manor has Knud arrested.

Like most other films from 1907, the action is photographed in long shot and the interiors are generally theatrical
in appearance, that is, composed of static frontal shots with
painted backdrops. In contrast, the exteriors are beautifully
composed and shot around real Danish castles. One sequence
in particular stands out. It is made up of a short series of
shots in which Knud cuts the rope on which Kuno is climbing.
The montage is based on the dramatic logic of the action,
carefully blending exterior and interior scenes. (An alternate
version of this film exists in which the interiors and exteriors
are not intercut as described here. At present, neither version can be completely authenticated.) The sequence shows
unusually intricate construction for 1907 and is worth describing in detail.

1. Exterior   Low angle long shot of Inger lowering a
    rope from a high window.

2. Exterior. Medium long shot of Kuno on the ground
    next to the castle wall. The rope enters the frame
    from the top, and he begins to climb.

3. Interior. Medium long shot of Knud at a window.
    He cuts the rope.

4. Exterior. Long shot of Kuno falling thorugh the
    frame.

5. Exterior. Low angle long shot (as in shot one) of
    Inger as she reacts in horror and withdraws into
    her room.

6. Interior. Medium long shot of Inger reacting at
    the window. (The cut from shot five is made on
    Inger's movement.)

7. Interior. Medium long shot (as in shot three) of
    Knud as he leaves the window.

8. Exterior. Medium long shot of Kuno lying on the ground. Some women rush into frame.

The entire sequence takes very little screen time and stands out quite dramatically in an otherwise conventional film.

Related to these costume dramas are several films that involve fantasy, adventure, and the exotic. Two of these, Flugten fra Seraillet (U.S. title, The Flight from the Seraglio) and Zigeunerens Haevn (U.S. title, The Countess' Wedding Day) exist for us only as plot descriptions and credit information.

Flugten fra Seraillet is the story of a young Englishman, Mr. Hopkins, who falls in love with a caliph's favorite wife, Sulejma. When he breaks into the harem, the caliph chases him off. He makes another attempt and Sulejma escapes with him. Hopkins's friend, Jackson, helps the couple by killing the caliph and sacrificing his own life so that the lovers can get away.[40]

Zigeunerens Haevn is about a count and an old baron who are rivals for Countess Rose. The baron has her kidnapped by gypsies, but the count kills the baron and rescues the countess.

Three other films of this type have survived: Fyrtøjet (The Tinder Box), based on the story of the same name by Hans Christian Andersen; Røverens Brud (U.S. title, The Robber's Sweetheart, though literally The Robber's Bride); and Løvejagten (U.S. title, Lion Hunting).

The surviving fragment of Fyrtøjet contains the following action. A young soldier meets a witch by a tree. The witch gets him to climb inside the tree where there are three creatures each sitting over a treasure. He takes two bags, climbs out of the tree, and has an argument with the witch. He hits her with his sword; she explodes, and the soldier walks off.

The film is done in a tableau style of head-on single-take long shots, much as Georges Méliès's films. Although one is tempted to see the film as primitive, Ebbe Neergaard makes a case for its basic faithfulness to the spirit of the Andersen original.

> Viggo Larsen who ... plays the soldier, permeates
> the scene with a lively mood, and the tricks with the
> suddenly appearing and disappearing dogs are pre-
> cise and amusingly done. These tricks in themselves
> create a cinematographic Hans Andersen mood....
> There is complete agreement with the spirit, if not
> with the letter of the poet, when the soldier wields
> his sabre, and, pouf, a cloud of dust rises and the
> witch is gone! That is as it should be: funny.[41]

In R\u00f8verens Brud, a wife tries to keep her husband
from his lawless life as captain of the robbers. Another robber is in love with the wife, but she rebuffs him. To get
even he betrays the robber chief to the police. The wife
gets her own revenge by killing the informer, after which
she succeeds in freeing her husband. He is caught, however,
and she must free him again. They escape to the woods, but
soon the police arrive and both are killed in the ensuing fight.

R\u00f8verens Brud is one of the best of the surviving 1907
films, primarily because of its sophisticated treatment of space.
The opening interior in the robber chief's house utilizes the
diagonal camera placement characteristic of Nordisk Films.
A door is set in the right rear wall, and all entrances and
exits are made through it, giving a sense of the exterior narrative space that lies behind it. Much of the film is shot in
outdoor locations, and even though the exteriors are in general more convincing and more interestingly composed, they
have a definite feeling of being spatially linked to the interior
scenes.

The opening scene contains one of the few cuts within
a scene found in the early Danish cinema. The "bad" robber
is trying to force his attentions on the wife. At the moment
that the drama intensifies, a title (missing in present day
prints) intervenes, marking a change from the opening long
shot to a medium long shot as the wife fends off the man's
advances. Later, when the "bad" robber goes to the police
to betray his chief, the action is photographed in medium
shot, befitting the dramatic importance of this scene.

Toward the end of the film, police are coming along a
road in order to set up an ambush. They stop and begin to
disperse. There is a cut to a reverse angle showing the road
from the opposite direction. It is a particularly effective cut

since the robbers will come down that road; it also gives the
viewer a stronger sense of the 360-degree reality of the space.
Unfortunately, this is followed by another reverse angle cut
returning to the soldiers who are once again dispersing. The
break in continuity caused by this cut may have been partly
covered by a title in original prints. In general, however,
the continuity of the film is clear and direct, enabling the
viewer to follow the action easily, even without explanatory
titles.

By far the most interesting and famous of the 1907
films is Løvejagten. It caused considerable notoriety in its
time and helped establish Ole Olsen's reputation as a producer.
In addition, it was very successful, selling 257 copies.[42]

In his autobiography Ole Olsen tells how he wanted to
make a film about lion hunting, but that he could not afford
to "travel to Africa and see it in reality."[43] This desire
was prompted by the success of another hunting film he had
made at the beginning of 1907. He had purchased a polar
bear from Hamburg, set it loose on the ice and, along with
Viggo Larsen as another hunter, set about to shoot it in front
of the camera. This was accomplished with the help of some
unseen riflemen.[44] Since the "reality" of the bearhunting
film was sufficient to sell 191 copies,[45] Olsen decided, even
if he could not go to Africa, that "with two lions, used in
the right manner, perhaps an illusion could be created."[46]
So from the same Hamburg source he had acquired the polar
bear, Olsen bought two lions and prepared to make his film.
The island of Elleore, which is in Roskilde Fjord not far from
Copenhagen, was chosen for a location. News of the film and
the presence of two lions, however, aroused enough opposition to cause the state secretary of justice, Peter Adler Alberti, to issue an order prohibiting the filming, an order
which Olsen ignored. Despite Olsen's audacity, the showing
of the film was blocked and Olsen was brought to trial. He
was finally acquitted by a high court, but not before Alberti
had revoked his license to make films.[47] The ultimate result
of this legal activity and the accompanying newspaper coverage of it, rather than negative, was to increase Olsen's business and move him further along the road to dominance in the
Danish film industry.[48]

The noteriety of Løvejagten has long since been forgotten, of course, but its aesthetics has gained in interest.

Because of its montage, the film anticipated the experiments
of Lev Kuleshov over a decade later, although the montage
ideas in Løvejagten were arrived at pragmatically rather than
theoretically and, as far as can be judged from surviving
Danish films, were never followed up by either Larsen or any
other Danish director. The need to create an illusion of being in Africa forced the filmmakers into creative montage con-
structions. Olsen and Larsen were faced with the problem
of making the space of the lions appear as contiguous with
that of the hunters, and of having other African animals in
the film while not having to transport them to Elleore. The
solution they hit upon, commonplace today, was unheard of
in 1907.

The film begins as two hunters come into a clearing in
the "jungle" and sit down to rest.[49] They look about them,
and cuts to shots of ostriches and zebras create the illusion
of the hunters' subjective point of view.[50] Another shot of
the hunters glancing is followed by a shot of a hippo. Cut
back to the hunters. One runs off camera and returns with
a small monkey. Both hunters then exit frame. Following
this are a series of high-angle shots of the hunters on the
march. They usually emerge out of the "jungle" and walk
out of frame near the camera. As they travel, they repeatedly
point to off-screen space which we either see in the following
shot as their point of view or as the space which they are
about to enter.

The actual spotting and killing of the lion and the excitement that these scenes are meant to generate rely heavily
on an intricate montage that cross-cuts between lions and
hunters, develops a chase, and utilizes subjective point of
view.

1. Hunters bed down.

2. Lion

3. Hunters asleep.

4. Lion.

5. Hunters asleep.

6. Lion (this time nearer camera with animal prey in
   mouth).

7. Hunters. One of them sits up, looks to left, grabs
   his gun, aims, and fires.

8. Lion with prey.

9. Hunters. The other jumps up, grabs his gun, and fires.

10. Lion leaves frame.

11. Lion. Enters frame near dead animal. Runs around.

12. Hunters firing. They exit frame left.

13. One hunter crosses through frame.

14. Lion in water (seen in long shot).[51]

15. Lion (seen in long shot, though different angle from shot fourteen). Hunter enters from right, aims, and fires. (This is the first shot in which hunters and lion are seen in the same frame.)

16. Close shot of lion on shore, dead.

17. Medium long shot of lion, dead. Hunter enters right, goes over to lion, and stands by it.

18. Other hunter with black guide comes toward camera. Guide points, and hunter exits frame in that direction.

19. Hunter by dead lion (as in shot seventeen). He exits.

20. Medium shot of hunter crossing frame. (Not clear which hunter it is.)

21. Long shot. Hunters enter right, kneel, and fire. They get up and exit left.

22. One hunter near dead lion. Other hunter enters. They examine body and begin to skin it.

23. Close shot. Hunters examining lion.

24. Hunters walk into frame in "jungle" followed by black guide dragging two lion skins. They hold up one skin and examine it. All have cigarettes.

25. Medium close shot. Hunters and guide looking toward camera.

Although these scenes are often awkwardly shot and edited, it is important that they were done, that at an early

stage in film history the ideas of montage juxtaposition to
create an artificial geography and establish subjective point
of view were introduced. Whether these ideas had any significant effect on other filmmakers is unknown, but Lǿvejagten
was widely distributed, including in the United States,[52] and
the Nordisk films, in general, were highly regarded from
their first appearance.[53]

        A number of contemporary dramas were also filmed in
1907. En moderne Sǿhelt (U.S. title, A Modern Naval Hero)
is about two naval officers on a mission to steal enemy papers.
One of them is caught, but the other escapes and takes the
stolen papers to the admiral. He then returns and rescues
the captured officer. Both receive medals for their bravery.

        Haanden (U.S. title, The Hand) is a crime film in which
a thief breaks into the home of a famous actress. Terrorized,
she faints, while the thief goes about his work. Her lover,
a lieutenant, arrives and subdues the thief.

        Testamentet (U.S. title, The Will) concerns a guardian
who steals the property of a dead friend and tries to marry
his own ward. He is found out and punished in some tragic
manner. The plot summary does not make clear how.

        Mesalliance (U.S. title, A Misalliance) is the old story
of a marriage between a man and a woman of different social
classes. Baron d'Alroy marries Kitty, a music hall performer
who does an act with her sister Daisy. The two sisters also
must support their father. Two years after their marriage,
the baron is called off to Africa with the colonial forces where
he is mistakenly reported dead. Kitty and her daughter are
forced to return to the home of her father and sister. The
baron's mother takes steps to have the child taken away from
Kitty, but d'Alroy returns and prevents this.

        None of these four films are known to have survived,
and for many other films from 1907 only titles remain to indicate their type and subject matter.[54]

        In addition to the fiction films, Nordisk Films produced
about forty nonfiction films, covering a variety of subjects:
royalty, the military, sports, scenic views, education, animals,
geography, travel, and industry. At least five of these were
distributed in the United States:

Steinindustri i Sverrig. (U.S. title, Stone Industry in
   Sweden)

Hundedressur (U.S. title, Dog Training)

Verdenssport (U.S. title, Sport from all the World)

Lapperne (U.S. title, The Laplanders)

Bornholm (U.S. title, The Isle of Bornholm)

Peter Elfelt also produced about forty nonfiction films in 1907
with a concentration of films about socially significant individuals, a kind of subject not normally found in the Nordisk
nonfiction films.[55]

   In 1908 there was an increase in the total number of
films produced by Nordisk, although the number of fiction
films declined by anywhere from two to six. Ebbe Neergaard
gives the number of fiction films produced in 1907 as sixty-
two and the number of nonfiction films as fifty-one. For 1908
he claims sixty fiction and seventy-five nonfiction.[56] Marguerite Engberg lists sixty-five fiction and forty-six nonfiction
films for 1907 and fifty-nine fiction and seventy-five nonfiction
films for 1908.[57]

   Peter Elfelt does not appear to have been active in 1908,
but Thomas S. Hermansen, mentioned earlier in this chapter
in connection with film activity in the city of Aarhus, made
three films under the name of his company, Dansk Kino-Foto-
Film-Industri. All three were actualities: Landbrug i Danmark (Agriculture in Denmark), Kongebesøg i Randers (The
King's Visit to Randers), and Hans Broges Begravelse (Hans
Broge's Funeral).[58] All other films in 1908 were produced
by Nordisk Films.

   The 1908 nonfiction films included a typical range of
subjects: sports, military events, commercial fishing, a ship
launching, animals, child welfare, wine growing, famous
places, travel, etc. Unlike 1906 and 1907, however, there
was a wider interest in far off places, indicating that Nordisk
either sent out cameramen to other countries as the Lumières
and others had done or bought films from other sources. In
1908 there were films on Moscow, St. Petersburg, Budapest,
Belgrade, Khartoum, Egypt, Siam, and a series of four films

with titles modeled on the following one: Berlin paa Kryds og Tvaers (Berlin Criss-Crossed). The other three were on New York, Nuremberg, and Tronhjem. At least sixteen of the nonfiction films reached the United States.[59] Unfortunately, none of Nordisk's nonfiction films from the period are known to have survived.

The foreign location films were made by two director-cameramen that were probably not part of the regular Nordisk staff, Ludvig Lippert and Langhoff. Lippert was responsible for the North African films, Orkenliv, Khartum, Dromedareksercits (Drilling of Camels), Ægyptens Storbyer (Egyptian Cities), Siam-Kongyubilæym, Oldtidens Ægypten, and for a film on the city of Belgrade. Langhoff covered Eastern Europe and Russia and is credited for Moskva, St. Petersburg, Nischni Novgorod, Budapest, and also the industrial Grev Zeppelins Luftskib.[60]

The survival rate for the fiction films of 1908 is hardly better than that for the nonfiction films. Only three are known to us today: Capriciosa (U.S. title, The Magic Purse), Natten før Christians Fødselsdag or Ole Lukøje (The Night Before Christian's Birthday), possibly released in the United States as The Chimney Sweep's Birthday Dream), and Motorcyklisten (U.S. title, The Non-Stop Motor Bicycle). All three were directed by Viggo Larsen and photographed by Axel Sørensen, who continued to be responsible for the entire Nordisk output of fiction films for the year.[61]

Capriciosa is one of the least interesting of the surviving Nordisk films. It is a fantasy-drama done entirely in long shot and using painted sets. Peter quarrels with his family and then dreams that he receives an inexhaustible purse from a woodland spirit, but only on the condition that he does not share the money with anyone. His actions offend his family. In the end he throws away the purse, awakens, and is taken back by his family. The film utilizes trick photography, as spirits appear and disappear, but with no special charm, such as that which endeared the Hans Andersen Fyrtøjet to Ebbe Neergaard.

Natten for Christians Fødselsdag is based on a tale by Hans Christian Andersen about a young man who dreams that he finds money and becomes successful, though he becomes progressively unhappy. When he wakes from his dream, he

tells his family about it.[62] Like many fantasy films of the
period, it utilizes trick photography to make people appear
and disappear; in addition, it uses dissolves to unite the
dream sequence with the framing story. Typically, it is
photographed in long shot and uses rather primitive painted
sets, in contrast to the painted sets of Georges Méliès which,
in the same period, showed a great range of imaginative
power. Only one scene has a cut within it. While spirits
are dancing around Christian, there is a cut from long shot
to full shot of the action. In original prints the spirits are
hand colored while the rest of the scene is black and white.
Although more interesting than Capriciosa, Natten for Christians Fødselsdag does not measure up to the dramas of 1907,
such as Røverens Brud, Et Drama fra Riddertiden, or the
adventure film Løvejagten. Both the strength and the future
of Nordisk production were in the direction of those basically
realistic films.

    Motorcyklisten is a typical chase film of the period,
much like Griffith's The Curtain Pole (1909), Ferdinand Zecca's
Cheval Emballé (1907) (The Runaway Horse), and Emile Cohl's
La Course des Potirons (1907) (The Pumpkin Race). The film
begins on the interior of a motorbike shop; a studio set with
painted buildings in realistic perspective is visible through
the window. Three men in the shop are polishing a bike.
Outside the window a man walks by, adding to the realistic
effect by relating interior to exterior. One man gets on the
bike which begins to leave frame right. Cut to outside bike
shop, a real street exterior. The man on the bike comes out
of the shop door, moves diagonally across the frame, and
exits left. Another man runs out of the shop gesturing wildly.
Cut to another street seen in diagonal composition. A man is
standing on a ladder which leans against a light pole. The
motorbike comes around the corner and knocks over the ladder. The man on the ladder joins in the chase. In subsequent shots set on different streets, the motorbike continues
to knock people down. All join in the chase. Finally, the
bike smashes through a window, and several people end up
beating the cyclist.

    Each scene is approximately the same length, so that
the building of the chase has little to do with the montage.
Neither does the chase escalate in violence or speed. It is
built primarily on increasing the number of people involved,
which is one of the simplest ways of constructing this kind of

film.[63] Basically, one shot of people running is followed by
another shot of people running, the camera itself remaining
stationary. Some minor exceptions to this structure occur
when a few times the camera makes short, jerky pans to follow the action and when once there is 180-degree cut from
people running toward the camera to people running away
from camera.

Compared to the best 1907 films, the three surviving
1908 films are rather mediocre and must give a poor idea of
the overall quality of Nordisk films in its third year of operation. Although film reviews can be misleading, especially
those of the early period of film history, comments on the
American release of Nordisk films indicate the high regard
in which Nordisk films were held as early as 1909. De To
Violiner (U.S. title, The Two Violins), a drama about two
violinists, one a cripple and the superior player, the other
handsome, who vie for a girl's love, was called "a beautiful
film" in which "the photography is remarkably clear and
snappy ... an eminently satisfactory picture."[64] Wilhelm Tell
(U.S. title, Wilhelm Tell), which tells the story of the famous
Swiss liberator, was considered.

> a good example of the excellent progress this con-
> cern [Nordisk Films Kompagni] is making in cinema-
> tographic art. We happened around while the Board
> of Censors were sitting in judgment on the film and
> the opinion expressed by one member of the Board
> was that it was the "best film that he had yet seen."
> The actors are well adapted to their parts and the
> scenes are well laid and the photography up to their
> usual high quality.[65]

Herremandens Barnebarn (U.S. title, The Farmer's
Grandson) is a drama that includes the abandonment of a young
wife by a brutal husband, years of struggle as she raises her
child alone in the city, and an eventual reconciliation of the
girl with her estranged father whom she had left years before.
It also has a scene in which the grandson of the title kills
his own father in order to save his grandfather, a scene
which, for one critic, added "a touch of tragedy ... which
transforms the whole into an admirable film."[66] Svend Dyrings
Hus (U.S. title, The Stepmother), which deals with the mal-
treatment of a child, was called "masterly" in its handling of
the subject, and, after commenting on the clarity of story and

action, the "excellence of the photography and the evident
care which they give to the details of the senario," the re-
viewer went on to say:

> The style and class of the subjects issued by this
> company are so different from that of any other
> manufacturer that they should make a welcome oc-
> casional change of program.[67]

At least thirty-six more of the fifty-nine or sixty Nordisk features of 1908 were released in the United States, most
of them during 1909. Fifteen of these were contemporary
dramas, two were adventure dramas, one was an adventure
fantasy, three were detective films, two were costume dramas,
twelve were comedies, and one cannot be classified.

The three detective films continued the policy of series
films begun by Nordisk in 1907 with the Happy Bob and the
Ripp and Rapp films, and became the first in a long line of
crime dramas of various kinds. These three were all based
on Conan Doyle's character Sherlock Holmes and bore the
titles Sherlock Holmes I or Sherlock Holmes i Livsfare (U.S.
title, Sherlock Holmes), Sherlock Holmes II or Raffles Flugt
fra Faengslet (U.S. title, Sherlock Holmes-2, Raffles Escapes
from Prison), and Sherlock Holmes III or Det hemmelige Dok-
ument (U.S. title, Sherlock Holmes-3). Viggo Larsen, in addition to writing and directing the films, played the detective.
The first of the series premiered on November 20, 1908 at
Olsen's Biograph Theater in Copenhagen.[68]

The first three films of the series must have been
planned from the beginning since their stories are continuous.
In Sherlock Holmes I Raffles, the criminal enemy of Holmes,
steals a diamond necklace but is captured and imprisoned.
Sherlock Holmes II begins with Raffles in jail and shows how
he manages to escape. In Sherlock Holmes III Raffles tries
several plans to kill Holmes but fails and is recaptured.[69]
The success of these films (selling 103, 119, and 87 copies
respectively), paved the way for a continuation of the Sherlock Holmes films until nine were made in all, the final one
being released in January 1911. Viggo Larsen was both director and star of the first six Holmes films, the last of which
was released in August 27, 1909.[70]

Moving Picture World was enthusiastic about the Sherlock

Holmes series even though it was often critical of crime films.
It called the series "remarkable" and mentioned its "excellence
of photography," a quality of Nordisk films that "cannot be
excelled."   It also commended the series for its acting, comparing it to "what you would expect to see at the famous
'Comédie Française' of Paris."   In reviewing Sherlock Holmes
II, it noted that it "is as much a masterpiece as its predeces-
sor, and Sherlock Holmes III promises to hold the same
rank."[71]

The New York Dramatic Mirror also extolled Nordisk photography in its review of Sherlock Holmes I, finding it to be
of "superior quality."   In addition, it found

> the scenic effects quite ingenious and novel. The
> plot is also interesting and is developed with consid-
> erable skill and with reasonable lucidity, although
> it might have been made a little more clear in the
> early scenes.

On the negative side, the Mirror thought that too much of
the action depended on the viewer's knowledge of "the personalities of Sherlock Holmes, Raffles and Moriarty," and,
in contradiction to Moving Picture World, that "the acting
appears oddly stiff."[72]

Less successful were two other 1908 crime dramas,
Mafia (U.S. title, Mafia, the Secret Society or Sicilian Family
Honor), which sold only thirty-eight copies,[73] and Livsslaven
(U.S. title, The Convict for Life), which sold forty-seven.[74]
No plot descriptions or reviews of Mafia have survived, but
Livsslaven is a story about a young man who accidentally kills
a rich farmer who has been trying to seduce his wife. He is
sentenced to life imprisonment but is saved by his brother,
an inspector at the prison, who unbeknownst to anyone else
takes the young man's place. As was often the case in early
films, the sensationalist aspects of the melodrama were tempered by a sentimental morality. The life sentence is changed
to death, and the self-sacrificing brother is shot "in the presence of all his brother officials. While dying he sees in a
vision his brother and his wife showing his picture, which
hangs on the wall in the little room, to their little child."[75]

This sentimental sensationalism also dominated Nordisk
love stories throughout the period. Two 1908 examples are

typical. Although these particular films have not survived, their plots were reenacted many times and will be encountered again later in this study.

Tiggersken (U.S. title, The Beggar Woman) sets up an opposition between passion and home life common in Danish films. A young girl, Maggie,[76] has been reduced to street begging in order to buy medicine for her sick mother. While doing this she meets Dr. Holmes who tries to help her, only to discover it is too late. Returning to Maggie's home, they find the mother dead. Maggie then becomes Dr. Holmes's housekeeper and eventually his wife, though out of gratitude to him rather than love. Her love she gives to one of the doctor's friends who eventually deserts her, forcing her to turn to begging. Some time later she meets her husband on the street and in remorse tries to drown herself. He rescues her and, after some soul-searching, takes her back.

Pierrot (U.S. title, The Prince and the Actor) tells the tragic story of an actor, Henry B., and his lover Jeannette, a dancer. She leaves him for a rich man. Two years later he meets her again and finds himself still passionately in love with her. She, however, has a prince for a lover. In a rage Henry B. insults the prince by destroying a portrait of him which is hanging in Jeannette's apartment. The prince has Henry B. imprisoned. Twenty years pass, and, while visiting the prison, the prince comes across the aged actor and has him released. A short time later the actor is near death. A minister arrives to give him the sacrament. Accompanying the minister is Jeannette who is now a deaconess. Henry B. dies happily while Jeannette weeps.

Hopeless love, separation, infidelity, remorse, unbridled passions--these are the characteristics of the Danish love stories that gave rise to the better-known erotic melodramas of 1910-14, such as Asta Nielsen's first film Afgrunden (The Abyss). This type of film appears to have been especially important to the development of a similar kind of film in Italy, Assunta Spina being a good example.[77]

Not all the love stories were tragic, of course, or even serious. Many romantic comedies were made throughout the period, though none from 1908 have survived. One for which a brief description is available, however, is called De fire Kaerester (U.S. title, Four Sweethearts). It concerns a

kitchen maid who conceals her four sweethearts in various
places about the room, including one in the washing tub, only
to have them continuously appearing at the wrong time until
all but one are driven out of the house. The film used actors
from the Frederiksberg and Nørrebro theaters.[78]

Judging by their titles, at least two other 1908 comedies
also revolved around a love theme, Urmagerens Bryllup (U.S.
title, The Watchmaker's Wedding), starring one of Denmark's
best comic actors, Carl Alstrup,[79] and Den Romerske Model
(U.S. title, The Artist's Model's Sweetheart). And perhaps
to these two should be added Othello (U.S. title, Othello),
also starring Carl Alstrup. The film apparently concerns an
actor who played Othello, although the relationship of this
plot idea to the love story of Shakespeare's play, if any, is
not known.

As there were comic counterparts to the dramatic love
stories, there were also comic counterparts to the dramatic
adventures. Kaliffens Eventyr (U.S. title, The Caliph's Adventures), starring Carl Alstrup and another of Denmark's
major comics, Oscar Stribolt, is the story of a bored caliph
finally cured of his boredom by obtaining a magic ring that
instantly transports him to any place he desires. This, as
can be expected, gets him into trouble, which he finally gets
out of by instantly transporting himself home.

Another Alstrup-Stribolt comedy from 1908 also concerns
fantastic adventures. Havkongens Datter (U.S. title, Neptune's Daughter or The Shoemaker's Dream) is about a young
man, fond of playing tricks, who has a dream in which he
ends up on the bottom of the sea because of an explosion related to a fight with pirates. There, Neptune's daughter falls
in love with him, but he refuses her offer of marriage and
a kingdom. She then has him imprisoned in the kingdom's
treasury. The young man fills his pockets with jewels and
escapes to the surface where he is rudely awakened by a
beating from his master.

In a more serious vein, Nordisk produced a film which
stands as an early example of a genre that has since become
a staple in motion pictures and which found its best Danish
example in Benjamin Christensen's first film, Det hemmlighedsflude X (The Mysterious X) in 1913. Spionen (U.S. title, The
Spy) combined treason and a love triangle. Lieutenant Duval

steals important papers and sells them to an agent for a foreign country. With the money he intends to flee abroad with
his sweetheart. Another officer, Joubert, discovers the treason and brings the spy to justice. Duval's girl helps free
him, but only in order to leave him forever. Joubert catches
Duval again, however, and kills him in a fight, after which
Joubert proposes to the girl, whom he has loved all along,
and is accepted by her.

Most of the remaining films from 1908 appear to have
been dramas. The titles of some of them indicate their sub-
jects: Gennem Livets Skole (U.S. title, The School of Life),
Blind (U.S. title, Blind), Synderinden (U.S. title, A Sinner),
Alene i Verden (U.S. title, The Blind Foundling), En Moders
Kamp med Døden (A Mother's Struggle with Death). There
was at least one historical drama, Falkedrengen (U.S. title,
The Brave Page Boy), and one based on Sardou's play La
Tosca, released in the United States as The Queen's Love.[80]

In 1909 Nordisk Films decreased its production of nonfiction films from seventy-five (1908) to sixty-two and increased its production of fiction films from fifty-nine (1908)
to eight-one.[81] Of the nonfiction films at least twenty-four
were distributed in the United States, and of the fiction films,
at least seventy.[82] The American-released nonfiction films
covered sports, travel, vaudeville, theater, occupations, and
personalities.[83] Among the American-released fiction films
were thirty-two contemporary dramas, six crime dramas, four
historical dramas, twenty-two comedies, three trick films, and
two which cannot be identified as to type.[84]

In 1909 competition to Nordisk Films Kompagni made its
appearance. Peter Elfelt, the first Danish filmmaker, released
six short nonfiction films, and Thomas Hermansen, who had
made his first film in 1904, released one nonfiction film. Hermansen also produced one fiction film, Den lille Hornblaeser
(The Little Bugler), based on a well-known Danish poem by
H. P. Holst about the 1864 war with Germany, and a ballet
film, De fire Aarstider (The Four Seasons), based on a ballet
of the same name.[85] In addition, a new company, Biorama,
produced four fiction films, Stormen paa København den 11
februar 1659 og Gøngehøvdingen (The Storm in Copenhagen
on February 11, 1659) and Apachepigens Haevn (The Apache
Girl's Revenge), both directed by Carl Alstrup, Faldgruben
(The Pitfall), based on Zola's L'Assomoir, and De onde Veje
(The Evil Roads).[86]

Of these films made by Nordisk's rivals only Den lille
Hornblaeser has survived, though contemporary prints are
less than half the original length.   It was directed by Eduard
Schnedler-Sørensen, who became an important director at
Nordisk, and photographed by Alfred Lind, whose career took
him to several different film companies both as cameraman and
director, and whose name is connected with some of the most
interesting work of the period.

The film begins with some children playing. Two soldiers enter from behind a building, move toward the camera,
and post a notice on a wall. The camera pans slightly and
smoothly to follow them. A boy, after reading the notice,
signs up with the army as a bugler. The boy then bids
good-bye to his family. His sister's boyfriend also shows
up in uniform and bids good-bye. Then, in a scene that
apparently came later in the original film, the mother in the
family receives bad news. Finally, after another apparent
gap, a rival suitor for the daughter is arrested by soldiers
and is shot by the bugler boy when he tries to escape. The
actors use a very broad acting style and are always seen in
long shot. In general the exterior scenes are photographed
in a more interesting manner than the interiors.

Nordisk released a film with a similar title in September
1910 called Napoleon og hans lille Trompetist or Napoleon og
den lille Hornblaeser (Napoleon and His Little Bugler--U.S.
title, The Little Drummer Boy). The American title is confusing although the plot summary given in Moving Picture
World clears up the confusion. A drummer boy for Napoleon's
army is caught by the enemy. After being questioned about
the whereabouts of Napoleon's army, he escapes, but is recaptured. On hearing enemy officers discussing a plan of
attack, the drummer boy steals a bugle and blows an alarm
which alerts the French army. The boy is shot, however,
though he manages to salute Napoleon before dying. Napoleon
then places a medal for bravery on the dead boy's chest.

This film has not survived, so its artistic merit cannot
be measured against the mediocre quality of the Schnedler-
Sørensen film. Moving Picture World, however, commended
the film's artistic merit as "undeniable," noting that "the actors perform their parts admirably." It also described the
emotional effect of the film, stating that

as the film disappears leaving only the impression of

the poor little dead body, decorated with the coveted cross, one cannot prevent a choking sensation. The picture is so realistic that this occurs entirely unbidden.[87]

The film was directed by Viggo Larsen, who also played Napoleon, and was photographed by Alex Sørensen.[88] Throughout 1909 Larsen and Sørensen continued to be responsible for most, if not all, of Nordisk's feature output.

At least three other historical dramas were produced by Nordisk in 1909. Madame Sans Gêne (U.S. title, Madame Sans Gêne or The Duchess of Danzig) was based on the play by Sardou concerning Napoleon's laundress, who became the Duchess of Danzig when her husband, Sergeant Le Fevre, was made a duke for his bravery at the battle of Danzig. Et Revolutionsbryllup (U.S. title, A Wedding During the French Revolution) was based on a play by the well-known Danish playwright Sophus Michaelis which was being performed at the New Theater in New York at the time of the film's American release.[89] The story concerns a love triangle complicated by the politics of the revolution. Alaine, wife of the Marquis Erneste de Tressailles, is in charge of the castle while her husband is away with the royalist army. He returns, only to flee when the revolutionary army takes the castle. Soon captured, the marquis is condemned to death. Alaine appeals for help to her former lover, Colonel Marc-Arron, who is now with the revolutionary forces. Out of love for her, he takes the marquis' place awaiting execution and, even though this ruse is discovered, allows himself to be killed.

Moving Picture World was quite impressed with Et Revolutionsbryllup, citing its photography as having achieved "perfection" and noting:

> The adequate presentation of films of this character does much to overcome the adverse criticism aimed at the motion picture theater by ignorant and misguided critics. The Great Northern people [the name used by Nordisk Films Kompagni in America] deserve commendation for their good service in producing this film.[90]

The New York Dramatic Mirror took a different tone,

however. While praising some of the situations in the film,
the review criticized the acting, saying that the players
"fail utterly in putting any life or feeling into the action,"
and complained that were it not for the intertitles, the story
would make no sense.[91]

The film was only moderately successful, selling sixty-
one copies,[92] twenty-two of which had gone to the United
States.[93] Nordisk returned to the subject in 1914, however,
with a feature-length remake starring Valdemar Psilander.

The only surviving film of these historical dramas is
Et Budskab til Napoleon paa Elba (U.S. title, A Message to
Napoleon or An Episode in the Life of the Great Prisoner of
Elba). The plot concerns a planned rescue of Napoleon from
Elba by a group of friends. They send a messenger to tell
him of their plan, but a traitor informs Napoleon's enemies of
the plan, and an attempt is made to stop the messenger.
After a difficult journey the messenger succeeds in reaching
Napoleon.[94]

The film has little structural or stylistic interest, certainly less than the best of the surviving Viggo Larsen films,
such as Løvejagten and Et Drama fra Riddertiden. It does,
however, share the basic stylistic traits of earlier Larsen
films: camera kept in long shot, straight chronology of
events, a fair amount of location shooting (in this case more
than usual, including wooded areas for the horse chase and a
rocky sea coast for the Elba scenes), and even the joining of
exterior and interior shots to present one action. Here an
interior of the messenger climbing out a window onto a ladder
is followed by an exterior showing the messenger on the ladder. The film is shot mostly in exteriors, dynamically and
interestingly composed. Despite this positive aspect, however, the scenes are little more than illustrations of the intertitles.

Two other dramas from 1909 have survived, Pat Corner
(U.S. title, The Master Detective or The Attack on the Strong
Room) and Barnet som Velgører (U.S. title, Child as Benefactor), different in subject matter but stylistically similar and
typical of Nordisk productions in this period.

With Pat Corner Nordisk continued its production of
detective films begun with the 1908 Sherlock Holmes series.

Also like that series, the action is set in England, the favorite
location for Nordisk crime films, even those made at a later
period. In Pat Corner criminals attempt to break into a bank
vault by digging their way through a wall. A bank guard
hears the digging noise and calls the master detective Pat
Corner who, on investigating the noise, discovers the criminals and, with the help of the police, arrests them. The
film has no suspense and very little action. Each scene is
covered from one camera position, and the action is seen in
long shot, though there is one exception to this, a scene in
which Pat Corner enters close to the camera and walks away
from it. The sets are painted backdrops sometimes photographed at an angle. In the scenes in which the criminals
are digging through the wall, both sides of the wall are
seen at the same time by using a divided set. This essentially theatrical device stands in marked contrast to the
interior/exterior cutting pattern that was one of the stylistic
traits of early Nordisk films.

At least seven other detective films were made in 1909.[95]
Two of them concerned the master detective Nat Pinkerton.
In Nat Pinkerton I (U.S. title, Nat Pinkerton I or The Lost
Child) the detective encounters a professional bigamist who
tries to have the younger brother of one of his victims killed
to prevent him from telling his sister about her future husband. Pinkerton, of course, saves the boy and apprehends
the criminals. In Nat Pinkerton II (U.S. title, Nat Pinkerton
II) he foils a band of anarchists who plan to assassinate a
governor with a bomb. Moving Picture World commended the
film for having "plenty of action in it, and what is better than
that, it has no killing."[96]

Three more Sherlock Holmes films were also made that
year. In Droske 519 (U.S. title, Cab. No. 519) Holmes saves
a man who has been kidnapped in order that someone else can
take his place and so come into a fortune left by a recently
deceased uncle. A forgotten money purse and a quickly noted
cab number provide Holmes with the clues he needs to apprehend the criminals, one of whom is caught as he is about to
dump the drugged body of his victim into the ocean.

Den graa Dame (U.S. title, The Gray Dame) is set in
an English castle and concerns a legend about a ghost, the
Gray Dame, whose appearance always coincides with the death
of the oldest son of the house. A visitor takes advantage of

the legend and plans to kill both the lord of the castle and
his son in order to get the title and estate for himself.
After a series of encounters involving secret doors, a dun-
geon in which Holmes is left to die, and a final confrontation
in which Holmes impersonates the threatened son, the criminal
is captured and unmasked.

From its plot description Sangerindens Diamanter (U.S.
title, The Theft of the Diamonds) appears to have been the
most action-packed of the three Sherlock Holmes films. The
apprehension of the thief is accomplished in last-minute rescue
style as Holmes arrives at the scene of the crime, an actress's
apartment, just as the criminal has left via a rope to the
roof. Holmes gives pursuit by himself climbing the rope,
only to have it cut from above. After saving himself from
a fall, Holmes succeeds in reaching the roof where a chase
from rooftop to rooftop ends in the fall and capture of the
villain.

The enthusiastic reception accorded the 1908 Sherlock
Holmes films by Moving Picture World was repeated for the
1909 films. Den graa Dame, the most commercially successful
of the three, having sold 100 copies, was especially well-
received.[97]

> The story is full of exciting movements, and the
> plot is worked out with decision and sureness of
> attack. There is not a lingering moment in the story,
> which moves rapidly, tensely and convincingly, as all
> detective stories should. Above all it is exceedingly
> well acted and then it has been very nicely set and
> mounted. The furniture of the castle, the uniforms,
> the carriage and the horses, everything, in fact,
> are provided to give the romance an aspect of ver-
> isimilitude.[98]

The reference to the verisimilitude of detail is particularly
noteworthy since this became increasingly important at Nordisk and is characteristic of the best of their dramas throughout the period under consideration.

Neither part of a series nor based on a famous detective is the 1909 Museumsmysteriet (U.S. title, The Somnam-
bulist). It is also atypical of the detective film in that it
has no criminal opponent to test the detective's skill, though

it does have a mystery. The supposed thief turns out to be
the former director of the museum of the title, who steals
things while sleepwalking, much to the relief of his daughter
and son-in-law, the new director of the museum. Perhaps
in keeping with its lesser status as a detective film, it sold
only thirty-one copies.[99]

Not much more successful than Museumsmysteriet was
a crime series about a master criminal named Dr. Nicola,
played by August Blom who was soon to become the most important director at Nordisk. The series was ended after only
three films, most likely because of poor sales.[100] In all only
123 copies were sold.[101] Moving Picture World mentions only
the second and third film of the series as having been released in the United States, although Nordisk Films shipping
invoices show that twenty-two copies of Dr. Nicola I (The
Hidden Treasure) were sent to the New York branch office
in August and October of 1909. This first of the series is
about a band of criminals who attempt, in vain, to stop Dr.
Nicola from finding a treasure.[102]

From the plot description, it is unclear whether Dr.
Nicola II (U.S. title, How Dr. Nicola Procured the Chinese
Cane) is a continuation of Dr. Nicola I, although the third
film in the series, Dr. Nicola III (U.S. title, Mystery of the
Lama Convent or Dr. Nicola in Tibet), does continue the
story of part two. Together, parts two and three sound
like an early version of The Maltese Falcon. A cane belong-
ing to the monks of a Lama monastery is lost, eventually ending up in the possession of an old sailor named China Peat.
This cane was originally intended as an insignia for a high
priest who had been chosen as one of three elders of the
monastery. Becoming one of the elders also means gaining
the secrets of life and death. Dr. Nicola, after spending a
fortune tracking down the cane, discovers it in the possession
of an English solicitor named Mr. Wilrey. By kidnapping Mr.
Wilrey's daughter, and after an adventure that takes them
all to the South Seas, Dr. Nicola procures the cane. In Dr.
Nicola III the villain gains entrance to the monastery through
the use of a disguise and the cane. Having fooled the monks
and having gained the secrets of life and death, Dr. Nicola
is then unmasked as an impostor by an old Chinese. Despite
this, Dr. Nicola escapes, taking with him a case of valuable
data and objects. Apparently this ending was meant to pave
the way for further installments in the series, which, as already mentioned, were never made.

More successful than the Dr. Nicola films was another
crime film with an Oriental flavor. Den gule Djaevel (U.S.
title, Tsing Fu, the Yellow Devil) is set in England and concerns a Chinese magician named Tsing Fu who makes lecher-
ous advances to Daisy, a music hall singer. Daisy's sweetheart, Joe Belling, punishes Tsing Fu by knocking him down,
and, in revenge, Tsing Fu has Daisy kidnapped. The kidnapping, typically for films involving Oriental criminals, is
planned in an opium den. When Belling discovers that Daisy
is missing, he questions Tsing Fu, who, of course, denies
any knowledge of the girl's whereabouts. Not believing him,
however, Belling follows Tsing Fu home, after first informing
a well-known detective where he has gone. Belling is over-
whelmed by Tsing Fu's associates and dropped through a
trap door. The detective shows up disguised as a Chinese
and, after gaining admittance to Tsing Fu's house, finds Belling and releases him. The two men then find Tsing Fu, release Daisy, and take Tsing Fu prisoner.

The racial overtones of this film and the stereotypic
manner in which the Chinese are apparently treated are quite
common for films not only of this period, but throughout the
history of the western cinema. Certainly, this treatment of
the Chinese did not hurt the film's reception. Moving Picture
World was quite impressed:

> A thrilling and convincing detective story worked out
> with all the care and attention which characterizes
> the Great Northern films. The same qualities of
> acting and the same effort to make the acting sym-
> pathetic is shown here that were such prominent
> factors in the success of the Sherlock Holmes series.
> It is a thrilling story, wonderfully told.[103]

Ebbe Neergaard's opinion of the crime films probably
sums up their function in Nordisk Films output:

> The crime films undoubtedly had their importance in
> the training of directors and actors for something
> like modern social depiction of contemporary milieus.
> They are also characteristic of the international line
> of production with an eye on the foreign market,
> which Ole Olsen steadily upheld.[104]

The international importance of the crime film in Nordisk

planning is attested to by the fact that from one-third to one-half of the copies of each crime film were sold in the United States alone, [105] which was not generally the most important of the Nordisk markets. [106] That many of the crime films, including parts of the Dr. Nicola series and later films in this genre, were set in England may also indicate how important the British market was for this type of film.

The other surviving contemporary drama from 1909, Barnet som Velgører (Child as Benefactor) is as moral and conventional as the crime films are sensational. It tells the story of a newsboy who saves a down-and-out man from suicide. After the man gets a job delivering groceries, the man and the newsboy find a room to share. One day, as he is working outside his employer's house, the man saves his employer's daughter who has fallen out of a window. In gratitude, the employer gives the man money and a better job and buys him furniture for his room. His new position allows him to marry as well as provide a place in his new home for the newsboy.

This sentimental story is handled in a routine way. The actors are always seen in full length, the interior sets are generally quite fake, with painted street scenes outside of the windows, and the scenes are made in uninterrupted takes, related to each other in a simple and straightforward continuity. One scene, however, the girl's fall, is cut in that interior/exterior pattern characteristic of Nordisk films of these early years. As the girl falls out the window, there is a cut to an exterior shot of the building. The girl falls into frame and is caught by the man. The action then returns to an interior as the girl's mother and father rush into the room from which the girl has fallen. Finally, there is a cut back to the street scene showing the man and girl lying on the ground and the entrance of the mother and father. In general, the social and moral characteristics of Barnet som Velgører are typical of many of the contemporary dramas made by Nordisk throughout the early period. Although these characteristics are not well-developed in this film, they appear to have been more clearly central in many of the others, at least as they are outlined in the surviving plot descriptions and reviews.

The class divisions so easily bridged in Barnet som Velgører are the main concern of En Kvinde af Folket (U.S. title,

A Woman of the People). A wealthy manufacturer falls in love
with one of his employees, but the girl's father, also an em-
ployee, objects. Because of his attitude he is discharged.
Soon the manufacturer becomes tired of the girl and casts
her off, paying her a sum of money which apparently satis-
fies her. When the girl's father discovers the source of the
money, he is angry. In the meantime, the manufacturer becomes engaged to another girl, but the father confronts and
denounces him for his former behavior. A turn in fortunes
has the manufacturer's business ruined by fire and the workman becomes wealthy through the sale of an invention. The
bitterness between the two men is finally dissolved through
the intervention of the workman's daughter, ending in a reconciliation of the former lovers.

Moving Picture World cited En Kvinde af Folket as "an
international moving picture drama," the kind of film that
could be "understood at a glance by epople in all parts of
the world":

> Think of it, now! This Great Northern picture was
> made in far off Copenhagen, the capital city of Den-
> mark, and to us, in the ultra modern metropolis of
> the New World, the action of the piece is as clear as
> daylight. Now this is what is wanted in moving pic-
> ture story telling--no ambiguity, doubt or obscur-
> ity.... The photography of this picture is up to
> the fine standard which the Great Northern Company
> have set for themselves, the tints and tones being
> judiciously chosen. What we like about it, however,
> is the intense realism of the acting. Every word,
> every gesture of the principal characters in this
> piece is a masterpiece of carefully studied histrion-
> ics. This is another case where the illusion is so
> perfect that one seems, as it were, to be looking at
> scenes from life itself. Great Northern films, which
> are going from success to success, have a polish
> and finish about them which give them that distinc-
> tion of quality which lifts the moving picture onto
> the plane of the pictorial.[107]

I have quoted from this review at length because it
illustrates several important points in relation to both Great
Northern and Moving Picture World. First, it shows Moving
Picture World's commitment to film as an international medium,

a commitment based on the box office potential created by the
various nationalities presented in the United States. "Nom-
inally American," wrote the editors, "the United States is
without doubt the most cosmopolitan country in the world."
After citing several specific national groups, they went on
to remind their readers that these groups "constitute so many
great publics for moving pictures made specially to appeal
to them." Finally, they saw the competition arising from production in countries throughout the world as "the soul of
trade" that would result in "nothing but good to the moving
picture as an international method of graphic and pictorial
expression...."108

Second, Moving Picture World's belief in clear story
telling that leaves "no ambiguity, doubt or obscurity," though
part of an overly conservative attitude toward the aesthetics
of the medium, represented a demand for a high standard of
production at a time when the medium was struggling for respectability. Moving Picture World constantly fought for quality by direct address of the producers and exhibitors while
it defended them from attacks by the representatives of official culture and the protectors of public morality who sought
to denigrate and restrict the medium.

The third point contained in the review of En Kvinde
af Folket is that of "the fine standard [of photography] which
the Great Northern Company have set for themselves." This
is the characteristic of Nordisk films most commented on by
writers for Moving Picture World, and is all the more noteworthy since the magazine often condemned pictures for poor
photography.109 The emphasis that Ole Olsen placed on the
photographic quality of his productions was recognized early
in his career when Nordisk Films was awarded a gold medal
at an international film exposition held in Hamburg in 1908.110
Ebbe Neergaard cites the photographic quality of Nordisk films
as "one of the two characteristics of N.F.'s production that
acquired for it a world market";111 and it is clear from later
Nordisk films that Olsen continued to stress this characteristic. During the peak years at Nordisk the company's films
maintained very high photographic standards, so much so
that even the films' weaknesses are often obscured by their
visual brilliance.

Another quality of Nordisk films, and the fourth point
of the review, is the "intense realism," not only of the acting,

but of the production as a whole. Judging from the surviving
Nordisk films made between 1906 and 1909, this claim for realism is overstated. However, it is a quality of Nordisk films
that continued to gain in importance and is clearly seen in
the major melodramas of the second decade of the century,
especially in their acting, decor, and treatment of space--
qualities which will be examined in detail in the next chapter.

Finally, the review mentions the "going from success to
success" of the Great Northern films. In general, this is
true of the great period of expansion of the Nordisk Films
Kompagni, not only in the United States but also, and perhaps especially, in continental Europe. The critical and financial success of the company is indisputable, though in the
case of the American operation, not as simple as Moving Picture World's statement makes it appear. Business correspond-
ence between the Copenhagen main office of Nordisk and the
New York branch office qualifies the impression that consistently emerges from reading Moving Picture World, giving a
picture of less than satisfactory financial success.

In another working-class drama of 1909, Bomben (U.S.
title, The Shell), a worker is fired after standing up to a
foreman who unjustly accuses him of laziness. Fear over his
future and the welfare of his family drive the worker insane.
In his madness he plots to blow up a new ship being built
by his former company. His wife tries to prevent this by
fetching a doctor, but while she is gone the worker goes to
the shipyard and plants the bomb. The foreman, however,
sees him leaving the yard and, being suspicious, tries to stop
him. A chase in boats ensues, resulting in the apprehension
of the worker after a fight in the water. The worker is revived and with his last energy reveals the place where the
bomb has been planted. After learning that the bomb has
been disposed of, the worker dies with a smile on his face,
happy that his plot has not succeeded.

Although En Kvinde af Folket and Bomben share a concern with injustice toward the working class, which Barnet
som Velgører does not, all three films finally present the em-
ployers as essentially good characters. In Barnet som Velgører
this is never in question, while in En Kvinde af Folket the
goodness takes some time to manifest itself and in Bomben
the worker's repentance for his attempted sabotage effectively
puts the blame on him for the original conflict with the foreman.

The apparent social and economic characteristics of all three
films are essentially depoliticized through sentimentality and
moralizing.

The moralizing that creeps into these films is at the
heart of another group of 1909 melodramas that are typical
not only of the Danish cinema, but of most national cinemas
in this period.

Heltemod Forsoner (U.S. title, Heroism Reconciles)
combines elements of the temperance melodrama, the idea of
duty, and the sensational theatrics of a person tied to the
railroad tracks. A railroad worker is tempted by an evil
companion to have a drink. The first drink leads to others,
and the man reports to work intoxicated. This, of course,
results in his being fired and, eventually, in the ruin of his
family. At this point the film changes genres and has the
man overhear a plot to rob a train. Responding to his sense
of duty which has remained intact, he sets out to prevent
the robbery. The crooks, however, subdue the hero and tie
him to the railroad tracks. Through a supreme effort the
man still manages to change a switch and prevent the accident
that the crooks had planned. Shortly after, he is freed by a
railroad guard and taken to the company traffic manager to
report. His heroism is rewarded by the reinstatement of his
job, after which the man hurries home to his family.

Another, less melodramatic, type of heroism is represented in En lille Helt (U.S. title, A Boy Hero or The Fisherman's Son). A fisherman has two sons. One day the father's
boat does not return and, despite a storm at sea, the favorite
son sets out to find him. He finds his father clinging to an
overturned boat and brings him safely to shore. The next
day a government official gives the son a medal of heroism.

The most intriguing part of this plot is the sea rescue,
a scene which certainly presented an opportunity for exciting
location shooting. Since neither the film nor its reviews are
available, it is impossible to determine how this scene was
handled. It is a type of scene, however, that appears in
later Danish films concerned with realistic representation of
the sea and its dangers. That many Danish films from this
period use the sea as a dramatic element is not surprising,
given the importance of the sea in the history of the country.

A good example is another 1909 moral drama, Praestens Sønner (U.S. title, The Sons of the Minister). A minister has two sons, John and Abel. One of them is following in his father's footsteps and is himself studying to be a minister. The other is a sailor, and in temperament is just the opposite of his more sober and conventional brother. Both love their adopted sister Cassie, though she loves John, the sailor brother. After a fight at a village dance, for which John is arrested, the minister makes him leave home. Cassie marries Abel and several years pass, during which time the minister dies. On one of his voyages John is shipwrecked along the coast near his old home. He saves himself and manages to stagger to the house which now belongs to Abel who has taken over the father's ministry. Cassie is alone when John arrives, and she helps him. Afraid that Abel will discover John, however, she makes him leave, though not soon enough to prevent Abel from discovering his visit. In a rage Abel takes a gun and goes to the sea cliff to find John. Just as he is about to shoot him, Abel slips and falls off the cliff. John carries his brother's body back to the house, where Abel lives just long enough to realize the injustice of his attempt to kill John and to ask him to take care of Cassie.

The roots of this story, of course, are to be found in the story of Cain and Abel; the idea of the black sheep of the family being sent away is common. In Danish film history the subject appeared again in a much more elaborate form in the 1913 feature Under Blinkfyrets Straaler (Under the Flashing Light's Beams), which will be discussed in the next chapter.

Another story with Biblical roots is told in Den vanartede Søn (U.S. title, The Prodigal Son). Once again, the son in a family, Gus, must leave home, but this time because he is convicted of theft and sent to prison, an event which causes his father to die of a broken heart. Gus's sister, Helen, marries Howard, a grocer who has long been in love with Helen but whom she had previously rejected. The mother moves in with them, and the three live happily until Gus's release from prison. Not knowing that the grocery store belongs to his brother-in-law, Gus plans to rob it. During the robbery, however, he realizes where he is and tries to leave. Howard and Helen catch him and, although Howard is willing to let Gus go, the police arrive and take him away. For the purpose of identification, Gus's mother must go to the police

station. Gus is so shocked at seeing his mother that it
changes him. He is convicted, but after serving his time,
he decides to go straight. Helped by an ex-convict's society
Gus sets off for a new life in a foreign country.

Many of the plots of Danish films are rooted in the
actions of dishonest, wayward, and ungrateful sons, who
often, however, change their ways and make up for their
previous misdeeds. In Arvingen til Kragsholm (U.S. title,
Ruined by His Son) an old squire leaves his estate in the
hands of his eldest son when his doctors prescribe a long
sea voyage to restore his health. No sooner is the father
gone than the son begins to squander the family fortune,
despite the efforts of his mother and sister to dissuade him.
The squire returns to find the estate in the hands of cred-
itors. He sends his son away, and the young man decides
to kill himself. A neighbor girl, who has long been in love
with him, persuades him to go to America instead and begin
a new life. He agrees, provided she goes with him as his
wife. After achieving success in America, he returns home,
buys back the estate, turns it over to his father, and is
reconciled with his family.

The idea of duty common to many of the films I have
described is nowhere more sharply set off than in Laegens
Offer (U.S. title, Doctor's Sacrifice). The plot and moral
structure of this film are quite similar to those of D. W. Griffith's 1909 drama The Country Doctor. Dr. Kramer has a
comfortable home in which he is seen with his wife and two
children, a boy and a girl. The children are brought in by
the nurse who is about to put them to bed. The doctor
notices that the boy looks ill and begins to examine him.
Before he finishes the examination, a message arrives that the
child of a poor workman is seriously ill. Although Kramer
hesitates to leave his own child, he does so out of a sense
of duty. While attending the workman's child, the doctor's
son dies. Inconsolable at his loss, Dr. Kramer sinks into a
deep melancholy from which not even his daughter can rouse
him. One day he is in the park with his daughter when the
workman sees him and tries to thank him again for what he
did. To the workman's surprise the doctor does not respond,
partly because he blames the workman for the death of his
own son. As he is about to leave, the workman sees the
doctor's daughter playing with a poisonous snake and quickly
acts to save the child, though he is bitten in the process.

This awakens the doctor from his lethargy, and he moves to save the workman's life. Because of this incident, the doctor's life is renewed, and he becomes good friends with the workman and his family.

On the level of the narrative Laegens Offer is more conventional than The Country Doctor. Griffith concludes his plot with the doctor's depression over the child's death and then carries this narrative element over to a treatment of the landscape around the doctor's home. Whereas the film opens with a long pan across the sunny countryside, it ends with a reverse pan across the same landscape, but now shrowded in shadows. We do not, of course, know how Laegens Offer looked, but the additional narrative material concerning the poisonous snake, the chance meeting of the doctor and the workman, and the sudden change of mental attitude on the doctor's part do indicate a much less tightly structured work and certainly a more artificial and dramatically weakened story.[112]

The intensely suffering individual is common enough in film and finds numerous antecedents on the stage and in literature. A familiar example is seen in Faderen (U.S. title, A Father's Grief). It is the sentimental story of a man who is called away from his happy home on an urgent business trip. While away his son becomes ill and dies, despite the efforts of two doctors. The father rushes home but arrives too late. His grief makes him insane, and he is placed in an asylum, unable to recognize even his wife. One day the wife sees a boy who looks very much like her dead son. Since the boy's parents are extremely poor, she is able to make arrangements to adopt the boy. The father is then brought home to a scene like that which opens the film, the child playing on the lawn while the mother sews under a tree. He is so startled by what he sees that his sanity returns and he is reconciled with his wife and new son.

Although it did not give this film a major review, Moving Picture World found it to be "a touching heart story [sic], sympathetically acted, adequately staged and intelligently photographed." It saw the film as having wide audience appeal and noted that "a mist will gather in front of the eyes before all the scenes are passed."[113]

Often these personal melodramas were given a social

dimension, as in En Livsroman (U.S. title, Never Despair).
A doctor's housekeeper is liked by everyone and admired by
a number of young men. Although the doctor is also in love
with her, he does not propose until it is too late. On the
day that he finally proposes, she accepts a young man who is
a painter. They marry and have a child, but soon after, the
painter is brought home dead from a fall. The girl struggles
to make a living for herself and the child by sewing, using a
machine she bought on an installment plan. She cannot meet
the payments, however, and the machine is repossessed. Des-
perate, she tries to kill both herself and the child by closing
the damper on her coal-burning stove. A neighbor smells the
fumes and finds the mother and child unconscious. She calls
a doctor who turns out to be the girl's former employer. The
doctor revives them and once again asks the girl to be his
wife. She accepts and for a second time finds happiness.

Despite the Cinderella ending of the film which bridges
class distinctions, the portrayal of the woman's struggle to
make a living and of the callous treatment she receives from
the sewing machine man provides a basic link to social reality,
one that Ole Olsen himself knew from first-hand experience.
Olsen's poverty-stricken childhood and his need to make his
own way in the world must have given him an understanding of, and probably a sympathy for, others in the same condition. D. W. Griffith, who was certainly masterful in his
treatment of the suffering and the poor, also knew these conditions from his own life and, through his films, gave his
audiences some of the knowledge he himself had gained. Of
course, both these men, and other movie pioneers who also
grew up in hard circumstances, were equally capable of creating upper-class milieus and the life of ease, often having
the acquisition of this state act as a means of forgetting the
past, and along with it, its reality as a social condition.

The castoffs and the forgotten of society do not always
get taken in, however, and sometimes even have no wish to.
Landstrygerliv (U.S. title, Vagabond Life) concerns a family
of gypsies who are hounded by the police when they try to
perform at a fair. When they cnanot produce their papers or
a permission to perform, the police take away the grandfather
who is the guardian of his fourteen-year-old granddaughter
and ten-year-old grandson. He cannot pay the fine levied
against him and is thrown into jail. His grandchildren visit
a judge who is touched by their devotion to the grandfather.

The judge orders the release of the old man and sends the
gypsy family on their way with some money. Once again they
enjoy the life of the road.

    In Fredløs (U.S. title, An Outcast's Christmas) a young
tramp "cast out by society and moved on from place to place
by the police," finds himself at the farm of a rich family on
Christmas Eve. Peering through the windows, he watches
the joy of the family inside. Comparing himself with the tired
old horse of the postman that is tied outside the door, he
shares his last crust of bread with the animal, and creeps
inside the stable to sleep. He is soon discovered by the
farmer's little girl, however, who in pity has brought the
old horse out of the cold. The girl, finding out that the
tramp is hungry, runs to the house for food. No sooner
has he eaten it, than he realizes the police are coming. He
kisses the girl on the forehead and runs out into the night.
The girl returns to the house and cries in her mother's arms,
"having had the first glimmer of a cold, cruel world."

    As usual, the basic social content of both films is
softened by the sentiment, though this may not have affected
their drama. What Moving Picture World said about Fredløs
would probably apply to Landstrygerliv and other similar
films:

> Dramatically strong and powerfully suggestive, this
> film, pathetic in its appeal to humanity, deserves a
> wide circulation.... It surely must do much good
> wherever it is shown.[114]

    The idea that Fredløs, and indeed the film medium as
a whole, could do good was very important to the philosophy
of Moving Picture World. The magazine often countered ad-
verse criticism of the movies with claims for their educational
and uplifting value, a claim also made by Ole Olsen. Ebbe
Neergaard refers to this quality of Olsen's thought by quot-
ing Olsen's own statements regarding movies' educational task.
Although Neergaard does this with specific reference to Olsen's desire to give the masses a view of how the upper classes
live, it is not unreasonable to apply this same educational zeal,
no matter how naive it may appear, to the films which taught
little moral lessons, as well as to those which showed the
masses "how the society members behaved, how they lived,
and how they ate!"[115]

More sensational are two moral dramas of 1909, both of which arrive at their moral lessons via sexual desire and attempted murder. To Guldgravere (U.S. title, Temptations of the Gold Fields or The Two Gold Diggers) tells the story of two friends, one much older than the other, who both work the gold fields. The older man, who has been the more successful of the two, has developed a fatherly affection for his friend. The younger man becomes attracted to a half-breed girl who convinces him to kill his friend and steal his gold. Afraid of losing the girl, the young man sneaks into his friend's cabin in order to kill and rob him. The older man, knowing that something is wrong, has made a dummy out of his blankets and watches as his friend enters the cabin. At the last minute, however, the young man realizes he cannot go through with his plan and quickly leaves. Returning to his own cabin, he discovers the girl trying to steal the little amount of gold he has found. Realizing that she has only been after money, he rushes at her but she flees. Later the two friends are reconciled.

Haevnen (U.S. title, Vengeance or The Forester's Sacrifice) concerns a forester whose wife is having an affair with the nobleman who employs him. One evening, in order to be with the wife, the nobleman tells the forester that he has been assaulted by a poacher. The forester leaves to catch the man and, as soon as he is gone, the nobleman and the forester's wife embrace. The forester sees them, however, and plans to kill his employer with the help of the notorious poacher the employer complained about. Claiming he could not find the poacher, the forester convinces the nobleman to join him in the search the next day. The nobleman's mother and wife, however, fearing for his safety, try to dissuade him from going, but to no avail. The nobleman's wife tries once again to stop her husband by following him. Seeing the woman's love, the forester repents of his scheme and persuades the nobleman to exchange clothes with him. As they come to the place of the planned murder, the poacher fires and kills the forester. Now that he is dead, the forester's wife realizes how deeply she really loved him.

Love, of course, whether true or mistaken, is the motivating force in many film stories, and one of the most common forms of the love story is the triangle, which gains in typicality when it ends in death and tragedy. Ørneaegget (U.S. title, The Eagle's Egg or The Rival Lovers) and

Konflikter (U.S. title, The Jump to Death) are classic examples
of this kind of melodrama. Ørneægget takes place in Corsica
and involves two friends, Carlo and Enrico, who are both in
love with the same woman, Marietta. Ultimately, their friend-
ship suffers, and they almost have a knife fight, which Marietta stops by telling them she will marry the one who can
first bring her an eagle's egg from a spot high in the cliffs.
Carlo gets the egg first but falls to his death. Enrico takes
the egg from Carlo's hand and returns to Marietta. They
are married, but Enrico's happiness is marred by the memory
of how he got the egg. One night Carlo's image rises up
between Enrico and Marietta, and in his fright and anguish
Enrico rushes out of the house. The next day Marietta finds
his body at the bottom of the rocks.

Konflikter's triangle is composed of one man and two
women. Pierre and Marcelle are circus performers in love
with each other. While performing at the Hippodrome, Lola,
an Italian singer, becomes jealous of Marcelle's success and
decides to steal away Pierre's affections. She does this but
soon drops Pierre who now learns the mistake he has made
in giving up Marcelle. In despair he agrees to try a dangerous leap, hoping not to survive it. He writes to Marcelle
telling her what he is about to do and asking her forgiveness.
The letter reawakens Marcelle's love, and she rushes off to
stop Pierre. She arrives just as Pierre falls to the circus
floor; thinking him dead, she throws herself over his body.
He shows signs of life, however, and after a period of time,
with careful nursing from Marcelle, Pierre recovers. "Realizing the value of true love," they marry and once again work
as a team.

One significant element of Konflikter is its circus setting,
frequently used as background for Danish dramas of the early
period. Ebbe Neergaard has noted that circus was "one of
the sweeping fashions of the time,"[116] and Ole Olsen, as well
as other producers, ever sensitive to popular taste, made
sure this taste was satisfied. Among the circus films are a
number of notable ones: Afgrunden (The Abyss) and Den
sorte Drøm (The Black Dream), Asta Nielsen's first two films;
Dødsspring til Hest fra Cirkuskuplen (Death Jump on Horse
from the Circus Dome), which sold at least 245 and perhaps
as many as 295 copies;[117] De fire Djævle (The Four Devils),
based on a short story of the same name by Herman Bang,
and cited by Ebbe Neergaard as "the most important circus

film of the period";[118] and <u>Den flyvende Cirkus</u> (The Flying
Circus), directed by Alfred Lind, who had been cameraman
on <u>De fire Djævle</u> and <u>Den hvide Slavehandel</u>, one of the most
influential of the white slave films, produced by Fotorama and
imitated by Nordisk the same year.

Less common than the films with contemporary settings
are the costume and adventure films which were a significant
part of the total output throughout the period under consideration. The reason for this may be revealed in the following
statement from a 1910 <u>Moving Picture World</u> review of <u>Kærli-
ghed i Orienten</u> (U.S. title, <u>Saved from the Sultan's Judg-
ment</u>):

> An Oriental film of great merit and absorbing in-
> terest.... Anything which adequately illustrates any
> of the features of the mysterious Orient, with its
> wealth of imagery, appealing directly to the curios-
> ity, is certain to be popular, and this picture is no
> exception to the rule.[119]

This appeal to the curiosity of people about things of
which they know little is the same justification that Ole Olsen
used for the upper-class subjects that characterize much of
Nordisk production. He tells us in his autobiography:

> I knew people's taste well enough to know that they
> wanted to see something from life around them, as
> it is lived in places where they could not themselves
> go. The young people wanted to see beautiful par-
> ties and elegant dresses.... They also liked to see
> how a count, a baron, or a king lived and how he
> ate his dinner.[120]

<u>Kærlighed i Orienten</u> centers its story around a harem,
a feature of the Orient that has been appropriated numerous
times by American and European films. It tells the story of
a young girl, Suleika, who becomes one of the wives of the
sultan. Unhappy about her life in the harem, she attempts
to get help from a young American diplomat with whom she
has fallen in love from afar. She sends a note to the young
man by way of the daughter of another diplomat. Unfortunately, this woman is also in love with the young man and,
in jealousy, sends the note to the sultan. In his anger the
sultan orders the death of his wife by drowning in the river.

One of Suleika's servants tells the American about this sentence. Waiting that night by the river, the American sees
the girl, bound in a sack, thrown into the water. Through
a great effort he saves her, and they leave the Orient together.

Although the conception of the Orient in this film is
naive, it probably did appeal to popular notions, as well as
help form them. In any case, Moving Picture World was convinced and found the film to be "of great merit and absorbing
interest," noting that "the players have performed these parts
to perfection and the photographer has not been dilatory in
his portion."[121] Seven years later Nordisk Films made a
feature-length film that exploited interest in the harem. Entitled Maharadjahens Yndlingshustru (The Maharaja's Favorite
Wife), it tells the story of a European girl who falls in love
with a Maharaja and marries him, only to find herself part of
a harem. This film will be discussed in chapter three.

Less exotic, though equally romantic in conception,
are three other dramas that take place outside the conventional
social milieu that characterizes most of the 1909 dramatic films
described so far.

Grevinde X (U.S. title, The Red Domino) has an aristocratic setting used for intrigue rather than for satisfying class
curiosity. The action takes place during a masked ball given
by a prince. Prior to the ball, Baron Lerche had overheard
Countess X and a friend planning to take revenge on the
prince. Both the countess, in Spanish costume, and the
baron, in red domino, attend the ball. The baron's plan is
to watch the countess and expose her plot, thus saving the
prince's life. The countess, however, notices that the red
domino is watching her and has him taken aside by some
friends who gag and tie him. The baron gets free from his
bonds, goes for the police, and returns to the party in time
to apprehend the countess who has poisoned the prince's
drink. After explaining everything to the prince, the baron
makes all the guests unmask and points out the rest of the
culprits. According to Moving Picture World's description,
the prince calmly reassures his guests with the line: "My
dear guests, don't let this little incident disturb our pleasure;
it was only an attempt on my life."

The film was both tinted and toned, processes which

apparently added to the effect of the masked ball. Moving
Picture World commented:

> ... the producer had many opportunities for a great
> spectacular display, of which he has taken full ad-
> vantage; and then the photographic colorist has done
> some excellent work on the film....

Also, in catering to an audience's attraction to the unusual,
the magazine suggested that "as an illustration of court life
and intrigue, the film will doubtless please many moving picture audiences in this country."[122]

The New York Dramatic Mirror, too, praised the photography of Grevinde X but was displeased with both the acting
and the narrative organization, citing "indifferent pantomime
and lack of clarity in the telling of the story."[123]

En Røvers Død (U.S. title, The Death of the Brigand
Chief) treated the audience to a view of bandit life. After
a group of bandits have preyed upon the inhabitants of the
neighboring villages, a company of soldiers succeed in round-
ing them up. Due to the laxity of the army sergeant and
sentries who had been assigned to guard the bandits, their
chief escapes. The sergeant is arrested for negligence and
sentenced to die before a firing squad. The sergeant's sweetheart, who had earlier been kind to the brigand chief by
bringing him food in prison, sets out to find the bandit in
hope of persuading him to return. Finding him, she begs for
his help. Though he first hesitates, he finally agrees to go
back, and they arrive just as the sergeant is to be shot.
The brigand takes the sergeant's place "knowing that he had
done one good deed in his life."

The storybook ending of En Røvers Død, though con-
tradicting the overall realistic aspirations of Nordisk films,
is typical of the period and indicates that the realism was to
be found more in production values than in story. Forlist
(U.S. title, The Captain's Wife) is a clear example of this
characteristic. The story is fantastic, but the use of setting,
judging from Nordisk sea stories that have survived, was
probably well within believable bounds. Captain Burns leaves
his wife and children to go on a long voyage. In the past,
the family had often gone with him, and the captain's wife
has learned a good deal about navigation from these voyages.

She uses this knowledge to plot her husband's course on a map at home. One night she has a vivid dream that her husband's ship is wrecked. She takes this dream as real, and sets out in search of her husband. She goes to the spot she had charted on her map and there finds her husband on a desert island. She arrives just in time to save him from death.

According to Moving Picture World, one of the most original of the 1909 dramas, one which also uses the sea, was Anarkister om Bord (U.S. title, Anarchists on Board). Citing it as "a picture story strong in plot, convincing in its rendering and, of course, excellent in photography," the magazine predicted that it would be "very popular among the independent houses."[124] The story concerns a group of anarchists smuggled aboard a ship in order to plant a bomb. Traveling on the ship is Prince Albert, who is on a diplomatic mission for the king. The police on shore learn of the assassination attempt and send a wireless message to the ship. During a search for the bomb, the anarchists escape in a small boat, though not without being spotted. Some of the crew give chase and capture the anarchists. On their return to the ship, the anarchists are forced, at gunpoint, to reveal the location of the bomb. The wireless operator, who has been leading the search, picks up the bomb and throws it into the sea. Exhausted by the search, he faints, though he soon revives and is rewarded by the prince. That the film was photographed aboard a real ocean liner strongly impressed the critic for Moving Picture World.

Although so few dramas have survived from 1909, all but one were made by Viggo Larsen for Nordisk Films. Since they are similar to Larsen/Nordisk dramas produced in preceding years, it is fair to assume that they are representative of the total Nordisk output of dramas in that year. The same assumption may apply to the comedies as well, although only two of them are definitely known to have been directed by Larsen. In addition, the five surviving comedies represent the three principal categories of comedy made by Nordisk. Vidundercigaren (U.S. title, The Wonderful Cigar), directed by Viggo Larsen, and Den nærsynede Guvernante (U.S. title, The Short-Sighted Governess) are farces; Tryllekunstneren (U.S. title, The Conjuror) and Heksen og Cyklisten (U.S. title, The Witch and the Cycle) are trick films; and Menneskeaben (U.S. title, The Human Ape or Darwin's Triumph) is a music hall act.

Present day prints of <u>Vidundercigaren</u> are incomplete.
About one-fourth of the original material is missing; apparently
most, if not all, from the end. The film begins in a café; the
set is a painted background. A man is smoking a cigar that
is so obnoxious that it not only repels people but knocks them
down. He gets onto a real street car, and there is a change
to a studio interior of the street car with a painted scene
visible thorugh the windows. Using his cigar he clears away
his fellow passengers in order to get a seat. In the next
scene, entered into without any transition from the previous
one, he is in a tailor's shop. Again using his cigar, he
forces the tailor to give him a suit. Next he goes to a house
and is met by a servant. Here the fragment ends.

The humor of <u>Vidundercigaren</u> is rather crude, the situations unimaginative, and the performance by the cigar
smoker is more mugging for the camera than acting, though
not unlike much of early Mack Sennett. Overall, the surviving material gives enough sense of the whole that the missing
material is only of academic interest, despite the fact that
<u>Moving Picture World</u> found the film to be "lively" and pre-
dicted it would "keep your audience good natured from beginning to end."[125] More sophisticated, however, are the
1906 comedies, <u>En ny Hat til Madammen</u> and <u>Anarkistens
Svigermoder</u>, also directed by Viggo Larsen.

Still not as interesting as the two earlier comedies, but
superior to <u>Vidundercigaren</u>, is <u>Den nærsynede Guvernante</u>.
The scenes are entirely exteriors, mostly done in long shot,
although the film ends with a close shot of the governess
crying, a shot which functions as a comic bow to the audience. A nearsighted governess is walking through a park
with her charge and holding a newspaper up to her face.
During the course of this walk a number of comic things happen to her: a man grasps her hand as if he were the child;
she bumps into an old man; she sits down on a bench under
a "wet paint" sign and ends up by attacking the painter who
tries to "help" her by painting designs on her back using
the lines caused by the bench; and finally, she walks away
with someone else's child.

Although the incidents are common enough and the
governess's unaware attitude too forced, the film still elicits
a humorous response and, like many early films, benefits from
the inherent interest of the real settings. Even in its own

time, however, Den nærsynede Guvernante was only moderately successful, selling fifty-five copies.[126]

In the tradition of Georges Méliès, though without his
skill and imagination, is Tryllekunstneren, a typical trick
film, but with the tricks obviously and poorly done. The
film opens as a landlady is showing a man a room that is for
rent. Both use broad gestures. He begins playing tricks
on her, making himself vanish and reappear in another part
of the room and causing himself to suddenly appear on the
balcony, then back in the room again. These tricks make
the woman frantic. Later, the man shows himself capable of
magically fixing broken items and rearranging the furniture
in his room without touching it. In another scene the landlady breaks her dishes after taking several falls. She asks
the conjurer to fix them, a request which she begins to make
continually, finally causing great annoyance in her boarder.
Ultimately, she proposes marriage to him, and he responds
by making her spin around the room and fly out the window
landing on the street below, the only real location used in
the film. She flies back up into the room and begs him to
stop. Like Méliès's scenes, with the exception of the one
mentioned, all are studio interiors using obviously fake sets
and photographed head-on.

Heksen og Cyklisten is superior to Tryllekunstneren
in both execution and conception. Angered by a cyclist's
response to her, a witch causes his bicycle to change into
various wheeled vehicles before it is eventually taken by a
pretty girl. A scene of the bicycle riding into the air and
back to earth is especially successful. In the end the cyclist
has only been dreaming. Moving Picture World found the film
to be "a very fantastic picture which is bound to amuse and
delight an audience.... Full of ingenuity in the way of trick
work."[127]

Different from the trick films is Menneskeaben, a
straightforward recording of a music hall act. Utilizing one
sparsely furnished set and a head-on camera, the film shows
a variety of tricks being performed by an ape. A man is
having dinner with the ape who is wearing men's clothes.
The ape eats with a fork and the two dinner companions appear to be talking. Three shots are used to cover this action. The scene begins in medium long shot, cuts to long
shot, and returns to medium long shot. The ape offers the

man a cigarette, then lights it for him. They pick up the
table, carry it out of camera range, and return without it.
A smaller table is brought in and they play cards. The ape
undresses, picks up a chamber pot, sits on it, and then goes
to bed. Dressed again, he conducts an imaginary orchestra,
roller skates, and rides a bicycle. Great Northern boasted
that this was "the greatest illustration of animal intelligence
ever given in a film,"[128] a claim that is, at best, exaggerated
for an audience today, though in 1909 was supported by the
strong sale of 173 copies.[129] Even The New York Dramatic
Mirror, usually reserved in its enthusiams for film, called
Menneskeaben "one of the most interesting films it has ever
been the good fortune of the writer to witness."[130]

Of the comedies that have not survived, all but one can
be classified as farces. The lone exception is a trick film
called Fart Paa (U.S. title, Hustling Mr. Brown) in which the
title character makes things move magically at great speed, to
the dismay of his victims. The farces offer a variety of subjects standard for the period.

Tøffelhelten (U.S. title, The Henpecked Husband),
called "a delightful comedy subject" by Moving Picture World,
concerns a man "who is scorned by his wife for surreptitious
smoking." In order to get back in her good graces he plans,
with the help of some fellow club members, a fake attack on
his wife from which he, of course, saves her. This appears
to succeed until she finds "an article of feminine attire" in
his coat pocket, at which point she proceeds to give him a
sound beating, to which the critic for Moving Picture World
rsponded: "God forbid that we should have a wife like
that."[131]

En indholdsrig Spadseretar (U.S. title, A Pleasant Walk)
and Et nyt Tyverialarmeringsapparat (U.S. title, A New Burglar Alarm) also pit their male protagonists against quick-fisted
wives. The former concerns an old gentleman who loses his
hat while on a walk and replaces it with a cap he buys from
a porter. Thinking he is a porter, numerous people try to
enlist his services, including two young women who ask him
to accompany them home. While doing so, he meets his wife,
who immediately suspects infidelity and, after getting home,
"takes vigorous measures to convince him of her displeasure."
The latter film has a businessman who, when his wife enters
hastily, hides a whiskey bottle in the safe. His wife then

forces him to spend a quiet evening at home, during which
time burglars break into the man's office. While robbing the
safe, they discover the whiskey and promptly get drunk,
eventually falling asleep on the floor. The next morning the
businessman discovers the burglars and calls his wife, asking
her to come with the police. After the police take charge of
the burglars, the man points with pride to the bottle as his
new burglar alarm.

The sexuality implied in Tøffelhelten (The Henpecked
Husband) is more directly stated in two other farces, Et
forfriskende Bad (U.S. title, Refreshing Bath) and En Bryllupsrejse (U.S. title, A Quiet Honeymoon). The first is the
story of a man who decides to sunbathe. After undressing
he finds it necessary to hide behind some bushes when he
hears footsteps approaching. From his hiding place he becomes witness to "an intimate rendezvous" which he interrupts by sneezing, resulting in a series of difficulties for
him. En Bryllupsrejse also deals with interruption, this time
of a couple's attempt to enjoy their honeymoon. Moving Picture World called it "an uproariously funny film," noting that
its depiction of the situation was "very graphic."132

Of the four remaining 1909 comedies two use overindul-
gence in alcohol as their principal plot element. Tyksakkernes
Ølgilde (U.S. title, The Club of the Corpulent) begins with
four friends, calling themselves The Club of the Corpulent,
who go to a restaurant and begin drinking heavily. One of
them, Heinze, remembers a business engagement and leaves.
Later, his three friends bring him steins of beer, though in
an attempt to get the beer through a small opening in Heinze's
door, it gets drunk by a passing tramp. Thinking his friends
have given him an empty stein, Heinze proceeds to beat them.
Naar Djaevleer paa Spil (U.S. title, How Brother Cook Was
Taught a Lesson) is about a monk who has one fault, a fond-
ness for wine. His colleagues try to cure his indulgence with
"a very unique and amusing method."

Another kind of cure is attempted in Den vidunderlige
Haarelixir (U.S. title, A Marvelous Cure or The Wonderful
Hair-Growing Fluid). A man, unhappy over his baldness,
sees an advertisement in a newspaper for a new cure for the
ailment. He buys a bottle of the hair-growing fluid that has
such "effective" results for him and his family that he regrets having used it.

In En Friday (U.S. title, A Day Off) the main character also gets something he had not expected. A man takes a day off from work, but instead of enjoying it he becomes the victim of a series of what Moving Picture World called "moving accidents that either met him or overtook him during the day." The nature of these moving accidents is not specified.

Eight additional Nordisk films of 1909 were not released in the United States. Three are identified by Nordisk records as comedies: Den store Gevinst (The Big Lottery) concerns a man who wins a big lottery; Blind Alarm (False Alarm) tells of a husband upset over the intended visit of his mother-in-law, a visit which she cancels; and Selvmorderlunden (The Suicide Grove), for which there is no plot information. Two others appear to be comedies from their titles: Gasrøret or Det løbske Gassrør (A Gas Pipe or The Runaway Gas Pipe) and Svigermoderen or Den musikalske Svigermoder (The Mother-in-Law or The Musical Mother-in-Law), distributed in England as The Mother-in-Law Crazy After Music. One film is identified by the Nordisk records as a drama: Barnet (A Child), in which a husband and wife, who have been separated by an imagined infidelity, are reconciled by their child. The remaining two are difficult to classify because only their titles are available: Rivaler (The Rivals) and Arrestation med "ekstraforplejning" or En behagelig Arrestation (Imprisonment with a Special Diet or A Pleasant Imprisonment).[133]

That so few of the Nordisk films were not distributed in the United States indicates the growing importance of the foreign market in 1909 and points to an even greater emphasis on this market during the next few years, an emphasis which was an important cause of both the phenomenal success and the final decline of the early Danish cinema. The next chapter continues the history of Danish film in its golden age.

NOTES

1. Ebbe Neergaard, The Story of Danish Film, trans. Elsa Gress (Copenhagen: Det Danske Selskab, 1963), p. 1.
2. In Italy, for example, the Lumières were the major influence in cinema until 1905 when Filoteo Alberini made his first film, a historical subject celebrating the unification of Italy in 1870 brought about by King Victor Emmanuel's army. See Pierre Leprohon, The Italian Cinema, trans. Robert Greaves and Oliver Stallybrass (New York: Praeger Publishers, 1972).

3. Marguerite Engberg, Dansk Stumfilm, 2 vols. (Copenhagen: Rhodes Internationalt Forlag for Videnskab, Kunst og Debat, 1977), p. 23.   Engberg also quotes Elfelt as saying that he obtained his first motion picture camera from the Lumière Company in Lyon, a camera that had been built by the Frenchman Jules Carpentier (see p. 21).   Lengths on this and other Danish films cited are given in meters.

4. Marguerite Engberg, Registrant over danske film, 1896-1914, 3 vols. (Copenhagen: Institut for Filmvidenskab, 1977).   In addition to film titles, this catalog contains other important information including lengths and release dates.

5. Danmarks Radio Praesenterer Elfelt Film, compiled by Ole Brage (Copenhagen: Danmarks Radio, 1975).

6. Danmarks Radio Præsenterer Elfelt Film, pp. 39-49.

7. Peter Elfelt films have been preserved and made available for study at Danmarks Radio and Hos Peter Elfelt in Copenhagen.

8. The original length was ca. 40 m.   Current prints are ca. 28 m.

9. Engberg, Registrant, I, p. 23.

10. According to the testimony of Ole Olsen, however, at least one foreign filmmaker did make some short actuality films in Denmark.   A Thomas S. Lorenzen invited the German producer Oscar Messter, who had begun making films in 1896, to come to Copenhagen.   Olsen said he was with Lorenzen and Messter when they photographed outside of Rosenborg Castle. See the Copenhagen newspaper Ekstrabladet, October 1, 1942.

11. Gunnar Sandfeld, Den Stumme Scene (Copenhagen: Nyt Nordisk Forlag.   Arnold Busck, 1966), p. 69.

12. Ebbe Neergaard, The Story of Danish Film, trans. Elsa Gress (Copenhagen: Det Danske Selskab, 1963), p. 23.

13. Olsen's copying of the Fotorama film The White Slave Trade was only one example of this practice.   Ebbe Neergaard suggests that Olsen was responsible for the demise of Kosmorama which had produced one of the most successful films of the period, Afgrunden (to be discussed in the next chapter).   After the making of Afgrunden Kosmorama went out of business and its managing director, Hjalmar Davidsen, was soon hired by Olsen.   "The claw of the lion, or polar bear [the Nordisk Films Kompagni trade mark], seems to have been stretched out once more, and the competitor was quietly annihilated" (The Story of the Danish Film, p. 44).

Although she agrees that this method of operating was characteristic of Olsen, Marguerite Engberg (Dansk Stumfilm, p. 260) suggests that Davidsen was himself responsible for

the annihilation of Kosmorama because he sold the rights to
Afgrunden (except for the city of Copenhagen) to Johan
Christensen of Skandinavisk-russike Handelshus, who himself
later sold the rights to a German distributor. Whatever the
reason for Kosmorama's closing, Olsen did put Davidsen (as
a director) and the two male leads in the film, Robert Dinesen and Poul Reumert, under contract to Nordisk although,
according to Marguerite Engberg, he never put Asta Nielsen
under contract. A letter from Nordisk to the Great Northern
Film Company in New York, however, responding to a question from Ingvald Oes, indicates that Nielsen was under contract but that she broke her contract in order to accept an
offer from a German producer. (Letter dated December 30,
1911 in the files of the Danish Film Museum.) Whether she
was under contract or not, Nielsen made one film for Nordisk
in 1911, Balletdanserinden.

    14. In The Early Development of the Motion Picture,
1887-1909 (New York: Arno, 1973, pp. 184-92), Joseph North
suggests that the dime museums and arcades were an important
place for the exhibition of films during the decline of their
popularity as parts of vaudeville programs. He speculates
that the real audiences for movies were developing in these
places rather than in the vaudeville houses. North cites the
rapid acceptance of films in place of vaudeville during the
White Rats' strike as an indication that there had been a film
audience all along.

    15. See Lewis Jacobs, The Rise of the American Film
(New York: Teachers College Press, second printing, 1969),
pp. 52-66, 81-94 for a fuller discussion of some of these developments.

    16. Ole Olsen, Filmens Eventyr og Mit Eget (Copen-
hagen: Jespersen og Pios Forlag, 1940), p. 9. Olsen's autobiography is the principal source of information on his life
used for this section. The title of this book carries a double
meaning. In Danish the word eventyr means adventure and
also fairy tale. Hans Christian Andersen's fairy tales, for
example, are called eventyrs. Olsen's title can then mean
either The Film's Adventure and My Own or The Film's Fairy
Tale and My Own. The way in which Olsen writes about the
growth of film in Denmark and the transformation this meant
in his own life indicates that he, indeed, considered both the
histories of Danish film and of his life as kinds of fairy tales.

    17. Olsen, pp. 9-20.

    18. Olsen, pp. 20-48. Although the sources for these
specific films are not known, it is known that prior to the

beginnings of Danish production, most films imported into
Denmark came from France, England, and the United States.
Even after Olsen founded the Nordisk Films Kompagni, he
continued to import films and buy negatives for Danish distribution. Among those Olsen had dealings with were Georges
Méliès, Arturo Ambrosio, Cecil Hepworth, Gaumont, Pathé
Frères, and the Warwick Trading Company. See Engberg,
Dansk Stumfilm, pp. 41-44. One of the leading Danish im-
porters and distributors of foreign films was Kinografen. Of
the American films Kinografen distributed the vast majority
were from Vitagraph and Biograph. Vitagraph, especially,
was successful in Copenhagen. See Nordisk Biograf Tidende,
January 1910.

    19. Olsen, pp. 49, 50. Olsen says only that his cam-
era came from France. Axel Sørensen, one of Olsen's early
cameramen, said Olsen bought two Pathé cameras. See Engberg, Dansk Stumfilm, p. 54.

    20. Neergaard, p. 9.

    21. Court photographer Peter Elfelt also recorded the
proclamation of Frederick VIII and continued his documenting
of the royal family until at least 1907.

    22. Engberg, Registrant, I, pp. 45-55.

    23. Engberg, Registrant, I, pp. 48, 49. The titles
of these two films were Konfirmanden paa Frederiksberg (The
Confirmand at Frederiksberg) and Et Opløb paa Frederiksberg
(A Gathering at Frederiksberg).

    24. Neergaard, p. 10.

    25. Neergaard, pp. 13, 14.

    26. Engberg, Registrant, I, pp. 51-103.

    27. Eileen Bowser, in her notes for the 1978 FIAF
Congress in Brighton, England, cites two American Mutoscope
and Biograph Company films from 1906 which contain similar
cuts, The Silver Wedding and The Lone Highwayman.

    28. Engberg, Dansk Stumfilm, pp. 105-8.

    29. Ebgberg, Registrant, I, pp. 104-99.

    30. Moving Picture World, the major American trade
periodical of the period, began including Nordisk films in
April 1908, listing forty-seven titles during that year. Nordisk Films Kompagni's own records indicate that films were
sent to the United States as early as May 1907.

    31. Engberg, Registrant, I, pp. 120-80.

    32. Nordisk Films Kompagni copybook recording trans-
actions with the American Mutoscope and Biograph Company of
New York.

33. Nordisk Films Kompagni shipping invoice dated August 13, 1908.

34. Many films exist as titles only or with descriptions too general to positively identify them as to types.

35. Information regarding U.S. titles and plot descriptions comes primarily from the early trade periodicals Moving Picture World, Moving Picture News, The New York Dramatic Mirror, and The Nickelodeon. Also used was the British publication The Kinematograph and Lantern Weekly, although British and American titles are not always the same.

36. Engberg, Registrant, I, pp. 139-88.

37. The Danish Film Museum has a print with English intertitles that is 87 m. in length.

38. Engberg, Registrant, I, p. 161. According to a Nordisk Films Kompagni invoice, fifty-five copies were sent to Miles Brothers in New York on October 1, 1907. Miles Brothers was at that time acting as an American distributor of Nordisk films.

39. I have not had the opportunity to see Kameliadamen and so cannot comment on it. Marguerite Engberg, however, as part of her discussion of Viggo Larsen, devotes seven pages to the film in her Dansk Stumfilm, including a shot-by-shot description. It apparently is done in a "theatrical" style and follows the five-act structure of the play. She gives similar, though not necessarily as extensive, treatment to Anarkistens Svigermoder, Den hvide Slavinde, Røverens Brud, Løvejagten, Heksen og Cyklisten, Et Budskab til Napoleon, and Barnet som Velgører, all surviving Viggo Larsen films from the 1906 to 1909 period.

40. The names and identifications of nationality may not be the same as the original Danish release prints. They were often changed to suit the countries of distribution. However, Nordisk Films did make many films with English settings and characters.

41. Neergaard, p. 21.

42. Engberg, Registrant, I, p. 169.

43. Olsen, p. 56.

44. Neergaard, p. 17.

45. Neergaard, p. 17.

46. Olsen, p. 56.

47. Olsen, pp. 56-73. Also helpful to Olsen was a political scandal in which Alberti was sent to prison for the embezzlement of large sums of money. See Stewart Oakley, A Short History of Denmark, p. 202.

48. Neergaard, p. 18. Neergaard also estimates that

sales of Løvejagten must have brought Olsen about 50,000
kroner. Marguerite Engberg, in a note to me, challenges
Neergaard's calculations, saying he forgot to take into account the cost to Olsen for the raw stock on all the copies
sold. Nevertheless, Engberg cites Løvejagten as "the biggest
success Nordisk had yet had." She also notes that it was
not until 1911, with Ved Faengslets Port, that Nordisk had
as economically an important film. See Dansk Stumfilm, p.
142.

    49. The jungle setting is suggested by the use of palm
leaf plants set among the natural vegetation of Roskilde.

    50. The shots of animals, other than the two lions,
are from high angles because they were photographed in the
Copenhagen Zoo, and it was necessary to avoid getting un-
wanted background.

    51. Lion-killing scenes take place on the beach.

    52. Nordisk Films shipping invoices indicate that
seventy-five copies were sent to Miles Brothers on October 3,
1907. Moving Picture World listed Løvejagten in its issue of
April 11, 1908 along with a one-line plot description which
certainly does not do justice to the film: "Two hunters and
their servant go hunting and kill two lions."

    53. Marguerite Engberg told me that in an interview
she had with Viggo Larsen shortly before his death, Larsen
had no conception of the significance of the editing in Løvejagten, but simply said that they had to photograph and edit
the film that way in order to get the story across and give
the impression of a real hunt.

    54. See Appendix B for additional titles not mentioned
in the text.

    55. Engberg, Registrant, I, pp. 104-99.

    56. Neergaard, pp. 18-19.

    57. Engberg, Registrant, I, pp. 114-290.

    58. Engberg, Registrant, I, p. 200.

    59. See Appendix B for a list of titles and descriptions.

    60. Engberg, Registrant, I, pp. 238-90.

    61. Engberg, Registrant, I, pp. 204-88.

    62. Among the actors are Holger-Madsen (who later
became an important Nordisk director) and Aage Brandt (who
also became a director).

    63. Although this device is simple, it can be extremely
effective. Witness Buster Keaton's use of it in Seven Chances.

    64. Moving Picture World, February 26, 1909.

    65. Moving Picture World, March 17, 1909, p. 483.
Comments on the high quality of Nordisk photography are

common in the reviews of the period. An article in The New
York Dramatic Mirror, comparing American and foreign films
and how to recognize films of specific producers, notes that
"Great Northern Films ... are distinguished by clearness and
perfection of photographic quality." See issue for November
14, 1908, p. 10. This issue also contains the Mirror's first
Great Northern advertisement and a brief notice that cites
The Bear Hunt (probably the 1907 Isbjørnejagt, the success
of which stimulated Ole Olsen to make Løvejagten) as a recent
release.

66. Moving Picture World, May 29, 1909, p. 713.
67. Moving Picture World, January 16, 1909.
68. Engberg, Registrant, I, pp. 236, 254, 288.
69. Moving Picture World, February 27, 1909, pp.
239-40.
70. Ebbe Neergaard implies that all nine Holmes films
were directed by and starred Viggo Larsen (Neergaard, p.
19), but Marguerite Engberg credits him with only six. Since
her work is based on actual Nordisk Films reocrds, and since
Larsen left Nordisk Films and Denmark at the end of 1909,
Marguerite Engberg should probably be taken as correct.
71. Moving Picture World, February 27, 1909, pp. 239-
40.
72. The New York Dramatic Mirror, December 19, 1908,
p. 7.
73. Engberg, Registrant, I, p. 239.
74. Engberg, Registrant, I, p. 211.
75. Moving Picture World, June 12, 1909, p. 811.
76. The names are those used in the American version.
77. Pierre Leprohon, The Italian Cinema, trans. Robert
Greaves and Oliver Stallybrass (New York: Praeger Publishers, 1972), p. 34.
78. Engberg, Registrant, I, p. 272.
79. Engberg, Registrant, I, p. 204.
80. Engberg, Registrant, I, p. 224. In its issue of
December 5, 1908 The New York Dramatic Mirror called Synderinden "an interesting story of a reformed girl who enlists
as an army nurse, and later impersonates a young woman who
she supposes has been killed in battle." The issue of November 28, 1908; referred to La Tosca as "admirably done, both
as to acting and photography...." An ad in the Mirror of
November 21, 1908 says Blind is the story of a blind beggar
boy.
81. Engberg, Registrant, I, pp. 291-418.
82. These figures are based on the Nordisk films listed

in The New York Dramatic Mirror and Moving Picture World
issues of 1909 and 1910.   In addition, another six fiction films
and four nonfiction films are listed as Nordisk products but
cannot be identified by reference to Nordisk Films records and
other primary sources.

83. See Appendix B for titles.

84. See Appendix B for titles.

85. Engberg, Dansk Stumfilm, pp. 215, 216.

86. Engberg, Registrant, I, pp. 291-94.

87. Moving Picture World, September 3, 1910, p. 632.

88. Engberg, Registrant, I, p. 397.

89. The play was bought by the Shuberts and was
being performed under the title A Son of the People.   They
had also purchased the rights to another Michaelis drama,
Napoleon at St. Helena.   Moving Picture World, March 5, 1910,
p. 342.

90. Moving Picture World, March 19, 1910, p. 426.

91. The New York Dramatic Mirror, March 19, 1910,
p. 18.

92. Engberg, Registrant, I, p. 414.

93. Nordisk Films Kompagni shipping invoice dated
February 12, 1910.

94. Judging by the plot description in Moving Picture
World, present day prints are missing a sequence in which
the messenger gets a boat in order to reach Elba and is sunk
in a storm.   Except for that the prints seem complete.

95. A later British Nat Pinkerton series was produced
by the Charles Urban Trading Company.   The first film of
the series was released on February 1, 1911.   See The Kinematograph and Lantern Weekly, January 5, 1911, p. 535.

96. Moving Picture World, April 24, 1909, p. 676.

97. Engberg, Registrant, I, p. 324.   Droske 519 sold
sixty-one copies (Engberg, p. 312) and Sangerindens Diamanter sixty-three (Engberg, p. 374).

98. Moving Picture World, September 11, 1909, p. 344.

99. Engberg, Registrant, I, p. 366.

100. Neergaard, p. 19.

101. Engberg, Registrant, I, pp. 327, 335, 371.

102. Engberg, Registrant, I, p. 327.

103. Moving Picture World, March 26, 1910, p. 599.

104. Neergaard, p. 19.

105. These percentages were determined from the figures given in Nordisk Films shipping invoices.

106. Neergaard, p. 48.   The most important markets
were in Europe, particularly Germany, where Nordisk also

owned sixty theaters and a production company. In addition,
Nordisk had branch offices in Vienna, Prague, Budapest,
Zurich and Amsterdam.

107. Moving Picture World, June 9, 1908, p. 871.

108. "Internationalism and the Picture," Moving Picture
World, September 17, 1910, p. 621.

109. A sufficient number of original prints and high
quality prints made from original and fine grain master negatives are available at The Danish Film Museum to corroborate
Moving Picture World's opinion.

110. Olsen, pp. 88-90.

111. Neergaard, p. 12.

112. It is tempting to think of a connection between
Griffith's film and the Nordisk production. Although the
Danish release date of Laegens Offer is not known, Nordisk
shipping invoices indicate that nineteen copies were sent to
the United STates during December 1909 and January 1910.
Moving Picture World printed the plot synopsis in its issue
of February 26, 1910. According to the records of the American Biograph Company, The Country Doctor was photographed
on May 29 and 31 and June 7, 1909; it was released on July
8, 1909. It is not possible, therefore, that Griffith saw
Laegens Offer before making his own film. It is possible,
however, that Griffith's film was seen by Albert Gnudtzmann
who wrote the scenario for Laegens Offer. See Dansk Stumfilm, p. 169. Biograph Company films were regularly distributed in Denmark by a company called Kinografen which
also handled films of Vitgraph, Lux, Edison, Selig, Essanay,
Bison, Kalem, Lubin, Imp, Thanhauser, Reliance, Rex, and
Solax. I have not been able to find any evidence, however,
that The Country Doctor was shown in Denmark.

113. Moving Picture World, May 21, 1910, p. 942.

114. Moving Picture World, December 25, 1909, p. 17.

115. Neergaard, p. 14.

116. Neergaard, p. 32.

117. Engberg, Registrant, II, p. 361.

118. Neergaard, p. 40.

119. Moving Picture World, April 30, 1910, p. 785.

120. Quoted by Ebbe Neergaard in The Story of Danish
Film, p. 14.

121. Moving Picture World, April 30, 1910, p. 785.

122. Moving Picture World, October 16, 1909, p. 570.

123. The New York Dramatic Mirror, October 23, 1909,
p. 17.

124. Moving Picture World, January 22, 1910, p. 128.

125. Moving Picture World, July 9, 1910, p. 194.
126. Engberg, Registrant, I, p. 339.
127. Moving Picture World, September 4, 1909, p. 344.
128. Moving Picture World, May 12, 1909, p. 695.
129. Engberg, Registrant, I, p. 313.
130. The New York Dramatic Mirror, June 5, 1909, p. 15.
131. Moving Picture World, September 4, 1909, p. 344.
132. Moving Picture World, March 19, 1910, p. 510.
133. Engberg, Registrant, I, pp. 320, 350, 364, 382, 383, 386, 389, 395.

CHAPTER TWO:

1910-1914*

The years 1910-14 were "great and golden years"[1] for
the Danish cinema. They saw the introduction of the long
film, the economic expansion of Nordisk Films Kompagni,[2] and
the first work of the three best known and most significant
Danish film artists--Asta Nielsen, Carl Dreyer, and Benjamin
Christensen. In addition, a number of other influential directors and actors made important contributions; among them
were August Blom, Eduard Schnedler-Sørensen, Robert Dinesen, Peter Urban Gad, Vilhelm Glückstadt, Alfred Lind,
Holger-Madsen, Olaf Fønss, Vlademar Psilander, Clara Pontoppidan, Lau Lauritzen, Oscar Stribolt, Hjalmar Davidsen,
A. W. Sandberg, and Carl Alstrup.

The economic success of Nordisk Films in 1912-13 has
been seen by Ebbe Neergaard as the major impetus for the
expansion of Denmark's film industry from 1911 to 1916. According to Neergaard, so many new companies came into existence that Carl Dreyer, then a journalist for the Copenhagen
newspaper Ekstrabladet, gave up trying to keep track of them
and resorted to the ironic device of naming them by the date
and time of their appearance.[3] Most of them were short-lived
and of little importance, while a few, Kosmorama, Kinografen,
Det Skandinavisk-russike Handelshus (The Scandinavian-
Russian Trade Company), and Dansk Biografkompagni, made
significant marks in the industry, though all but one of these
were also short-lived. Two other companies, Biorama, founded
by Søren Nielsen, and Fotorama, started by Thomas Hermansen

---

*Unless otherwise noted, all the Danish films discussed in this
chapter have survived and their descriptions come from my
own viewing.

and Fred Skaarup and located in the city of Aarhus, had begun production in 1909. Both were of some importance throughout the period under consideration.[4]

There is general agreement among Danish film historians
that the most significant of these companies, in terms of its
effect on the entire Danish film industry, was Kosmorama, an
assertion that is especially interesting since Kosmorama produced only one film. That film, however, had a major effect
on other producers and on the relationship of Danish theater
people to the cinema. The film was Afgrunden (The Abyss,
750 m.--circa 2½ reels. These are original lengths; when the
surviving material is significantly shorter than the original,
it is so noted.) It starred Asta Nielsen (in her first screen
appearance), Robert Dinesen, and Poul Reumert, and was
written and directed by Peter Urban Gad. Alfred Lind did
the photography. Kosmorama was headed by Hjalmar Davidsen who was to become an important director at Nordisk.

Afgrunden, made in 1910, played a key role in convincing Danish theater people that film was a legitimate medium.
As in America, established Danish stage artists would have
nothing to do with the cinema. It was the younger stage people, without reputations, who were willing to work in film,
and such was the group that made Afgrunden. Hjalmar Davidsen, who had met Asta Nielsen at the Dagmar Theater, arranged a special afternoon screening of the film for an invited
audience of theater artists who were so impressed by what
they saw, that they changed their minds about the possibilities of film as a dramatic medium. This helped make such
well-known theater people as Otto Rung, Sophus Michaelis,
Betty Nansen, and Dr. Karl Mantzius into defenders of the
cinema.[5] With this change came a strong influence from the
theater on the style and subject of films. Unlike the American
cinema, however, the theatrical influence was not from melodrama but from a more naturalistic drama, in line with the
changes brought about by the plays of Henrik Ibsen. The
film subjects were still melodramatic, but their focus was on
the erotic and psychological rather than on action. Afgrunden
became the prototype for this kind of film.

Much of the success of Afgrunden was due to Asta Nielsen's performance. Her acting capacities have been well described by Bela Balasz in his Theory of the Film, but her
great emotional power was already evident in her first screen

appearance, which Ebbe Neergaard has called "a shockingly
realistic rendering of a human fate." Neergaard also notes
that prior to this performance she had played only minor
parts at The New Theater in Copenhagen of which, had they
seen her, those theater artists present at that momentous
special screening would have taken little notice.

> Because of her the aristocratic, sceptical actors of
> the Copenhagen Royal Theater could admit the artis-
> tic possibilities of the movies. It is told that when
> the film was shown ... for people from the Royal
> Theater, Olaf Poulsen, probably the greatest comical
> genius of the Danish stage, started making jokes--
> then he fell silent, and at the end, when the film
> was over, he said merely: "I'll be damned!" The
> brilliant director William Block whose acting school
> is partly responsible for the fact that Danish actors
> made such important contributions to the films, also
> had to admit the great possibilities of the new art.[6]

Asta Nielsen made only two more films in Denmark before she
left for Germany where her worldwide reputation was established.[7]

Although the recognition afforded Afgrunden by the
theater world was remarkable, it apparently did not impress
the film's writer-director, Urban Gad. In an interview in the
theater review Masken Gad took an aggressive stance for the
film as a medium separate from the stage.

> The picture-theater gives the audience just what it
> wants: a short and impressive action, the opportu-
> nity to see the often excellent facial expressions of
> the actors without being forced to listen to the tir-
> ing lines, so destructive to the imagination, an in-
> tense feeling of personally and closely taking part
> in the course of the action, the greater probability
> of the story, the rapid change from place to place in
> the development of the drama, the almost simultaneous
> contemplation of and identification with the different
> situations created by the development of the conflict,
> and last but not least the deliverance from "theater":
> the avoidance of the lengthy explanations, the speeches
> to the audience so disturbing to the illusion, the read-
> ing of letters--which in the picture-theater is done

by the onlooker himself--and the initiation into the
difficulties of the script-writer to introduce the per-
sons and situations necessary to the action.
    In those fields the "real" theater can in fact learn
something from the moving picture. For these are
considerably closer to life and reality than the stage
and the expressive possibilities of the stage in general....[8]

Gad's belief in the cinema found expression, not only in his
productions in both Denmark and Germany, but also in his
writing of one of the first major books on the film medium,
a relatively comprehensive text on film production and aesthetics.[9]

    Born on February 12, 1879, Gad came from a well-known
Copenhagen family. His father was an admiral and his mother,
Emma, a writer. Paul Gauguin was his uncle, and this may
have influenced Gad to study painting, a field which he soon
gave up for the theater.[10] With the success of Afgrunden
Gad's theater work gave way to a commitment to the cinema.
He made five more films in Denmark before accepting an offer
from Deutsche Bioscop in Berlin, where he went in 1911 along
with Asta Nielsen who was then his wife.[11] Gad continued to
work in Germany until 1922 when he made his last German
film, Hanneles Himmelfahrt. He returned to Denmark and became manager of the Grand Teatret, a cinema in Copenhagen.[12]
In 1926 he made his last film, Lykkehjulet.[13] He died on December 26, 1947.[14]

    Afgrunden is the story of Magda, a piano teacher who
meets a young engineer, Knud, on the trolley. They soon
become engaged, and he takes her to meet his father (a minister) and mother in the country. While there she meets Mr.
Rudolph, a cowboy-clad performer in a traveling circus, and
immediately falls in love with him. They run away together
and later work as a dance team. He is unfaithful to her,
but she continues to love him. One day Knud sees her in
the city and follows her to a performers' boarding house. He
convinces her to return to him, pledging to come for her later
that day. On returning, however, he discovers that she is
still in love with Rudolph, despite his mistreatment of her.
Later, on stopping at a café, Knud sees Magda playing the
piano and arranges to see her. A waiter tells Rudolph that
she is with another man and, during the ensuing confrontation,

Magda kills Rudolph. The police are summoned to take her
away.

The importance of Afgrunden lies in its subject matter,
its portrayal of powerful emotions of sexual possession and
submission, and in the excellent acting of Asta Nielsen and
Poul Reumert, rather than in its formal execution. Except
for a few interesting exterior compositions, a trolley scene
that has a 180-degree cut, and some strong closeups using
natural lighting, the film is quite conventional in its use of
camera, cutting, and lighting. However, it transcends its
technique through its "shockingly realistic rendering of a
human fate."

This effect is nowhere more evident than in a famous
dance that Nielsen and Reumert perform showing clearly and
forcefully what the rest of the film implies. In this dance
Asta Nielsen ties up Poul Reumert with a rope and then proceeds to dance around him, rubbing her body constantly
against his. The strongly erotic character of this dance
helped make the film a great success, giving it a reputation
for being almost pornographic. Asta Nielsen singled out this
scene, and the last one in the film in which Magda is led away
by the police, for specific mention in her discussion of Afgrunden in her memoirs.15 Both scenes impress audiences
today in much the same way that they apparently did in 1910.

Gad and Nielsen followed this success with a second
film, Den sorte Drøm (The Black Dream, 1,206 m.--(4 reels),
made for Fotorama in 1911. This time Valdemar Psilander, the
leading male film star of the period, played opposite her, and
once again it was a story of strong sexual passions.

Stella (Asta Nielsen) is a circus performer who falls
in love with Count Waldberg (Valdemar Psilander). Hirsch, a
jeweler, also loves her and, at a party at Stella's house, tries
to force himself on her. Waldberg steps in, however, and
knocks Hirsch down. Later that evening, Hirsch gets Waldberg into a card game in which Waldberg loses heavily. Unable to pay his debt, Waldberg buys a gun with which to commit suicide. Stella discovers the gun and takes it from him.
She then plans to steal a necklace from Hirsch which Waldberg can sell to pay his gambling debt. Stella visits Hirsch
and makes an attempt to steal the necklace. Hirsch sees the
theft reflected in a mirror, but allows her to leave, following

her to a meeting in the park with Waldberg. After she gives
Waldberg the necklace, Hirsch confronts her and threatens
to have her arrested unless she meets him that night. She
agrees, and Hirsch leaves to follow Waldberg. After the
necklace is sold, Hirsch buys it back while getting a note
from the other jeweler that Waldberg had sold the necklace.
Later that night, Stella has to put off Waldberg in order to
keep her appointment with Hirsch. Searching through her
purse to get his gun back, Waldberg finds a card from Hirsch
stating the meeting time. He goes to Hirsch's house, surprises them, and shoots Stella. Just before she dies, she
reveals to Waldberg that she had gone there only to save
him.

The continuity of Den sorte Drøm is more fluid than
Afgrunden and utilizes a greater variety of camera angles
than most films of the period. A simple example involves a
scene between Stella and Waldberg which is also the most
passionate scene in the film. They are in her house where
he is pleading for her love; after an initial resistance, she
finally yields. They are seated on a divan, first seen in a
side angle medium shot. As his pleading becomes more passionate and the sexual tension of the scene increases, Gad
cuts to a frontal medium shot which helps to intensify the
scene and to prepare the way for her acceptance of him--
signified in a passionate embrace and a reclining position on
the divan.

The film also makes good use of mirrors in the sets,
not merely for decorative purposes, but as a way of expand-
ing the acting space. A particularly good example is the
scene in which Stella tries to steal the necklace. A mirror
allows us to see both Stella and Hirsch though they are in
different parts of the room, so that we experience the scene
from two viewpoints simultaneously. We get a view of Stella's
action which allows us to identify with her because we can
see how furtive she must be, while at the same time we see
that Hirsch is watching her in the mirror and so get a sense
of Stella being discovered. We steal the necklace with her,
and we catch her at the same time. A use of mirrors to
create a double viewpoint is common in Danish films of the
period, as other examples will demonstrate.

Another characteristic of Den sorte Drøm is its peculiar
lighting style. The film has strong frontal lighting that casts

heavy shadows on the walls of the set, much like old stage
footlights. These shadows serve a dramatic function, casting
"dark images" of the actions, making them menacing in an
almost expressionistic manner. The shadows also get heavier
as the film progresses and the action moves toward its tragic
end.

Den sorte Drøm was the last film that Gad and Nielsen
made together in Denmark, though he directed four more
films and she played in one more. All five films were made
for Nordisk Films Kompagni.

In 1911 Asta Nielsen played a ballet dancer (Camilla
Flavier) under the direction of August Blom, who had become
the principal director at Nordisk after Viggo Larsen's depar-
ture. The film is Balletdanserinden (The Ballet Dancer, 800
m.--circa 2½ reels) and appears not to have been shown in the
United States, even though two copies were sent to the New
York office of Nordisk. It concerns a young author, Jean
Mayol (Johannes Paulsen), who meets the ballet school's most
promising dancer and gives her a chance to go on when the
lead dancer gets sick. After her successful debut, Jean introduces her to his best friend, Paul Rich, a painter (Valdemar Psilander), and Paul immediately wants to paint her portrait. Meanwhile, Camilla, who is in love with Jean, sees him
with another woman, Yvette Simon, the wife of a rich manufacturer. Camilla is invited to perform at a party given by
Mr. Simon, who also happens to be a friend of Jean's. At
the party Camilla sees Jean kissing Mrs. Simon and, in anger,
denounces Jean before all the guests. Paul takes Camilla
away as Mr. Simon scorns his wife. Camilla stays at Paul's
studio that night, though in a separate bed. The next day,
Jean visits Paul and assures him that he loves only Camilla.
Camilla overhears and believes him, though shortly she finds
a note from Mrs. Simon that Jean has dropped and, once again,
doubts him. She goes to see Mr. Simon and shows him the
note, whereupon Simon takes a gun and goes to Jean's house.
Camilla, however, runs ahead to warn Jean and Mrs. Simon.
They manage to momentarily fool Simon, but he soon catches
his wife and shoots her. Camilla collapses when she hears
about it, and Paul takes her to his parents' house to recuper-
ate. Jean arrives to see Camilla, but she shows her new
preference for Paul. Here present day prints end and, although the film is almost complete, it apparently is missing
its dramatic resolution. No additional material has survived,
however.

Typical of Nordisk dramas of the period, the film is
shot almost entirely in deep focus, a technique which is especially useful at the party scene, where there is another use
of a mirror to expand the playing space. While Camilla is
shown performing, a mirror reflects Jean and Mrs. Simon kissing. This allows for two actions to take place simultaneously
while keeping the main attention on Camilla and strengthening
audience identification with her. The deep focus, combined
with the use of the mirror, allows the scene to play and the
character relationships to be drawn without interrupting the
spatial and temporal reality of the shot. This avoidance of
cutting, which is a general characteristic of Nordisk films,
is by no means a stylistic trait left over from an earlier period,
but rather a concern for mis-en-scène that has its roots in
the theater. The theatrical effect is tempered, however, by
devices like the mirror and the placement of the camera at
an angle to the set, thus avoiding the frontality so common
to earlier theatrically influenced films. In addition, the sets
are solidly furnished and convincingly real.

Another characteristic of this and many other Nordisk
films is the use of camera placement to emphasize off-screen
space. In the scene of Camilla's debut, the camera adopts a
backstage view from the side, with Jean standing in the foreground. Camilla's audience, to whom she is bowing and from
whom she takes flowers, is off-screen to the left. This im-
plication of an active space beyond the frame is common enough
in later films but much rarer in this period, though numerous
other examples can be found in Nordisk films.

As usual, Asta Nielsen's performance is quite strong.
The film as a whole however, lacks the emotional and erotic
intensity of Afgrunden and Den sorte Drøm, despite a plot
that easily allows, if not calls for, these qualities. This absence is probably due to the sensibility of August Blom and
the more conservative tendencies of Ole Olsen's company. The
fact that Olsen never put Asta Nielsen under contract seems
to indicate that he did not fully appreciate either her characteristics or potential. Ebbe Neergaard suggests that it may
have been her physical appearance that put off Ole Olsen:

> Maybe her appearance was too unusual--she had a
> wide mouth with narrow lips, a small nose, wide cheek-
> bones and very large eyes. She was not the conven-
> tional type of beauty. [16]

Urban Gad's four films for Nordisk all have love stories, yet with the exception of the last one, of a type less sensational than his first two films. In their story and treatment, they are in keeping with the general output of Nordisk Films and affirm the development in this period of a Nordisk style, even reflected in Carl Dreyer's first film, Praesidenten (1918-20).

Hulda Rasmussen or Dyrekøbt Glimmer (Dearly-Bought Tinsel, 1911, 855 m.--circa 3 reels) tells the story of a girl who becomes the mistress of her sister's lover, a wealthy man able to give her fine clothes and jewelry. He gets her a job performing at a variety theater where her old boyfriend sees her and tries to get her back by fighting the rich man. Since only two-thirds of the film has survived, the remaining continuity is unclear. We next see Hulda in Monte Carlo with the old boyfriend and the police after him. (Has he taken to stealing in order to get her the things she wants?) A detective apprehends him and, later (after his release from prison?), they both appear down and out and apparently go off to America.

The film is shot in much the same style as Balletdanserinden. Most scenes are done with single-camera setups, although a few have cuts within the scene. A particularly interesting one occurs in reel one as Hulda is about to enter the rich man's bedroom to try on some clothes. As she moves from one room to another, there is a cut that shows both Hulda in the bedroom and, through the doorway, the room she has just left. The actress (Emilie Sannon) pauses at the shot change just long enough to express the importance of the step the character is about to take. The movement from one moral plane to another, suggested in the scene by the two rooms, is emphasized by the real spatial relationship established between the rooms. Also characteristic of Nordisk, the rooms are solidly and realistically furnished and are photographed at an angle, a camera placement that works against the otherwise theatrical nature of the sets and actions.

After Hulda Rasmussen, Gad directed Den store Flyver (U.S. title, An Aviator's Generosity, 780 m.--2½ reels), made in 1911 but not released until December 1912. The story concerns a flyer, Arthur Vidart, played by Poul Reumert (Mr. Rudolph in Afgrunden), his sister Else, and Arthur's close friend Jean Aubert, another flyer. Arthur is in debt to a moneylender and can only pay the debt by winning an upcoming air race. Before the race Arthur introduces Aubert, who will also take part, to Else. They fall in love at once and meet frequently. Arthur discovers that Aubert has another sweetheart, and he forces his sister to break off her relationship. The two friends also separate on bad terms. Learning of her brother's debts and of his need to win the race, Else goes to Aubert and asks him to lose the race. At first Aubert refuses, but when he discovers that Else still loves him (she is wearing a locket he had given her), he agrees. The race takes place and Arthur wins. On the ground he finds Else with Aubert, and she explains how Aubert had purposely lost. She takes Arthur's winner's medal and pins it on Aubert, after which a reconciliation takes place.

The only existing prints of this film are from the Library of Congress paper print collection. The sequences are out of order and the photographic reproduction is poor, so it is difficult to make judgments about the film. In general, Den store Flyver appears to be well done, though it is less interesting than Afgrunden or Den sorte Drøm. Its most notable characteristic is the race sequence at the end of the film which contains several shots taken in the air, showing one plane in the foreground and another in the background. The synopsis of the film given by Moving Picture World made special mention of the aerial photography.[17]

Poul Reumert, who went on to become one of the great Danish actors, also played in Gad's Gennem Kamp til Sejr (U.S. title, Through Trials to Victory, 1911, 770 m.--2½ reels). In this film he is an army lieutenant who seduces a young girl and then leaves her. The girl, Mona (Edith Bueman), visits her uncle, a minister, in the country. Lt. von Platen is quartered with the family during Mona's visit, and they become lovers on the night before he is to leave. On her return to the city, she is attacked by thieves and saved by another officer, Seedorff (Henry Seeman). Seedorff courts her and they become engaged. Later, Seedorff meets von Platen and, while visiting him, sees a picture of Mona on the wall of his apartment. Seedorff confronts Mona, refuses to listen to her, and leaves. Mona returns to her uncle's for a rest. One night she sleepwalks in her bridal outfit. Her uncle goes to Seedorff and convinces him to forgive Mona; the couple are reunited.

Gennem Kamp til Sejr is excellently acted, as are the
other Gad productions, carefully staged, and beautifully
photographed and lighted. Especially noteworthy are the
lighting in the sleepwalking scene, which plays upon the
brightness of Scandinavian summer nights, and the lovely
exteriors in the minister's garden and on the streets of
Copenhagen. As usual the interiors are solid and convincing, realistically matching the exterior location shots.

Gad's final film for Nordisk before departing for Germany was Den hvide Slavehandel III (The White Slave Trade
III, 665 m.--circa 2 reels), the last of a line of White slavery
films produced at Nordisk. The plot is similar to those of the
other White slavery films. A young variety entertainer, Nina
(Lilly Lamprecht), is in love with a naval officer, Thompson
(Richard Christensen). One evening after the show, she
takes him home to meet her mother (Augusta Blad). Thompson shows them his sailing orders. The owner of the variety
theater has consistently made advances toward Nina and, after
her lover has sailed, she leaves the show. Seeing an ad for
a theater job in St. Petersburg, Nina applies and is accepted.
On arrival she is met by Cohn, the supposed theater manager
but in reality a white slaver. Not hearing from Nina in some
time, her mother becomes worried and writes to Thompson
seeking his advice. Fortunately, Thompson receives sailing
orders for St. Petersburg and, on his arrival goes to the
manager of the Empire Theater where Nina is presumably
working. When he discovers that she has never worked there,
he goes to the police who say they cannot help him (a characteristic response of the police in white slavery films). Meanwhile, a Russian officer invites the officers of Thompson's
ship to see the night life of St. Petersburg. Hoping to get
a line on Nina's whereabouts, Thompson goes along. The officers end up at the brothel where Nina is being held. Thompson and Nina contact each other and plan an escape that night.
The slaver overhears them, however, and has Thompson
knocked out and Nina locked in a secret compartment. The
next morning the police discover Thompson unconscious. The
slaver has taken Nina aboard a ship, but he unknowingly has
lost one of the passage tickets, which the police find at the
brothel. The slaver is apprehended and Nina returns to her
mother.

Two plot elements provide a minor variation from the
earlier white slavery films: Nina's occupation, which is more

glamorous than those of her predecessors, and a change in setting from England to Russia. However, the basic plot line, about a girl who leaves her fiancé or lover to work in another country, gets taken by white slavers, and is eventually rescued by the lover, remains at the heart of this and all white slavery films.

Typical of Danish films of the period, Den hvide Slavehandel III makes much of the photographer's skills in lighting. This is particularly true of evening interiors and, most strikingly, of the scene in which Thompson tells Nina and her mother of his sailing orders. The scene is lighted as if from one lamp on the table around which the characters are seated. The effect is very convincing. In addition, this film often uses panning shots to follow action, a shooting method not unknown in the period but still unusual enough to merit special mention.

This discussion of white slavery films suggests another of the influential occurrences of 1910 and another of Nordisk's rivals.

In April 1910 Fotorama, located in the city of Aarhus, released a film called Den hvide Slavehandel (The White Slave Trade). It was directed and photographed by Alfred Lind, who photographed Afgrunden and continued to be associated with significant projects throughout this period. It was not the first white slavery film, Nordisk having made Den hvide Slavinde (The White Slave Girl) in 1906, but it did have the distinction of being 700 m. in length with a running time of almost 40 minutes. It was also attracting large audiences that were standing in line to see it in Aarhus, despite the fact that it was four times the length of the average film. Ole Olsen's interest was aroused and, according to accounts, he sent his own filmmakers to see this film, four months later releasing his own version called Den hvide Slavehandel I (603 m.--2 reels) and directed by August Blom. That same year Fotorama began distributing Nordisk films in Denmark and soon after one of Fotorama's most important directors, Eduard Schnedler-Sørensen went to work for Nordisk.[18]

Only a short fragment of the Fotorama film has survived,[19] so its quality cannot be judged, though Ebbe Neergaard claims that the fragment shows "that it was not that bad."[20] The Nordisk film has survived almost in its entirety, however, and perhaps could be summed up as "not that good." It begins in the usual manner as a girl, Anna, sees a newspaper ad for a job in London. She takes the job, leaving her boyfriend, Georg, behind. On her arrival Anna is taken by slavers, one of whom had actually accompanied her on the trip, though, of course, she did not know that. During her imprisonment at the brothel, Anna convinces the maid to mail a letter for her. Her father receives it and goes to the police, but they tell him they cannot do anything about his daughter's plight. Georg goes to London, hires a detective, and sets out to find her. He sees the slaver whom he recognizes as having been on board the same ship as Anna. Suspicious, they follow the man and find the brothel. Entering as customers, they let Anna know of their presence. Later, Anna slips out of her room on a bed sheet and escapes with Georg. The slavers pursue them and recapture Anna. Georg and the detective get the police, but on a search of the brothel, can find nothing. The maid, however, tells them where the slavers have taken Anna and the police go after them. The final capture and rescue take place aboard a ship on which the slavers have been fleeing the country, and Anna returns home.

The story is clearly told even without the aid of intertitles, but it is also quite unimaginative. The scenes are arranged episodically in single-camera setups with the action generally seen in long shot. The interiors look like stage sets and have no real feeling of space beyond the doors and windows, a restriction which is not mitigated by the cutting. The two chases at the end of the film lack excitement because they do not last long enough, and there is no cross-cutting of the action.

One scene, however, stands out because it utilizes a split screen effect, combining three actions in one image. A slave recruiter telephones one of her confederates concerning Anna. The slavers are seen on the right and left portions of the screen talking into telephones, and Anna and her father are seen in the center with city traffic behind them. This splitting of the image was not rare in Danish film; it provided an alternative to crosscutting, but still allowed the drawing of narrative relationships between characters in different locations.

The introduction of the long film was of major importance

to the Danish film industry as it was to every other national
cinema. The fear of producers and exhibitors that films
longer than one reel would not be accepted by the public
was quickly overcome, especially in Denmark. That people
lined up to see the Fotorama Den hvide Slavehandel was an
early indication of this and must have helped push Ole Olsen
in the direction of longer films. His own recounting of the
selling of Nordisk's Den hvide Slavehandel in Germany, which,
characteristically, he claimed as "the first long Danish film,"[21]
conveniently neglecting the Fotorama film which was actually
100 meters longer, reveals his commitment to the promotion
of longer films as well as to his methods. He describes how
he threatened to withhold all Nordisk films from the largest
theater owner in Hamburg if the latter did not buy Den hvide
Slavehandel and premiere it the next day. Given the importance of Nordisk films in the German market at this time, the
theater owner had no alternative but to use the film. Olsen
then claims that the crowds that came by the third day of the
showing were so large that twenty policemen had to be used
to keep order.[22] In all, 103 copies of Den hvide Slavehandel
were sold, making it one of the biggest hits of the year.[23]

     Denmark's success with longer films apparently helped
break down prejudice against them in other countries. I have
already cited Robert Grau's remark in The Theater of Science
that gave Nordisk credit for the introduction of the multiple-
reel film into America. Ole Olsen implied this influence in his
account of the showing of Den hvide Slavehandel in Germany,[24]
and the same claim was made by The Kinematograph and Lantern Weekly for England and Italy. The British trade periodical specifically credited the success of selling Nordisk's long
releases on an exclusive rights basis for dissolving scepticism
about two- and three-reel films.[25] In another article Kinematograph told of the growing importance and public acceptance
of long films in Italy, citing the Pasquali Company as "the
first to follow the example of Nordisk...." Like Nordisk,
Pasquali also made social melodramas, circus films, and detective dramas, including one based on Sherlock Holmes called
Raffles on Top.[26] By October 1913 Kinematograph was claiming that "almost the whole of the films being prepared by the
Italian firms are much above the limit of 3000 feet, some even
reaching 6000 and 9000 feet."[27]

     In the spring of 1911 the manager of a British cinema
decided that his patrons would be satisfied with one long film

in an evening as well as they would with a program of short
films. The Nordisk film Den hvide Slavehandel II (under the
title In the Hands of Imposters) had shown to packed houses
and had received an enthusiastic audience response at Prince's
Picturedome in London during April. He reasoned that if the
long Danish film could be shown successfully, he would run
the three-reel Vitagraph film A Tale of Two Cities in one
evening. At the time it was usual to show each reel of a
multiple-reel film on separate evenings, thus requiring the
audience to return several times to see the entire film.[28]

Vitagraph produced a series of three-reel literary adaptations in 1911, including David Copperfield, Vanity Fair,
and Ivanhoe.[29] Edison and Kalem also began to release three-
reel subjects specifically meant to be shown at one time, rather
than in the reel-a-week format. In September 1911 Edison
came out with Foul Play and Kalem premiered Colleen Bawn.[30]

Soon long films from france and Germany also came on
the market. In August 1911 a three-reel Gaumont social drama
called The Outcast and a three-reel Eclair bandit adventure
called Zigomar opened in London.[31] In 1913 Eclair began a
nine-film series of Sherlock Holmes two reelers released at
monthly intervals and Pathé produced an eight-reel version
of Emile Zola's Germinal, with a running time close to three
hours.[32] In November 1913 the German four and a half reel
drama The Student of Prague, directed by a Dane, Stellan
Rye, opened in London to excellent reviews.[33]

Despite the popularity and success of long films in England and elsewhere, voices continued to be heard in the trade
calling for a return to the tried and trusted formulas on which
the industry had been founded. The case of the American
Biograph Company's opposition to long films and the con-
straints this policy put on Griffith's aspirations are well known.
In Italy, even when long films like Cabiria had become common, The Kinematograph and Lantern Weekly's correspondent
in Turin reported that many still believed long films would
ruin the industry.[34] As late as 1914 British detractors of
the long film were calling for a return to shorter films, re-
minding the industry that "the success of the picture theater
was founded on the unique variety of its program."[35] The
Kinematograph and Lantern Weekly itself expressed doubt
about the viability of long comedies. Although it found a recent five and a half reel comedy called Cupid Works Overtime

to be a success, most comedies, it maintained, should be con-
fined to one reel, noting that too much laughter brings on
pain--the opposite of comedy's intended effect.[36]

Although long films emerged in Denmark in 1910, it
was not until 1911 that other countries began to follow the
Danish lead. Once the trend started, it became irreversible
and changed the nature of the film industry. One observer
identified this development very clearly when he wrote, "One
Company [Nordisk] seems to have started what is likely to
be a new era in the trade...."[37]

The success of the white slave films inspired both Fotorama and Nordisk to make sequels. In September 1910 Fotorama released Slavehandlerens Flugt (The Slave Trader's Escape), or Den hvide Slavehandel II. Little is known about
the film, not even its length, and no prints have survived.
Nordisk made a second film, also called Den hvide Slavehandel
II or Den hvide Slavehandels sidste Offer (The White Slave
Trade's Last Victim, 930 m.--3 reels), which premiered in
January 1911. August Blom directed again, but this time
with greater success, producing a more complex and sensational film.

The story begins at a railroad station, the train diagonally
composed in the frame. The slave trader's agent is looking
for a prospect whom he finds in Edith von Felsen (Clara Wieth),
just boarding the train. The action changes to the train where
another agent, a woman, is seated next to Edith. Edith shows
the woman a letter from her aunt inviting Edith to stay with
her. (Edith's mother has just died.) The aunt is to meet
Edith at the ship she will be taking. The woman tells her
male confederate about Edith. The accomplice sends two tele-
grams, one to the aunt saying that her niece has been delayed and the other to another woman agent telling her to
pose as a friend of the aunt who will tell Edith that her aunt
had to go away for a few days. They take Edith to their
headquarters and one of the slavers calls another man. (This
is done using a split screen effect similar to that in Den hvide
Slavehandel I.) On the ship Edith had met a young engineer
named Faith (Lauritz Olsen). As she was leaving the ship,
Edith dropped her wallet and Faith found it. He goes to the
aunt's house to return it and, of course, discovers that something is amiss. Bright, who had been telephoned earlier by
the slave agent, arranges to buy Edith. Faith goes to the

police for help, but, as usual, they tell him there is nothing
they can do with the evidence he has. At a party Lord X
is attracted to Edith and also offers to buy her, but this
brings him into conflict with the other man who arranges to
abduct Edith in order not to lose her. The next day Edith
is alone in her room and Lord X arrives to take her for a car
ride. As soon as she gets in the car, the abductors drive
off with her, taking her to Bright's house. They refuse to
feed her until she yields to Bright. A Creole servant who
has been assigned to watch Edith takes pity on her, but
Bright beats her when she tries to give Edith help. Edith
defends her, however, and in gratitude the servant agrees
to take a note to Edith's aunt. The slave traders take the
note from the servant as she tries to leave the house, but
the servant manages to get to the aunt and tell her what has
happened to her niece. The servant also gives Faith a key
to Bright's house. Meanwhile, the slavers show up at Bright's.
Faith also arrives and subdues Bright, but as he is leaving
with Edith, the slavers grab her. A pursuit takes place, but
the slavers stop Faith's car and hold him at gunpoint until
they get away with Edith. The Creole, who had accompanied
Faith, manages to get on back of the slavers' car and so finds
out where Edith is being taken. Faith and the Creole go to
the police and this time get their aid. The slavers hide Edith
in a closet, however, so that the police are unable to find her.
After the police leave, Faith finds Edith and another chase
ensues, this time across rooftops where the police finally apprehend the slavers. With her rescue Edith is finally reunited
with her aunt.

     Not only does this film have a more complex plot and
more engaging action than Den hvide Slavehandel I, but it is
superior in a number of other ways as well. The sets are
done with greater attention to realism, an effect that the first
film was after but did not achieve. They are solidly constructed, fully decorated, and often quite elaborate, whereas
the sets for the earlier film are flimsy looking and only min-
imally decorated. As usual they are photographed at angles
and in deep focus, although the scenes, with two exceptions,
are still shot in single-camera setups, a technique which is
part of the Nordisk style. The realism of the interiors is
matched by a significant use of real locations for the outdoor
scenes, while the traveling scenes are done aboard real trains
and boats in motion.

Most interesting is the consistent use of available light
and of studio light that imitates, for expressive purposes,
the light of nature. In the first of the two train scenes Edith
and the slave agent appear to be lighted only by the light
that comes in from the window, through which the moving
landscape can be clearly seen. The conversation between the
two slave agents on the train is shot on an outside platform
and has a similar lighting effect. The scene of Edith alone in
her room just before Lord X comes for her begins very darkly,
but as Edith raises a shade, light from outside, apparently
intended to be a morning light, illumines her. It is a beautiful and quite convincing effect. The last scene of the film,
with Edith, her aunt, and Faith present, is given a sunset
effect as light coming through a window slowly fades. In
general, the lighting in Danish films was a major contribution
to the developing techniques of the cinema.

The success of Den hvide Slavehandel II was even
greater than that of Den hvide Slavehandel I; it sold about
260 copies. It was also more than 300 meters longer. The
third film in the Nordisk series, Urban Gad's version, has
already been discussed and appears to have been the last of
the white slavery films; it was released in November 1912.

Along with the success of the white slavery films went
controversy and censorship. In the United States the Danish
white slavery films were not even shown, at least at the time
of their initial release, although copies of Den hvide Slavehandel I and Den hvide Slavehandel II were sent to the Nordisk
agent in New York.[38] Other white slavery films also encountered problems. In December 1913 a court injunction was obtained against the showing of an American film called Inside
the White Slave Traffic, though the producers were able to
substitute a "European production" dealing with white slavery.[39] The following month an ad appeared for another white
slavery film called Curse of White Slavery. The distributor
of the film, All-Star Feature Company, was also calling for
the withdrawal of the most famous of the American white
slavery films, Traffic in Souls, on the grounds that its producers were making false claims when they said the film was
based on the recent John D. Rockefeller committee report on
white slavery. According to All-Star Features, Rockefeller
had denied there was any connection between his report and
Traffic in Souls.[40] At the same time, Oscar Hammerstein sued
to have Traffic in Souls removed from the Republic Theater

that the Hammerstein Opera Company owned and was leasing
to David Belasco. While this suit was in progress, Chief
Magistrate McAdoo in New York found another white slavery
film, A Victim of Sin, to be "gross, immoral and raw" and
threatened to take action against its producers if the film was
not withdrawn, which it shortly was. In another legal case
a grand jury indicted three men for their part in the production and exhibition of a film called The Inside of the White
Slave Traffic.[41]

The moral controversy surrounding white slavery films
prompted an interesting article in Motion Picture News which
discussed the effect of these moral questions on the film industry. The article mentions the great success of two such
films, The Fight and The Lure, neither of which is identified
beyond its title. Both films had been closed by the police
and reopened by the producers. As the publicity around
these actions grew, so did the crowds going to see the films.
Finally, legal pressure forced the producers to remove certain
objectionable scenes, after which attendance began to decline. [42]

The only American white slavery film currently available
is Traffic in Souls, directed by Richard Loan Tucker. Although this film may not be representative of the American
manifestation of the genre, it is typical of the differences
between American and Danish films and stands in contrast to
the Nordisk white slavery films. One of the most striking,
and unexpected, differences is that it is more graphic than
its Danish counterparts in making clear that the girls kidnapped by white slavers are used for prostitution. In general,
it was the Danish films that were more open about sexual content. Stylistically, Traffic in Souls shows a concern with
montage, especially in cross-cutting, that is rarely seen in
Danish films which put more emphasis on mise-en-scène.
Traffic in Souls also uses closer camera setups and has a more
complex plot structure than any of the Danish white slavery
films. Like the Danish films, however, it makes extensive use
of location shooting and should be considered an important
example of the early feature-length film.

The notoriety of the white slavery film in general and
the importance of Traffic in Souls in particular are attested
to by the appearance in early 1914 of a parody film called
Traffickers in Soles, released by Feature Photoplay Company
and billed as "a 3 reel Comedy-Travesty." Advertising for

the parody film also refers to the Rockefeller report, pro-
claiming that "Rockefeller and his millions could not do what
the two world-wide famous police inspectors, Levy and McGui-
ness, have done to reform the Traffickers in Soles."[43] The
ability of Traffic in Souls to generate a parody is certainly
evidence that the film had been widely seen, since for a
parody to be economically viable it must have a ready-made
audience already familiar with the original being parodied.

Fotorama, the company that started both the impetus
to longer films and cinematic interest in white slavery, made
at least thirty-one films in 1910-14.[44] Only eight of these,
however, exist in any form; in most cases the prints are
fragmentary, or at best out of sequence, and poor in photographic quality. Six of the eight are from 1910: Elverhøj,
Ambrosius, Holger Danske, I Bondefangerklør, Ansigtstyven,
and the already mentioned Den hvide Slavehandel.

Elverhøj (Elf Hill, circa 250 m.--1 reel) is based on one
of the most popular plays of the Danish theater, written in
1828 by Johan Ludvig Heiberg for a wedding in the Danish
royal family.[45] It tells the story of a girl raised by elves and
and is done entirely in long shot and with theatrical sets.
The play was also used as the basis for a film by Biorama in
the same year. The two versions are very similar, though the
sets of the Fotorama version are somewhat better and the Biorama film is over 100 meters longer than Fotorama's.

Ambrosius (Ambrose, 139 m. survived) is another theatrical adaptation, this time from an 1817 play of the same
name by Christian K. F. Molbech about an early eighteenth-
century poet named Ambrosius Stub who died unrecognized.[46]
The film was directed by Eduard Schnedler-Sørensen, soon
to become an important director at Nordisk. The fragment
that remains shows a troubador getting drunk at a social
gathering and then walking dejectedly down a street; both
scenes are shown in long shot and single-camera setups.

Holger Danske (Ogier the Dane), based on traditional
Danish tales, has survived in fragmentary form, though how
much of the film has come down to us is uncertain since its
original length is not known. The current prints are 64 m.
and show the old bearded warrior, Holger Danske, sitting at
a stone table. He has a vision of a young girl who is then
carried into a cave by the villain. Holger enters and kills

him and then reenters the room with the stone table and sits
down. Directed by Eduard Schnedler-Sørensen, the fragment
is insufficient to make any judgments.

I Bondefangerklør (In the Claws of Confidence Men,
50 m. survived) is out of sequence and incomplete, as is
Ansigtstyven (The Face Thief, 100 m. survived). Ansigtstyven is of interest because it is a crime film involving a double,
a device which is used in other crime films of the period, and
because in one scene the villains escape on a railroad handcar
they steal from two railroad workers. Although this scene is
treated simply (they only ride away from the camera), it brings
to mind Griffith's famous handcar chase in A Girl and Her
Trust (1912) and a similar scene from Nordisk's Gar El Hama
II (1912) directed by Eduard Schnedler-Sørensen. Ansigtstyven led to a sequel, Ansigtstyven II, the next month, following the pattern of series crime films established by Nordisk.

The only Fotorama film to survive in substantial form is
the 1911 En Hjemløs Fugl (U.S. title, Homeless, 962 m.--3
reels). It was copyrighted in the United States by Ingvald
Oes for Great Northern, and has been preserved in the paper
print collection of the Library of Congress.[47] Nordisk shipping records, however, indicate that only one regular print
and one paper print were sent to the United States, so that
it does not appear that the film was actually distributed here.
Also, the American trade journals make no mention of the film.

The story concerns an unfaithful wife who abandons
her husband and child after being caught twice with another
man, once by an old friend, who is also an admirer of hers,
and once by her husband. The woman and her lover run off
together, taking with them money he has stolen from his employer. The man is caught, but the woman escapes with the
money in her purse. The purse is stolen from her by another
woman who is run down by a car while escaping. The police
recover the purse and think its owner is now dead. Penniless,
she becomes a street singer, but is soon given a regular singing job. She becomes successful and returns home to find
that her husband has remarried. She kidnaps her daughter
but repents of her action and returns the child. She then
tries to commit suicide but is stopped by the old friend who
had originally caught her with her lover.

This rapid flow of sensational incidents, typical for

Danish melodramas of infidelity, unfolds mostly in terms of
the acting and action rather than the camera and editing.
In general, scenes are shot in single-camera setup and follow
each other in chronological sequence.

According to Ebbe Neergaard, Fotorama devoted itself
largely to sensational melodrama and was in competition with
Biorama which specialized in the same kind of material. As
Neergaard puts it regarding Biorama:

> No art talk there, but hard-hitting titles like The
> Revenge of the Apache Girl, Copenhagen By Night,
> In the Claws of Confidence Men [a title used by both
> Fotorama and Biorama], Dark Copenhagen, The Lersø
> Gang (based on a topical crime case), The Hyena of
> the Big City ... The Modern Messalina, The Last
> Victim of the Bird of Prey, The Carbuncle Queen,
> The Men of Dusk. If only the films had been as
> good as the titles! He [Søren Nielsen, the owner of
> Biorama] is said to have made one called The Mys-
> teries of the Skeleton Island.[48]

Biorama made at least seventy-seven fiction and nonfiction films in 1910-14, including those made under its new
name adopted in 1912, Filmfabrikken Skandinavien. In addition to the already mentioned Elverhøj, however, only six
others have survived: København ved Nat (1910), Bukseskørtet (1911), and Brudekjolen (1911), made under the Biorama name; and Lumpacivagabundus (1912), Gaardmandsdatt-
eren (1912), and Dødsvarslet (1912), made for Filmfabrikken
Skandinavien.

København ved Nat (Copenhagen by Night, circa 400 m.
--circa 1½ reels) is a comedy directed by Carl Alstrup and
includes Oscar Stribolt in the cast. It is a typical farce, not
unlike those produced by many American and European companies, in which some gentlemen go partying, only to get
themselves in trouble with the law and with their wives. Each
scene is shot entirely in uninterrupted long shots. The sets
are generally solid looking, especially in the men's homes, and
entrances and exits are made through doors built into the
sets. The acting style is broad with a great deal of slapstick
humor. Overall, the film has little to recommend it.

Bukseskørtet (A Pair of Trousers, length unknown) is

also a comedy, shot almost entirely on one interior set. It is about two women who get into trouble by wearing pants in public.

About half of Brudekjolen (The Wedding Dress, 450 m. --1½ reels) has survived, but even this amount makes it clear that this Cinderella story of a poor girl and the son of a rich family is of little interest.

Lumpacivagabundus or Haandværkersvendens Æventyr (The Journeymen's Adventure, 750 m.--2½ reels) is a slight comedy about three happy journeymen as they go from one roadhouse to another until they split up. Except for the presence of Oscar Stribolt the film has little to recommend it. Current prints, however, are missing almost half the original material, making it difficult to evaluate the film.

Gaardmansdatteren (The Farmer's Daughter, 475 m.-- 1½ reels) is primitive for a 1912 film. The camera is always in long shot with single takes for each scene and the story is told more through the intertitles than the images. In keeping with the theatrical look of the film, the actors take a bow to the camera at the end of the last scene. The story is quite conventional, telling of a poor farm hand who makes a fortune in America and returns to marry the daughter of a farmer who had originally dismissed him. Current prints are missing about one-third of the original material, though the missing scenes probably could do little to change the simplistic plot.

Dødsvarslet (A Death Warning, 700 m.--circa 2½ reels) is the only one of the surviving films that fits Ebbe Neergaard's description of Biorama's productions. It is also the only surviving film of genuine interest. This may be due to Aage Brandt's direction. Though only a fragment of one of his other films has survived, Skæbnens Dom (Fate's Judgment, 1915), it shows the same attention to setting and lighting that characterize Dødsvarslet. Brandt was a student of the influential theater director Karl Mantzius. He acted for several years for director Emil Wulff of the Frederiksberg Theater and later at the Centrateatret and the Odense Theater where he played Mefisto in Faust. He entered film work as an actor and became a director for Filmfabrikken Skandinavien.[49]

Dødsvarslet begins with a shot of people in a theater box apparently watching a performance. There is a cut to

a woman dancing in Egyptian costume. One of the men in the
box, a painter, invites the dancer to his studio where she
poses for him in costume. Her husband (lover?) finds out
about this and goes to the studio, forcing her to leave. A
half year later she gets a note from the painter, and he
visits her at home. Here we get a series of shots of them
(walking, in a row boat, and kissing) that have a freedom of
execution and a nonnarrative leisureliness that make them very
modern in feeling. She leaves her husband who is also a
stage performer. (Some material appears to be missing between the original meeting of the painter and the dancer and
these scenes at her house. Over 100 m. are apparently missing from present day prints.) The husband meets an old
friend, a hypnotist, who agrees to help him get even with
the painter. One day the dancer and the painter pass the
hypnotist on the street, and he does something to the painter
that causes him to begin seeing the hypnotist's face (a double
exposure effect). The painter gives a ball, and the hypnotist
shows up. Using a mirror to get the painter's eye, the hypnotist forces him to shoot himself.

The use of hypnotic control is common in early Danish
cinema and anticipates the hypnotic and supernatural powers
of such later characters as Dr. Caligari, Dr. Mabuse, and
Nosferatu. Other examples of this narrative device will be
discussed in this and the next chapter.

Along with Kosmorama's Afgrunden and Fotorama's Den
hvide Slavehandel as influential films from minor companies is
Kinografen's 1911 drama De fire Djævle (The Four Devils).
Ebbe Neergaard considered it "the most important circus film
of the period."[50] It became a great international success;
Jay Leyda, for example, mentioned it, along with Afgrunden,
as having played a significant role in influencing prerevolu-
tionary Russian cinema.[51] The film is based on a story by
Herman Bang, adapted for the screen by Carl Rosenbaum,
and directed by Robert Dinesen and Alfred Lind. At 880 m.
(3 reels) it is also one of the longest films made until that
time. Later, the story was adapted twice more for the screen,
first by the Danish director A. W. Sandberg in Germany and
then by F. W. Murnau in America.[52]

The film begins with a title stating that "the action takes
place in Copenhagen today." Two poor boys are sold to an
old man who trains children in dance and circus. He is also

training two girls at the same time. They make an appearance
in a suburban variety show, and after the show Fa'er Cecchi,
the trainer, invites a man to his place to drink and gamble.
Fa'er Cecchi gets mad at the man, however, and chases him
out. Six years later the foursome is seen rehearsing for the
circus, still under Fa'er Cecchi's training. Some more years
pass and Fa'er Cecchi has died. The act is without work,
and one of the girls, Aimée (Edith Buemann), donates her
jewelry to keep them going. Fritz (Robert Dinesen), another
member of the troup, gets an idea for a sensational circus
act. One day at the circus a countess slips Fritz a note asking him to meet her at her home. Aimée, who loves Fritz,
notices that something is up and follows Fritz to the rendezvous. He spends the night with the woman while Aimée
waits outside. The meetings continue until Aimée finally confronts Fritz; he just pushes her away, however. The aerial
act that the troupe performs does not use a net and Aimée,
who is supposed to catch Fritz, lets him fall to his death.
Aimée then jumps to her death.

De fire Djævle is a very ambitious film for 1911. It
utilizes a variety of camera distances and angles (unlike Nordisk films), a panning camera to follow the action in several
scenes, careful matching of the action from one shot to another
and, in one sequence, cross-cutting between Fritz as he tries
to decide whether to keep his appointment with the countess
and Aimée as she worries about Fritz's strange behavior.
The most famous and striking shot, however, takes place at
the end of the film. After Aimée has jumped to her death
and there has been a shot of the countess who has seen both
falls, there follows a close shot of the empty trapeze swinging
back and forth. In addition, the film has a restrained acting
style and excellent blocking of the actors in the mise-en-
scène.

The style of this film contrasts strongly with that of
most Nordisk films. The narrative structure is more complex
and the camera placements and cutting more varied and interesting. In the films of August Blom, for example, Nordisk's
principal director in 1911, there is a tendency to restrict the
narrative action to one location at a time with very little feeling of the extension of events beyond the frame. De fire
Djævle gives much more the feeling of a total world, of the
interaction of events. This is sometimes achieved by cross-
cutting, but also by staying with a character in two consecutive

shots and by varying the characters' distance from the camera. Ebbe Neergaard calls it "the first film told in reasonably modern film language," a statement which does not do
justice to the best work of Griffith in the same period, but
one which does indicate the sophistication of this film's tech-
nique.53

     It is difficult to know who should be given the most
credit for this achievement. The story itself, though from a
well-known author, is unremarkable, and even if it were
otherwise, this would not guarantee an interesting production.
Of the two directors only Alfred Lind had prior experience
in directing for film, including Fotorama's Den hvide Slavehandel. He was also an experienced cameraman and, in addition to sharing the direction, also photographed the film. In
fact, Lind's film experience went back to 1906 when he made
some of the technical installations for the newly founded Nordisk Films Kompagni. In 1906 he also photographed a workers'
May Day demonstration in Copenhagen and the following year
traveled around Scandinavia filming. He also operated the
first cinema in Iceland before returning to Denmark to work
for Fotorama in Aarhus and then for Kosmorama and Kinografen. Later, he set up his own studio in Ordrup, Alfred
Lind Film, and made films in Germany, Italy, and France.
In 1938 he returned to Denmark and set up a film school.54

     Robert Dinesen, on the other hand, had a theatrical
background. After spending three years at sea as a young
man, he studied acting with Nicolai Neiiendam, V. Herold, V.
Lincke, and at the Dagmarteatret school. He made his stage
debut on October 23, 1894 and worked at the Dagmar until
1905. After that he toured Scandinavia, returning in 1908-09
to Det Ny Teater and in 1909-10 to the Dagmar. In 1910 he
made his film debut as the engineer in Afgrunden. The same
year he moved to Kinografen and then to Nordisk where he
stayed through the teens. In 1920 he went to Palladium as
director. That same year he visited Berlin where he met Joe
May who offered him a contract to work in Germany. This
move to Germany, made by many of the best Danish film people, was justified in retrospect by Dinesen in an interview
on his eightieth birthday:

          At that time Berlin was for us Danes the gateway to
          the international life, a beautiful city, which, without
          exception, agreed with us all. Never were two days

the same, and the comradeship in the cinema was
unique. That is the only acceptable excuse why I
never went home.

When Goebbels took charge of theater and film in Germany,
Dinesen decided to quit entirely, though he remained in Germany. He died in Berlin in March 1972 at the age of ninety-
seven, having made his last film in 1929.[55]

The combination of Alfred Lind and Robert Dinesen,
given their respective experiences, may account for both the
cinematic boldness of the film and its restrained acting and
subtle mise-en-scène. Ebbe Neergaard, who does not credit
Lind with codirection of the film (this he assigns to Carl
Rosenbaum who wrote the scenario), acknowledges the influence that Lind probably had in "making this the first film
told in reasonably modern film language. In his own unre-
liable, roaming way he had a considerable influence on the
development of Danish film."[56] That Alfred Lind was connected with Den hvide Slavehandel, Afgrunden, and De fire
Djævle, the three most influential films of Danish cinema's
golden age, seems to justify Neergaard's evaluation of him.
As will be seen later in this study, Alfred Lind continued to
be associated with interesting film projects.

Although none of the other surviving Kinografen films
measure up to Den fire Djævle, they are not without interest.
Released about three months after Den fire Djævle was a one-
reel comedy called En Bryllupsaften (A Wedding Night, 290 m.
--1 reel), directed by Einar Zangenberg and with Robert
Dinesen as the bridegroom. On her wedding night a girl's
mother sends a note to the new couple's maid instructing her
not to let the daughter go to bed without her tea. The maid
continually interrupts the couple whose only thought is to
get to bed.

This short bedroom farce is a good example of erotic
subject matter, found so commonly in the dramas, treated comically, though still maintaining its basic character. Most of
the film takes place in one room and is seen in long and full
shots. In one scene the couple is shown from inside the
house through an open door arriving at their new home. This
same shot, incidentally, can be found in a number of Danish
films from the period, often providing for interesting silhouette
effects. In another scene the camera looks past the couple

into their bedroom from a slightly high angle which reveals
the corner of their bed, thus linking the characters with
their ultimate goal.

Ildfluen (The Firefly, 1913), also directed by Einar
Zangenberg, was originally 1325 m. (circa 4½ reels), though
present day prints are only about 960 m. It is well photographed, with a number of well-executed panning shots and
interesting camera setups. The story is a patchwork of conventional melodramatic situations, including children stolen by
gypsies, a nobleman in love with a circus entertainer, a
gambling, bomb-throwing villain, and a reuniting of the kidnapped children with their mother after many years have
passed.

The typical romance and melodrama of Ildfluen are common in the early cinema, and whether they work or not depends very much on the treatment given them. In this case,
although they are instructive because so conventional, they
are never very interesting. More successful is a different
kind of melodrama found in a serial-like adventure called
Den røde Klub (The Red Club, 1,185 m.--4 reels), also from
1913 and starring Einar Zangenberg; it is not known whether
he also directed the film. Its exaggerated situations, trap
doors, chases, and secret societies are well staged and sufficiently entertaining that the incompleteness of the print does
not destroy the film's effectiveness. What in 1913 demanded
clear story telling in order to be successful, today succeeds
on a more abstracted level of the conventions for their own
sake.

Prince Stanislao (Tronier Funder) and the Baroness
Sonia (Edith Buemann Psilander) are lovers, but politics demands that Stanislao marry Princess Ilka. Sonia sees an announcement of their engagement and, enraged, allows her
maid, Ziska, to take her to a secret association which is a
threat to the Prince. Boris, an army captain, sees Sonia
dressed as a man and follows her to the hideout of the Red
Club. After gaining entrance by force, he falls down a
chute into a room filled with electrical equipment. Boris
escapes by causing a short-circuit explosion. Sonia shoots
Boris with a gun containing some kind of spray. Next we
see her at a secret meeting of the Red Club.

Reel two of the film begins with Boris, in civilian clothes,

arming himself with a gun and flashlight. He ties up Sonia,
still in man's clothes, in the basement of her house and goes
for the police. When they return, Sonia is gone. While
looking for her, they fall into a pit and are shut in by Sonia
and a confederate who is wearing a police uniform. Boris
sets a small explosive charge that opens the trap door that
keeps them prisoner. He then follows Sonia and the president
of the Red Club through another trap door, but they catch
him and hang him from a hook by his hands which have been
tied together. They attach a gun to a clock and aim it at
Boris; at a certain time a string will be pulled tight, squeez-
ing the trigger. The police find Boris and save him just as
the gun goes off. Meanwhile, Sonia, now dressed as a soldier,
visits Stanislao with the intention of killing him. Boris arrives just in time to prevent the murder, though Sonia escapes,
with Boris and the police in pursuit. A gun battle takes
place throughout the chase. Boris finally catches up to
them, and another gun battle takes place in a cellar. As the
president of the Red Club is about to shoot Boris, Sonia
throws herself in the way of the bullet, saving Boris and
receiving a fatal wound. Just before the house explodes,
Boris carries Sonia outside where she dies.

Two other Kinografen films have survived: Det Indiske
Gudebillede (The Indian Idol) (1915), to be dealt with in the
next chapter, and Badhotellet (The Baths Hotel, 1,240 m.--
4 reels), of which only a fragment (about one-sixth) remains.
Little can be said about Badhotellet. The interiors have a
solidity and reality similar to that which characterizes Nordisk
films, and a few ship scenes at the end of the fragment were
shot on location. The story apparently involved a love triangle. Einar Zangenberg and Edith Buemann Psilander are in
the cast; the director of the film has not been identified.

In all, Kinografen made at least seventy-six films from
1910 to 1914, both nonfiction and fiction. Many, if not most,
of the fiction films were directed by Einar Zangenberg and,
judging from the titles, covered a variety of subjects: Menne-
skedyret (The Human Monster, 1912), Efter Dødsspringet
(After a Death Leap, 1912), Marconi Telegrafisten (Marconi-
Telegrapher, 1912), Moderkærlighed (Mother Love, 1913),
Skuespilleren (The Actor, 1913), Den store Circusbrand (The
Great Circus Fire, 1913), Livets Ubønhørlighed (Relentless-
ness of Life, 1913), Elskovsbarnet (A Love Child, 1914). The
nonfiction films were typically diverse: Dansk Industri (Danish

Industry), Den internationale Kaproning (The International
Boat Race), Den lanske Marine (The Danish Navy), Københavns Cirkusbrænder (Copenhagen's Circus Fire), Frederiksberg Have (Frederiksberg Garden), Christian den IV's Byg-
ningsværker (Christian the IV's Buildings), and Spejderkorp-
set (A Boy Scout Troop).[57]

In the nonfiction film Peter Elfelt continued to be active,
producing at least eighteen films, including scenics, coverage
of sports, public events, and personalities, and a six-part
series entitled Kalkbruddet i Limhamn (Limestone Quarry in
Limhamn).[58] Although he continued to document some of the
people and events of his time, his importance as a filmmaker
had passed, along with the importance of the nonfiction film
itself.

Despite the significance to the Danish film industry of
the Nordisk rivals cited so far, none of them produced works
which artistically deserve to be included among the major
films of the time. However, two other companies, and two
directors in particular, did emerge in this period that can
lay legitimate claim to a permanent place in film history on
the basis of artistic merit. That neither the companies nor
the directors are widely known only stresses the need to
bring them to light. In the case of one of these directors
none of his films were known to have survived until three
prints were found in 1975. The companies are Det Skandinavisk-
russike Handelshus (The Scandinavian-Russian Trade Company)
and Dansk Biografkompagni; the directors, Vilhelm Glückstadt
and Benjamin Christensen. Christensen, of course, is known,
though this films made before Häxan (U.S. title, Witchcraft
Through the Ages, 1918-21), have been seen by few people
outside Denmark and are not currently in distribution.
Glückstadt is hardly known even in Denmark, and until recently has been only a name for a few film historians.

Benjamin Christensen is second only to Carl Dreyer
among the ranks of Danish film directors. To say this is not
to link him to Dreyer, as some people have done, but merely
to ascribe to Dreyer an artistic preeminence that few filmmakers in the whole history of the cinema have equaled. As John
Ernst, in his monograph on Christensen, has pointed out, however, the comparison of Christensen to Dreyer is one of the
labels that Christensen has never been able to escape, a comparison which Ernst considers "superficial (and erroneous)"

and ultimately results in "a disservice to both Dreyer and
Christensen, even if it is meant as a compliment to them
both."59

     Benjamin Christensen was born on September 28, 1879
in Viborg, Denmark.60 His father, a well-established businessman, sent him to the best school in the city, Cathedral
School, where he studied Romance languages. After gradu-
ating he went to Copenhagen to study medicine, but in a
couple of years turned to opera singing, entering the students' academy of the Royal Theater in 1901. He made his
debut in 1902 in the part of Masetto in Don Giovanni. His
voice failed, however, because of a nervous disorder diagnosed
as incurable. With this he turned to acting and, after completing his acting studies, was hired by the City Theater in
Aarhus where he remained for three years and where he also
received his first assignments as a director. He then went
to the Folketeatret (The National Theater) in Copenhagen,
but there his acting voice failed as well. In 1907 he left the
theater and became a wholesaler in French wines. He continued to look for other opportunities, however, and in 1911,
encouraged by Robert Storm-Petersen, entered film work as
an actor for Dansk Biografkompagni. It is reported that,
along with many others, he had seen Afgrunden and had been
strongly impressed by the possibilities of film. When Dansk
Biografkompagni's president, Carl Rosenbaum, resigned,
Christensen took over and, in 1913, began production of the
first film under his own direction, Det hemmelighedsfulde X
(The Mysterious X--U.S. title, Sealed Orders, 1,977 m.--6½
reels). Until this film was completed Christensen continued
with his activities in the wine business. In 1915 he began
work on a second film called Manden uden Ansigt (The Man
Without a Face), which was never finished. This was followed
by Hævnens Nat (Night of Revenge, 1,950 m.--6½ reels),
which was his final production for Dansk Biografkompagni.

     Det hemmelighedsflude X and Hævnens Nat (U.S. title,
Blind Justice) were very successful in the United States and
brought Christensen an offer from Vitagraph to be its chief
supervisor. Hævnens Nat opened at the Rialto Theater in
New York on January 29, 1917 with accompaniment by a fifty-
piece orchestra. It had also been shown, with much success,
at Sing Sing prison, since the film deals with an ex-convict.
Christensen returned to Denmark after attending the opening
of Hævnens Nat and, incidentally, meeting Mary Pickford.

He was filled with admiration for the American cinema, stating that he would try to learn from it.[61]

Christensen's next project was for the Swedish company, Svenska Biografteatern. From 1918 to 1921 he worked on his most famous film, Häxan (The Witch, 2,500 m.--circa 8 reels). Although backed by a Swedish company, it was made in Denmark and had a Danish crew and cast. It was released in February 1922 and caused much controversy over both its content and form. It was originally planned as the first part of a trilogy about superstition through the ages, but parts two and three, to be entitled The Saint and The Spirits, were not made.

After Häxan Christensen went to Germany where he directed Seine Frau, Die Unbekannte (1923) for Decla-Bioscop and acted in Dreyer's Mikaël. He also began a picture for UFA entitled The Woman Who Did, starring Lionel Barrymore and Henry Vibart, which was left unfinished. Between 1926 and 1929 he directed six films in Hollywood: The Devil's Circus and Mockery for MGM; Hawk's Nest for First National; and The Haunted House, House of Horror, and Seven Footprints to Satan for Warner Brothers. At the beginning of the 1930s he returned to Denmark and between 1939 and 1942 made four films for Nordisk Films Kompagni, Skilsmissens Børn (Children of Divorce), Barnet (A Child), Gaa med mig Hjem (Come Home with Me), and Damen med de lyse handsker (The Lady with the Light Gloves). His last film was received very badly and he retired to become the director of the suburban cinema called Rio Bio.[62]

In a 1921 essay Christensen called for a new kind of author, a call which characterized his forward-looking thought about film and, at the same time, defined what he himself had already achieved and contributed to Danish cinema.

> ... this is what must be made clear to everyone, that the word and the picture are two separate arts, which speak to us differently. And therefore we must have two kinds of authors: the word's and the picture's! Let us soon find the picture's author, the film's artists, who work directly for the film and themselves make the films.[63]

Carl Dreyer, writing in 1922, recognized the visionary

qualities of Christensen and singled him out for special recognition among Danish filmmakers. Referring to Det hemmelighedsflude X and Hævnens Nat he noted:

> Certainly they meant a tremendous step forward at
> the time, but what was surprising then was a work-
> ing technique, dazzling in details, against which the
> manuscripts seemed pretty mediocre.
>   ... behind these two films one caught a glimpse
> of the outlines of a personality that is not common
> within the ranks of film people ... a man who knew
> exactly what he wanted and pursued his goal with
> unyielding stubbornness.... It created a stir that
> he took half a year to make a film (usually eight to
> ten days was the norm). People shrugged him off
> as a madman. The way things have turned out it
> is clear that he was the one in touch with the fu-
> ture.[64]

When Det hemmelighedsflude X opened in the United
States it was greeted enthusiastically:

> This feature is nothing less than a revelation in dra-
> matic motion pictures. It sets a new and hitherto
> but hoped for standard of quality. It emphasizes as
> no other film production the absolute superiority of
> the screen over the stage and opens up a vista of
> coming triumphs for the motion picture....
>   An extraordinary boldness of invention joined with
> a mastery of detail that approaches genius help to
> make this feature rise above all which has been
> filmed before.[65]

Bush's praise of the film was only surpassed by his praise
of Christensen whom he called "a man of inspirations ... an
artist who can do things with and on the screen the like of
which has heretofore been almost unknown."

The New York Dramatic Mirror and Motion Picture News
were no less enthusiastic in their praise of the film. The Mirror maintained that when "viewing the picture you are held
in the grasp of a master director's art,"[66] while the News,
going farther than either MPW or The Mirror, saw it almost
in apocalyptic terms:

If this, the first of the 'De Luxe Attractions [one
of the American distributors of the film] to be offered ... is a criterion of those that are to follow,
it may be said without fear of contradiction that the
day of the motion picture's perfection is close at
hand.
     ... as nearly flawless, considered from any angle
you choose, as any screen production can be. It is
a gem, beside which most other big features--even
the best--compare as tawdrily as would a tinsel gew-
gaw beside a diamond of purest water.
     Photographically, the production is a marvel ...
[it] will ... be recognized as one of the greatest
motion pictures which has ever been shown to the
American public.67

     The specific assertion that Det hemmelighedsfulde X
rises "above all which has been filmed before" is debatable,
but the general praise of the film is certainly valid. It deserves to be included among such early landmarks as Judith
of Bethulia, The Avenging Conscience, and Cabiria, and it
is only one of the accidents of film history and perhaps one
of the shortcomings of film scholarship that it is not as well
known as these films.

     Det hemmelighedsfulde X tells a story of honor and
suspected infidelity admidst a setting of war and spying.
When war breaks out, naval lieutenant van Hauen (Benjamin
Christensen) receives sailing orders from his father, the fleet
admiral. Prior to this time, Count Spinelli (Herman Spiro),
who is a spy for the enemy, had made advances toward Lt.
van Hauen's wife (Karen Caspersen). Although she had always rebuffed him, she did give him a photograph of herself
with a note on the back saying that she would never see him
again. Just before van Hauen is to sail, Spinelli visits the
wife again while her husband is out, but again she rebuffs
him. When van Hauen returns unexpectedly, his wife makes
Spinelli hide, fearing that her husband will misunderstand.
While van Hauen is saying good-bye to his children, Spinelli
breaks open the sealed orders that van Hauen had left on
the mantelpiece. He copies them and returns them to their
case. Meanwhile, van Hauen finds a fragment of a note that
Spinelli had written to the wife. The note is not incriminat-
ing in its entirety, but reading a portion of it leads van Hauen
to think his wife has been unfaithful. He accuses her and,

as he is about to leave in anger, discovers Spinelli hiding.
This, of course, only confirms his suspicions. A fellow officer arrives to get van Hauen, and they leave for their ship.

Knowing the content of the sealed orders, Spinelli com-
municates them to his confederates via carrier pigeon. The
pigeons are kept in an old mill, so Spinelli must go there to
send his message. After releasing the bird Spinelli goes
through a trap door into a lower portion of the mill. A gust
of wind blows the outer door of the mill shut which, in turn,
slams down and jams the trap door. Spinelli cannot get out,
and after some time in the room, he writes a note confessing
his deeds. While this is occurring, the carrier pigeon is shot
down by a soldier on van Hauen's side, and the contents of
the message are communicated to Admiral van Hauen. Intent
on finding out how the sealed orders have gotten into enemy
hands, the admiral summons his son. When they find that
the orders have been opened, the lieutenant is arrested.

During his trial for treason, the wife shows up with
Spinelli's overcoat, which the count had left behind. A copy
of the sealed orders is found in the pocket, but to save family honor van Hauen claims that the coat is actually his. This
brings about his conviction, and van Hauen is sentenced to
death. When fighting breaks out near van Hauen's home, the
wife seeks shelter in the old mill. Spinelli is discovered along
with his confession, and the wife races to save her husband,
arriving just as they are about to shoot him. With this the
husband and wife are reunited and the misunderstanding
cleared up.

As Dreyer had remembered, the script is mediocre, but
as Christensen had envisioned, the film was "written" in pictures and communicated by means other than words. Perhaps
the thing that is most striking about the film is its lighting,
and this is a cinema that is generally impressive for its use
of light. Christensen, however, takes the use of light as an
expressive tool farther than any of his contemporaries. Especially impressive are night scenes in van Hauen's house in
which only parts of the main room are lighted (either using
the room's electric lights or the bright Scandinavian summer
nights as the supposed source of the light) and the scenes
in the old mill in which much is made of silhouette effects
based on light that seems to enter only from windows and
doors. There are also some fine flashlight effects as the

spies move about inside the dark mill. A principal use of the
light is for the creation of interior frames, using only portions
of the screen to heighten dramatic effect. In the mill scenes
the lighting and interior framing are concrete expressions of
the spies' secretiveness, of the very nature of their activity.
The skillful use of mirrors to reflect action also plays a part
in these effects.

Although not as immediately startling as the lighting in
the film, the cutting and certain uses of the camera also demand close attention. Christensen appears to have been well
aware that the particular way in which a scene was shot and
cut was determined by the specific demands of the story. For
the most part a stationary camera was the general rule in
1913, especially in Danish cinema, which has few examples of
expressive camera technique. Christensen, however, was more
flexible and inventive than any of his colleagues and experi-
mented in ways that anticipated later developments in film
form.

The absence of an expressive camera technique in most
Danish films has been attributed to a specific source by John
Ernst. Comparing the 1913 Nordisk film Atlantis to Det
hemmelighedsfulde X, he makes the following observation:

> Where Atlantis is rather the culmination of a stylistic
> development, which began with photographed theater,
> Det hemmelighedsfulde X is the beginning of some-
> thing new. Benjamin Christensen introduces the ex-
> pressive in film art (not to be confused with a phil-
> osophically based expressionism ... even if the X
> also played a certain part for some film artists who
> created the expressionistic German film). The ex-
> pressive here should be understood as a form of film
> dynamics and film drama which came into being due
> to the film's own means, in this case, first and fore-
> most in the cutting, the camera movements and the
> lighting.[68]

One sequence in particular points out the expressive cutting
and camera techniques of which Christensen was capable.
It is also an extraordinary scene in terms of lighting, so
that it becomes a convergence of the three elements of "the
film's own means" that Ernst identifies.

The sequence is the one in which Spinelli is trapped in
the mill. A door blown open by the wind has jammed shut
the trap door that leads to the room in which Spinelli is working. Because the outer door stands open over the trap door,
Spinelli cannot lift the trap door when he attempts to leave.
Not knowing what has happened, he pushes frantically on the
trap door, but to no avail. Spinelli's growing frenzy is communicated clearly by Christensen's cross-cutting between shots
of Spinelli in the lower room and shots of the bottom of the
outer door with the trap door banging against it. In order
to clearly delineate the nature of Spinelli's predicament, Christensen shows the impossibility of ever opening the trap door
as long as the outer door remains in place. To do this he
photographs the full length of the outer door and, especially,
the hinges which hold it to the door frame, which, despite
Spinelli's pushing upward, cannot come apart, and so allow
the outer door to fall out of the way. Of the two ways of
doing this, cutting to a shot of the hinges or panning up to
the hinges, Christensen chooses the latter, giving a strong
sense of the cause and effect relationship at work in Spinelli's
entrapment while maintaining the tension built up by the image of the trap door banging against the bottom of the outer
door. This sequence provides one of the earliest and most
sophisticated examples of an action built from the juxtaposition of its constituent elements and compares favorably to the
policeman's interrogation of the newphew in D. W. Griffith's
The Avenging Conscience (1914).69

In some ways Vilhelm Glückstadt is an even more fas-
cinating figure than Benjamin Christensen, if only because
he is almost entirely unknown, while his films are among the
most interesting produced anywhere in the world. For Ebbe
Neergaard, Glückstadt was just a name in film history because
none of his films had survived. Even so, he mentions him
favorably a number of times in his discussion of The Scandinavian-Russian Trade Company.70 Since Neergaard's book
was written, three Glückstadt films have been found, and he
can now be put in some perspective.

Glückstadt was born on February 18, 1885, the young-
est son of a wholesale merchant, Moritz Glückstadt, and Pauline
Jacobsen. He was a student in Gammelholms Latin and Real-
skole, but left school early without taking his exams. Early
on he exhibited skill in writing and was in a position to devote himself to it. At age sixteen he was appointed a trainee

at Landmansbank's Frederiksberg branch and eventually advanced to assistant. In 1906 he established, along with Kay van der Aa Kühle and Johan Christensen, a wholesale firm called Det Skandinavisk-russike Handelshus, which at first dealt in wine, whiskey, and other goods, but later became an agent for foreign films, particularly those of the Vitagraph Company of America.[71] After the success of Afgrunden, they began to make films as well, building a studio in Hellerup, a suburb of Copenhagen. In 1913 the company changed its name to Filmfabrikken Danmark, with Glückstadt as director. In 1916 he left his work as a film director for reasons that are unclear.[72] In 1920 he appears to have been involved in film distribution since he was being sued, along with Christensen and a man named Ullberg, for fraud in regard to some American films to which they had received the Scandinavian rights, but which they were also selling to Germany. The suit was decided against Glückstadt and Christensen, who were fined 14,000 and 20,000 kroner respectively. Ullberg was cleared and the other two appealed their convictions.[73] Glückstadt died on April 3, 1939.

Glückstadt's first film, Det blaa Blod (The Blue Blood, 1912) froma scenario by Stellan Rye, was also one of Det Skandinavisk-russike Handelhus' first major productions according to Danish film historian Ove Brusendorff.[74] Between this and his earliest surviving film, Det Fremmede (The Stranger, 1914, 844 m.--circa 2½ reels), Glückstadt directed at least six other productions: De to Brødre (The Two Brothers, 1912); Konfetti (Confetti, 1912); Slaegten (The Family, 1912), after a satirical novel by Gustav Wied and codirected with Alfred Lind; De Dødes Ø (The Isle of the Dead, 1913), inspired by the paintings of Böcklin; Krigskorrespondenten (War Correspondent, 1913); and Den sorte Varieté (The Black Music Hall, 1913). In 1914 he also made a film called Ungdomssynd (Youthful Sin).[75] The year 1915 saw his last three films: I Storm og Stille (In Storm and Calm Weather) and Det gamle Spil om Enhver (The Old Play of Everyman), both of which have survived and will be discussed in the next chapter, and For Barnets Skyld (For a Child's Sake).[76]

In addition to Glückstadt, Det Skandinavisk-russike Handelshus or Filmfabrikken Danmark, as it became known in 1912, had at least six other directors: Alfred Lind, Kay van der Aa Kühle, Rasmus Ottesen, Johan Christensen, Stellan Rye, and Emanuel Gregers, who had started as an actor

for the company.[77] The scripts for at least two of Filmfabrikken Danmark's films, Bryggerens Datter (The Brewer's
Daughter, 1912), directed by Rasmus Ottesen, and Ballonek-
splosionen (The Balloon Explosion, 1913), directed by Kay van
der Aa Kühle, were written by Carl Dreyer. According to
Ebbe Neergaard, Ballooneskplosionen

> ... was the first of a series of sensational films, in
> which the courageous and lovely Emilie Sannom was
> relentlessly exploited in all kinds of acrobatic tricks
> in the air, which made her extremely popular and
> got her the name of "daredevil of the air."[78]

After Glückstadt left the company in 1916, this type of sensational film "became characteristic of the production tendencies," culminating in a serial called Panopta. In the 1920s
the company "settled down to nature films and suchlike...."[79]

The story of Den Fremmede, the earliest of the surviving Glückstadt films, revolves around Poul Wang (Emanuel
Gregers), a confidential clerk for a trading company. One
evening he goes to a nightclub with some friends while his
wife, Clara (Gudrun Houlberg), waits at home.[80] He cannot
pay his bill and, in his drunkenness, asks that it be sent
to his home the next morning. When the bill arrives, he still
cannot pay it; apparently it is for a rather large sum. Poul
visits Frandsen, a moneylender, and borrows the money to
pay the bill. Later, Frandsen goes to Poul's office to collect
and, when it still cannot be paid, Poul decides to burglarize
his employer in order to get the money. That night, Poul's
employer, Dahl (Rasmus Ottesen), is working late and watches
Poul's actions. At the last minute, Poul changes his mind and
returns the money to the safe. Poul continues to put Frandsen off. Then one night Dahl summons Poul to the office and
the latter reveals his financial problems. Dahl remembers a
time from his youth when he stole some money. After leaving
Dahl, Poul calls his wife and tells her he will not be home
until late that night. Alone in the house and feeling insecure,
Clara takes out Poul's gun for protection. Later, Poul sneaks
into his own house intent on stealing money that had been en-
trusted to him and which he has been keeping locked in a
desk drawer. Thinking he is a burglar, Clara shoots him,
wounding him in the arm. A strange bearded man, who has
appeared periodically throughout the film, enters their house
and gives Poul some money with which to pay his debt. The

film ends with the bearded man entering his own house, taking
off the beard, which was only a disguise, and revealing himself as Dahl.

Den Fremmede is an excellent film, particularly in its
cutting and camera placement which allow a development of
space that is at times more sophisticated than any other Danish film of the period and, indeed, must rank as one of the
most advanced films of the entire prewar cinema. The opening scene in the company office creates a thoroughly realistic
space for the action. It begins with the camera shooting from
one room to another through a set of glass doors to show the
part of the office occupied by Dahl who then walks through
the doors toward the camera, pauses in close shot, and gestures off-screen right. Poul enters frame and along with
Dahl walks back through the glass doors, after which Dahl
exits through a door in the right background of the set. The
showing of both office rooms simultaneously by use of the
glass doors expands the playing space without cutting it up
and gives a strong sense of the continuity of space, while
the gesturing off-screen, as well as the exits and entrances,
brings the off-screen space strongly into play, allowing the
viewer to believe that the office extends beyond the two rooms
we actually see. Then Glückstadt uses a 180-degree reverse
cut to show the space that had been occupied by Poul before
he entered the frame to talk to Dahl. Dividing the office into
different playing areas and showing the opposite angle, point
the way to a treatment of space that was more fully explored
by later filmmakers, including the great German director F.
W. Murnau.

Poul's attempted burglary of the office is handled in a
similarly interesting manner. The burglary is seen largely
through glass doors, first through the main entrance door,
then, as Poul enters the office, from behind his desk looking
through glass doors into the outer office, and finally, through
glass doors from a position in the outer office showing Poul at
the safe.

The film also contains one well-executed shot in which
Dahl is standing at the window of his office with what appears
to be a real exterior (not a double exposure) of a ship at
dock and people walking around. Both Dahl and the exterior
are in focus, and the interior and exterior light are balanced.
The film does contain an excellent double exposure, however,

in the sequence of Dahl's memories of his own youth. He is
standing next to a fireplace and staring into it. The fireplace opening is matted out and shows the memory events.

Deep focus photography characterizes most of the film.
In addition to scenes in the office and at the nightclub, which
are particularly effective because of the depth, one other
scene deserves special mention because the depth works in
conjunction with an object and a character for a strong dramatic effect. When Clara thinks there is a burglar in the
house, she goes for Poul's gun which she had earlier taken
out for protection and placed on a table in her bedroom. In
this scene we see the gun on the table in the foreground at
the bottom of the frame. Clara walks toward the gun from the
background with her hand stretched out toward it. Had not
both the gun and Clara been present in the same shot and
both in focus, the scene would not have been nearly as effective.

Finally, the recurring interruption of the main narrative
line by the unexplained shots of a bearded man deserve special mention. This figure actually opens the film and is seen
walking down a hill toward the camera. The story proper
then begins with the office scene described earlier. Later,
the bearded man appears putting on a cloak, then between a
shot of Clara waiting at home and Poul in the nightclub. He
also shows up at the nightclub, says something to Poul, and
walks on. His last appearance is at the end of the film after
Clara has shot Poul in the arm. Seeing the film today, we
simply suspend judgment of such scenes and wait to see what
they will lead to, but audiences in 1914 must have had quite
a different and more puzzled reaction to them.

After Glückstadt, the director at Det Skandinavisk-
russike Handelshus that deserves the most attention is Alfred
Lind. This is partly because no films have survived that
have been identified as the work of the other directors mentioned in connection with this company. But more importantly,
Lind's work is of interest, for whatever company it was produced.

According to Ebbe Neergaard, Den flyvende Cirkus
(U.S. title, The Flying Circus, 1912, 975 m.--circa 3 reels)
was Lind's first circus film,[81] although he had photographed
and probably codirected the 1911 Kinografen success, De fire

Djævle. Like the earlier circus film, Den Flyvende Cirkus
was quite successful, selling 228 copies, and was photographed
as well as directed by Lind.[82] It tells the story of a traveling circus and of the passions of a snake charmer who is in
love with the tightrope walker.

The circus arrives at a country town and sets up. Ula
Kiri-Maja (Lili Bech), the snake charmer, is cynical, almost
brutal, in her relations with other people and in her attitude
toward the world. (She smokes cigars and seems like a prototype for some of the women who appeared later in Erich von
Stroheim films.) Her love for Laurenzo, the tightrope walker,
is not returned. The young girls of the town visit the circus, among them the mayor's daughter, Erna. Laurenzo
shows an interest in Erna, and Ula reacts with jealousy. At
the performance Erna throws Laurenzo a flower and arouses
Ula's jealousy even more.

The next day a fire breaks out in the town, and Erna
is trapped on the top floor of a building. Laurenzo saves
her by walking a rope stretched from the burning building
across the street, returning with Erna in his arms. Two
days later, he visits her at home and after further visits,
asks the mayor for permission to marry her. The mayor
refuses to let her marry a circus man; however, he does
agree to marriage if Laurenzo can become prosperous and
give up circus life. Laurenzo gets an idea to tightrope
walk from the group to a church tower for a large sum of
money to be paid by the circus owner. Ula's snake escapes before the walk is to take place and gets itself up into
the tower. When Ula discovers this, she does nothing. Laurenzo goes ahead with his walk and, of course, confronts the
snake on the rope when he nears the top. Erna helps subdue
the snake by climbing to the top of the tower. The mayor
gives his consent for the marriage, and the circus leaves
town without Laurenzo. The film ends with a scene of the
circus caravan leaving town and Ula walking behind it. She
stops, turns around to face the town, and flips away her
cigar in a devil-may-care manner. Then she walks out of
frame.

In general, Den flyvende Cirkus is not as interesting
as De fire Djævle. The camera placements and cutting are
not as carefully controlled and the love relationships, except
for Ula's part in them, are rather pale and lacking in passion.

Even Ula's vengeance is weakened by the silly plot device of
the snake getting to the top of the tower. Lili Bech's portrayal of the character, however, is strong and really the
most successful aspect of the film, although some of the tightrope scenes, especially the fire rescue, are well staged and
photographed. Despite its shortcomings Den flyvende Cirkus
captures enough circus atmosphere, of a seedy kind, as op-
posed to the more glamorous circus settings of the Nordisk
films, to communicate a realism that is still engaging for a
modern audience.

     Less than two months later Den flyvende Cirkus was
followed by a sequel called Bjørnetæmmeren (The Bear Tamer,
1,103 m.--3½ reels), directed, photographed, and written by
Alfred Lind. Lili Bech again plays the snake charmer, but
the tightrope walker has been replaced by a bear tamer and
the love triangle has been reversed. This time the snake
charmer goes for a stage door Don Juan, and the bear tamer
is the injured party. The major change, however, is a switch
from a dramatic mode to a comic one. Lili Bech still walks
around with a cigar in her mouth and still has the same pet
monkey from the previous film, but she is a much weaker
character, almost as if the cynical shrug she gave at the end
of Den flyvende Cirkus was an act, and what she really wanted
was a husband and respectability. Her original fierce passions
and her willingness to kill her man rather than lose him have
been replaced by petty bickering and eventual submission.
In Bjørnetæmmeren she marries the bear tamer whom she has
convinced to join the traveling circus. The morning after the
marriage they begin fighting, in the manner of earlier Danish
domestic comedies. They are offered a job with a dance
troupe, and much of the second reel of the film is taken up
with a long, dull snake dance done by Lili Bech. After the
performance she leaves with the Don Juan, but her husband
follows them. Surprising them at the Don Juan's house, he
confronts them using his bear as a back-up threat. He takes
his wife home, and they are reconciled. Were it not for the
presence of the snake charmer, who is an obvious carryover
from the earlier film, it would be difficult to recognize this
as a sequel, so different is it in tone and interest. It should
be noted, however, that about 300 m. are missing from present day prints, and this may account for some of the film's
shortcomings. Den flyvende Cirkus seems to have been preserved in its entirety.[83]

Part of one other film made by Det Skandinavisk-russike
Handelshus in 1912 has survived. Entitled Kornspekulanten
(The Grain Speculator, 565 m. survived), it tells the story
of a grain dealer who is being unfaithful to his wife. His
girlfriend is a dancer, and the wife knows about her. One
day while at work, grain, which is stored on a platform above
the office, begins to spill out trapping the man. A fire starts
as well, and he calls home for help. His wife and a friend
rush to the rescue by car, but are delayed by an impassable
bridge. The dancer follows in another car. She tries the
bridge and is killed when her car crashes. Despite the de-
lay, the wife arrives in time to save her husband.

Kornspekulanten is one of the best examples of action
filmmaking in the early Danish cinema. The cross-cutting
between the trapped grain dealer and the rescuers is handled
with skill and builds real excitement. Part of the cross-
cutting pattern includes tracking shots of the cars as they
race along the roads. It may be the Danish film that is most
like the Griffith Biograph action melodramas of the same period, such as An Unseen Enemy and A Girl and Her Trust.
There are, of course, echoes of A Corner in Wheat as well,
though this element of the story may be traceable directly
to Frank Norris's The Octopus, in which a grain king falls
into the hold of a ship and is buried by wheat. Other films
about grain speculators were made in the same period, though
none earlier than this one. A 1913 Nordisk film, also called
Kornspekulanten, ends with a scene in which the speculator
and a confederate topple into a wheat bin and are drowned.
The Nordisk film was released in the United States and received with some enthusiasm, though not with much historical
perspective, by Moving Picture World:

> The real merit of this feature lies in the fact that
> it is not overdrawn for the sake of sensation and
> deals with a subject that is familiar on the surface,
> but never before touched upon in motion pictures.[84]

Obviously, in his liking for this three-reel film, the writer
had neglected Griffith's 1909 one-reeler.

In 1910-14 at least nineteen other small production companies were in operation, some of which lasted a very short
time and are merely names in forgotten records: Continental
in 1910; Imperial Films Co. and Ingvar Jorgensen Film from

1911; Copenhagen Film Co. and National Films Co., both from
1912; A/S Dansk Film, Heimdal, Kaulbach Kunstfilm, Record
and Selandia, all from 1913, though Record made a few films
in 1914 also; and Tivoli and Det nye Danske in 1914. Of
those mentioned in this list only three are represented by
surviving films.

Continental made Peder Tordenskjold in 1910. It is
composed mostly of single-shot illustrations of a text high-
lighting events in the life of Peder Wessel, a Danish naval
hero. An introductory title to present day prints states that
only thirty of the original fifty scenes have survived.[85]
Some of the scenes have interesting compositions utilizing the
ship's rigging and space at various levels to fill the frame.
In one scene there is a genuine point-of-view shot, very
rare at this early date, showing in an iris what Peder Wessel
sees though his telescope. The same scene contains a dialogue
title, "They are striking the flag," also a rarity in 1910.

Two films made by Selandia in 1913 have survived. I
sidste Sekund (At the Last Second, 600 m.--2 reels) tells the
story of a young man who saves a countess from a runaway
horse and later from the machinations of her inventor husband's assistant who also steals an important gunpowder discovery. Although the plot is typical of a certain kind of Danish film, its execution is quite primitive for 1913. The film
is done entirely in long shot and is devoid of drama. It has
no meaningful structure, but is simply one scene tacked onto
another. Formally, it looks more like a film from 1907 or 1908
than from 1913.

More interesting, though in no way exceptional, is the
second of the surviving Selandia films, Dr. Thürmers Motionskur (Dr. Thurmer's Exercise Treatment). It is a comedy
about a motion-producing vapor that a woman buys to cure
her husband of laziness. Based largely on stop-motion photography, it differs from earlier trick films only in its cutting
and changing camera placements, which are more sophisticated
than can be found in its predecessors. The film also contains
quite a few close shots and some 180-degree reverse cuts.
The story of Dr. Thurmer's Motionskur is confusing, probably
due to the nature of present day prints. Although the original length is not known, it is clear that the surviving material is incomplete.

Verdensgiften or I fremmed Havn (The World's Poison
or In Foreign Port, 725 m.--circa 2½ reels survived), produced by A/S Dansk Film in 1913, is an exercise in exotica
quite typical for the Danish film of this period, though it is
poorly done, especially in its lighting. The interiors are
lighted by harsh sunlight, an effect that is not often seen
at this period because either diffused sunlight or artificial
light was common. Like in other Danish films, however, some
backlighting is used. Overall the film looks unprofessional
when compared to the work of Nordisk or Filmfabrikken Danmark. The story is set in the Far East and concerns a young
ship's officer who gives up his homeland and his fiancé when
ensnared by an opium-smoking woman. The officer ends up
killing the woman's Indian servant after which he himself is
run down by a train.

Worthy of more attention are a number of other minor
companies, either because the amount of their production was
more substantial or they were related to some noteworthy individual or type of film.

Regia Kunstfilms Co. made a film d'art series in 1911,
including a film based on Oscar Wilde's The Picture of Dorian
Gray and another on the Danish novelist and dramatist Gustav
Wied.[86] Ebbe Neergaard suggests that these "were not real
films," though he apparently had not seen any of them. He
also suggests that the company was set up "merely to ensure
the license of an important movie theater. When that was
obtained the production stopped."[87] Whatever the reason for
the company's existence or the quality of its films, it is interesting that the film d'art movement existed in Denmark
also, as it did in France and the United States.

Thomas S. Hermansen and Alfred Lind (Alfred Lind
Film) had their own production companies in 1912. Hermansen produced and photographed at least six films that year,
each running between two and three reels.[88] Lind made at
least four films, also running two to three reels in length.
Two of them starred the famous Danish actor Olaf Fønss.[89]

Two other independent producers, though each made
only two films, deserve special mention because of their subsequent activities: Constantin Philipsen because he built the
largest movie theater in Copenhagen, the Palads, located in
the abandoned central station in Copenhagen;[90] and Carl

Rosenbaum because he became president of Dansk Biografkom-
pani, which employed and was later taken over by Benjamin
Christensen. More extensive in their output than most of the
other small companies were Dansk Filmfabrik and Dania Biofilm Kompagni, both founded in 1913.

Dansk Filmfabrik produced at least fifteen films during
1913, most of which were directed by Gunnar Helsengreen
and photographed by Thomas Hermansen. Generally, their
films were between one and three reels in length, though one,
Sexton Blake, based on a British juvenile Sherlock Holmes,
with an alternate title, The Detectives, was 1,167 m. The
subjects of all but three of the other films are unknown and
even for those three, there is just the barest hint. In Under
Kniven (Under the Knife, circa 600 m.--2 reels), a professor's neglected wife flirts with the captain of the horse guards.
Manden fra Heden (The Man from the Moors, 911 m.--3 reels)
is a three-part story of everyday life from the Danish moors.
Opdagelsen Sejr (The Successful Discovery, 496 m.--1½ reels)
is about an inventor whose father-in-law steals the invention,
a new car engine. No one of any significance in Danish cinema appears to have worked for Dansk Filmfabrik.[91]

Dania Biofilm Kompagni produced at least twenty-nine
fiction films and seven nonfiction films in 1913 and 1914.[92]
The quality of these films is not known since only a fragment
(231 m.) of one of the features, the 1913 Lejla or Skolerytter-
skens Roman (The Romance of the Equestrienne, originally
over 1,000 m.), has survived. The fragment tells a story
about Lieutenant Claes who loves a woman named Lejla. His
commanding officer does not approve, saying she is not worthy
of Claes. Lejla gets a job in a circus as a horse rider. An
accident occurs on opening night, and Lejla is afraid to go
on. Another scene disconnected from this part of the story,
shows Claes waiting for Lejla in a café. It is unwise to make
any definite judgments from this fragment, of course, but the
film does not appear to have been of much interest. For
eight of the company's other fiction films, which ranged from
1½ to 3 reels in length, there is minimal story information.
The first seven listed here are from 1913; the eighth is from
1914.

In Scenens Børn (Children of the Theater), an actor
becomes disabled and cannot go on. His wife, an actress,
falls in love with another actor.[93] Frøken Lilli (Miss Lilli)

is a comedy about a married man who comes home from a party
with a necklace that his wife thinks is for her.[94] In 3 "in-
dvendige" Jomfruer (3 "housemaids"), three housemaids are
dismissed one after the other, and the detested mother-in-law
comes to help.[95] The quotation marks in the title give it a
double meaning, since jomfruer by itself means virgin. Literally, the title translates as 3 "House" Virgins, explaining
why they were probably fired and replaced by the mother-in-
law. In Vingeskundt (Winged), an engaged count has a mistress who dies from grief when she learns about his engagement.[96] In Søstrene Corrodi (The Corrodi Sisters), two sisters love the same man who plays with the affections of both.
One sister commits suicide. In Dybet drager (Deep Breaths),
Eva loves a lieutenant, but is married to a rich merchant.
The lieutenant dies.[97] Det Syndens Barn (The Child of Sin)
is the story of an unwed mother who gives up her child for
adoption. Later, she becomes a well-known actress, and the
son shows up.[98] Juveltyven paa Eventyr (The Jewel Thief's
Adventure) is a comedy about a journalist who mixes up the
pictures of a big-time thief and a prince, causing much confusion.[99]

Dania Biofilm Kompagni also has the distinction of having hired Benjamin Christensen for his first film acting jobs.
He appeared in at least four films in 1913: Scenens Børn,
Lille Claus og store Claus (Little Claus and Big Claus, circa
3 reels), with Robert Storm Petersen who had originally convinced him to enter filmwork, Vingeskundt, and Søstrene
Corrodi. Dania Biofilm also employed Poul Reumert, who had
made his film debut in Afgrunden. Reumert appeared in
Juvetyven paa Eventyr, Ansigtet bag Ruden (The Face Behind the Window, 1914), and Flyverspionen (The Airman Spy,
1914), also starring Clara Wieth. Both Reumert and Wieth
worked extensively for Nordisk in this period also.[100]

Among the Dania Biofilm nonfiction shorts were films
on Albania, the asphalt industry, and the island of Bornholm.[101] As with all the companies in this period, however,
the nonfiction films were a small part of their business.

Despite the importance of some of the films, companies,
and individual directors discussed so far in this chapter, it
is still Nordisk Films Kompagni which dominated the Danish
cinema. According to company records it produced at least
569 films from 1910 through 1914, 392 of which were fiction

films and 177 of which were nonfiction.[102] By year, the
breakdown is as follows:

Year	Fiction	Nonfiction
1910	43	54
1911	57	28
1912	116	37
1913	87	14
1914	90	44

Most of the fiction films during 1910, 1911, and 1912 were
one and two reels in length, though a few three reelers were
also made. In 1913 and 1914 the three-reel feature became
more common and several films of four reels and longer appeared. A survey of the average lengths of these films reveals that the move was to the longer film, but that, in general, it was not yet the feature film as we know it today, or
even as it is normally defined for this period at four reels
or more. Some genuine features were made, but they were
the exception rather than the rule.

     As might be expected, 1910 was a transitional year for
Nordisk. Afgrunden did not immediately transform subject
matter, and Fotorama's Den hvide Slavehandel did not bring
about a total changeover to the longer film. And, of course,
films continued to be made throughout the early period that
were neither long nor concerned with strong passions. Of
the seven Nordisk films that have survived from 1910, only
Den hvide Slavehandel I points to the future, and only because
of its length. The other six are very much like the films
described in the preceding chapter.

     In 1910 Nordisk launched a series of comedies, similar
in concept to the Happy Bob series of 1907. They ranged in
length from 72 m. to 132 m.; all featured an actor named Victor Fabian and bore titles such as Fabian paa Rottejagt (U.S.
title, Fabian Hunting Rats), Fabian paa Kærlighedsstien (Fabian on Lovemaking), and Den nye Huslærer or Fabian som
Musiklærer (The New Private Tutor or Fabian as Music Teacher).
In addition to these three that have survived, the series included seven other titles, all bearing Fabian's name (see Appendix B). No director is listed for the Fabian films, but all
of them were photographed by Axel Sørensen who began working for Nordisk in 1906.[103]

All three of the surviving Fabian films show the same
characteristics. They are photographed entirely in long shot,
contain a very broad acting style, and depend largely on
slapstick for their comic effects. All are quite primitive for
1910.

Fabian paa Rottejagt begins with Fabian and his wife
eating dinner. He finds a rat in the food and they try to
kill it, but end up destroying the apartment instead. They
chase the rat out into the street and, at the same time, knock
down a woman passerby. A policeman arrests both Fabian and
the woman. While they are at the police station, the arresting
policeman visits Fabian's wife. When the police chief shows
up, she hides the policeman. When Fabian returns, she hides
the police chief. Fabian discovers both, however, and throws
them out, having finally caught some "rats."

Fabian paa Kærlighedsstien has Fabian, in a letter, ask
a girl to marry him. After a scene in which he has many
mishaps while dressing in formal clothes, and not noticing that
he has a tear in the seat of his pants, he goes off to the
girl's house where her parents fawn over him. When they
discover the tear in his pants, the father offers him a new
suit. The boys in the family, however, do not have such
high regard for the suitor and arrange for him to fall through
a trap door and into a wash tub on the floor below. Fabian
goes back upstairs and the father spanks the boys. Over half
the original film is missing. Den nye Huslærer has Fabian as
a live-in tutor who gets roughed up by his two charges.

Moving Picture World received the Fabian films favorably,
calling him "an addition worth while to the motion picture fun
makers and his work should be duly appreciated." In the
same brief review they praise Fabian paa Rottejagt as "funny,
so funny indeed, that more than one commented favorably
upon it."[104] Its review of Fabians Skovtur claims that

> Fabian has become a popular character in the motion
> picture world who will be watched for by audiences
> everywhere. His work is so genuinely comical and
> the acting seems so natural it is small wonder that
> the audience is laughing immoderately while the film
> runs.[105]

In comparison to other comedies of the period, the Fabian

films seem hardly deserving of this praise. Perhaps the best
indication of the difference in perception between this 1910
critic and someone looking at the film today is in the comment
on the "natural" acting to be found in the films, a characteristic that the present day viewer would be hard-pressed to
find.

Like the Fabian comedies, another 1910 Nordisk film,
Dobbeltgængeren (A Victim of His Double, 217 m.--circa 1
reel), illustrates the continuation of an earlier genre, the
detective drama. It, too, is characterized by long shots and
scenes done in single-camera setups with the actors shown in
full length. The narrative develops in a straight line and is
dependent on many coincidences, such as the detective finding a cigarette which turns out to be a clue, the crooks happening to have chloroform with which to subdue the detective,
and the detective's assistant having a hammer handy when a
trunk needs to be opened. Of course, such coincidences
were characteristic of the genre and have basically remained
so. Also characteristic of the genre, as it developed in Denmark, is the absence of cross-cutting to heighten the suspense and action of the final chase. There is actually one
scene in the chase where the action is implied by a title only.
The title says that the detective's car, which is chasing a
train, is traveling at 100 km. per hour, but only one long
shot of the car is shown, and the car is not traveling very
fast. No shots of the train are included.

One effect the film uses that was not used by its predecessors, but which I have already cited in another 1910
Nordisk film, Den hvide Slavehandel I, is the split screen to
portray a telephone conversation. When the victim of the
crime calls the detective to report a stolen necklace, the victim is seen at the right of the screen, the detective at the
left, and in the middle is a high-angle shot of a city street
to show the characters' spatial separation. It appears that
Dobbeltængeren was made first, and so used the split screen
first, since it was entered in the Nordisk negative book before Den hvide Slavehandel I.[106]

In keeping with its straightforward presentation and its
one-reel length, the story of Dobbeltgængeren is simple.[107]
A robber makes himself up to look like a rich man whom he
wants to rob. When the victim is out, the robber enters the
house and robs the safe, managing to fool the butler who sees

him. The next day the rich man discovers the theft and calls
a detective. The butler tells the detective how his employer
had returned the day before, but the rich man denies it.
The detective finds a cigarette that is different from the kind
the rich man smokes and keeps it as a clue. On the street
he sees a man who arouses his suspicions, and when the man
drops a cigarette, the detective picks it up, finding that it is
the same brand as the one he found in the rich man's house.
The detective follows the man to his hideout and breaks in on
him and his confederates. They subdue the detective, however, tie him up, place him in a box, and set a bomb. The
detective's young assistant rescues him after seeing the robbers leave their hideout. Searching the hideout, the detective finds a map the robbers left behind and uses it to follow
and capture them. This chase takes place using a train,
carrying the robbers, and a car, in which ride the detective
and his assistant.

Another of the surviving 1910 Nordisk films is the
single-reel Den sorte Domino (The Black Domino).[108] It is
a primitive film considering the year; the action is photographed in single-take scenes with the actors always seen in
long shot. The story goes back to Cain and Abel, pitting a
good brother against a bad one, and updating it with sex
and a secret organization that wears masks and cloaks and
uses skulls at its meetings.

The last of the extant 1910 Nordisk films is En uheldig
Jæger (U.S. title, A Would-Be Sportsman), though only 66 m.
of the original 116 have survived. It is a trick comedy featuring Oscar Stribolt as a gentleman sportsman who fails utterly at hunting and fishing. In length, content, and style
this film, too, continues the type of production that Nordisk
had developed during its first four years of existence.

In 1910 there was also a continuation of the Sherlock
Holmes films: Sherlock Holmes i Bondefangerklør (U.S. title,
A Confidence Trick), Sherlock Holmes or Den forklædte
Guvernante (U.S. title, The Bogus Governess), Milliontesta-
ment (U.S. title, The Stolen Legacy), and Sherlock Holmes
sidste Bedrifter (U.S. title, Hotel Thieves).[109] Moving Picture World was favorable in its evaluation of these films as
it had been for earlier titles in the series. Of Sherlock
Holmes i Bondefangerklør it said:

Some of the complications in it are more than ordi-
narily interesting and will keep the people guessing
until the denouement. The photography is clear and
the acting is excellent. There are a number of
thrills introduced which help in maintaining the interesting features at a high standard.[110]

Nordisk also made a topical crime film in 1910 based on
the well-known British murder case involving Dr. Crippen,
who murdered his wife and brought his mistress, Ethel Le
Neve, home to live with him, in the very house where Crippen had buried the body of his wife beneath a cellar floor.
Although suspicions were raised about the disappearance of
Mrs. Crippen (her husband said that she had gone to California where she died), the police were unable to find any
trace of her. When Dr. Crippen and Miss Le Neve suddenly
fled the country, however, a further search was made which
uncovered Mrs. Crippen's remains. Crippen was arrested at
sea and returned to London for trial. On November 23, 1910
he was executed at Pentonville.[111]

Nordisk released its one-reel film Dr. Crippen og Miss
le Nove on September 1, 1910, while police court proceedings
against the couple were just beginning and before they had
actually been brought to trial. Crippen was not even found
guilty until October 21, 1910. The Nordisk film, then, was
as current as the newspaper headlines, and must have been
made to appeal to the same audience that was reading about
the crime and its aftermath. Unfortunately, the film has not
survived, nor have I found any descriptions of it. How
closely the film followed the actual events of the case and
how much an appreciation of the film is dependent on a knowledge of the case, therefore, are not known. It was, however,
as successful as the Sherlock Holmes films of that year, selling 63 copies.[112]

A general review of the year 1910 produces a list of
typical comedies and dramas similar to those described in the
previous chapter. The following sampling is probably sufficient to represent the whole: a dog rescue drama (Boscoe,
U.S. title, Saved by Bosco); a domestic comedy about a henpecked husband (Christian Schrøder i Biograf-Teater, U.S.
title, Willie Visits a Moving Picture Show);[113] a melodrama involving a woman's infidelity, blackmail, murder, and a son's
first meeting with his mother (La Femme, U.S. title, Who Is

She?);[114] a detective drama in which a pupil of Sherlock
Holmes solves a diamond swindling case (Diamantbedrageren,
U.S. title, The Diamond Swindler);[115] a sentimental tale about
a lost child forced into street begging by an unscrupulous old
woman and later returned to her mother by a poor family that
had taken her in (Fødselsdagsgaven, U.S. title, The Birthday
Present); a comedy about a man who advertises for a wife in
order to get someone to do his sewing (Svendsen holder
Systue, U.S. title, Mr. Muggins Has His Sewing Done); a
moralistic Russian peasant drama in which charity toward an
enemy brings reform and reward (Den Livegne, The Life of
a Muschik); a love story about a gypsy girl's faithfulness
to her former aristocratic lover (Zigeunerskens Kærlighed,
U.S. title, The Love of a Gypsy Girl); and a comedy about
a banana seller who wins a lottery and begins to imitate a
gentleman (Den heldige Bananmand, U.S. title, The Lucky
Banana Seller).[116] (See Appendix B for more detailed descriptions.)

    While Nordisk continued to produce much the same kind
of film as it had in past years, new directions were beginning
to emerge. Coinciding with these changes at Nordisk was the
elevation of August Blom from actor to director and artistic
administrator. Blom's films, more than those of any other
director, might be said to epitomize the Nordisk style during
the golden age. He became the leading Nordisk director after
Viggo Larsen left the company, and he brought with him a
grounding in the theater that helped lend a certain obvious
respectability to Nordisk films. Along with Ole Olsen he "as-
sembled the best known names of Danish theatre by the score,
now when it was artistically acceptable to perform before the
camera."[117]

    Blom was born in 1869 and started his career as an ac-
tor in Kolding in 1893. He later joined the Folketeatret in
Copenhagen. In 1908 he joined Nordisk as an actor, appearing in a variety of films, including the three Dr. Nicola films
made in 1909: Tyven (U.S. title, A Society Sinner, 1910);
Kean (U.S. title, Kean or The Prince and the Actor, 1910);
and Forrædren (U.S. title, A Traitor to His Country). (All
three films were about one reel in length. No copies have
survived.) Two years later he began directing and continued
through the silent period. He stopped directing when sound
came in. At his death in 1947 he was manager of a Copenhagen cinema.[118]

In his first year as a director Blom began a series of
literary adaptations and social melodramas, types of productions for which Nordisk was to become famous. He made versions of Defoe's Robinson Crusoe, Robert Louis Stevenson's
Dr. Jekyll and Mr. Hyde known alternately in Denmark by
this title and as Den skæbnesvangre Opfindelse (The Fatal
Invention) and Shakespeare's Hamlet. Kean, in which he only
acted, was based on the Alexandre Dumas play. The longer
than average length of these films (from 324 m. to 429 m.),
suggests the cultural weight of the sources and the comapny's
high opinion of such projects. Unfortunately, no prints of
these early adaptations are known to exist.

Among the admirers of these literary adaptations was
the critical staff of Moving Picture World. They were amazed
by the "wonderfully enterprising and conscientious producers"
of Robinson Crusoe, particularly because of the film's "verisimilitude," how "when Robinson Crusoe arrived on his desert
isle, there were all the indications and appearances of tropi-
cals, vegetation and the like," noting also that Crusoe wore
"the traditional garb of the many stage Robinsons" they had
seen. Finally, they predicted the popularity of the film,
especially with young people, and how it would help the producer's business.119

Hamlet impressed them even more, first for the performance of Alvin Neuss in the lead role, and then for the
authentic use of Elsinore as a setting. They also singled
out the reported participation of the Royal Theater Company
of Copenhagen which they felt was "equivalent to saying that
Sothern, Marlowe, Mantell, the later Mansfield and like celeb-
rities, acted the leading parts." In conclusion, they gave
the film a strong recommendation:

> ... altogether the film is one which placed the Great
> Northern Film Company (Nordisk) in the front rank
> of the silent drama. The demand for the film will
> no doubt be great and exchanges should place their
> orders early to avoid disappointment.120

Hamlet opened in England when filmed Shakespeare was
the rage. Playing at the same time as the Nordisk Hamlet,
for example, were productions of Macbeth (990') and Julius
Caeser (1260') released by Co-Operative Cinematograph Co.
In the United States Hamlet received special notice because

of Alvin Neuss's performance in the title role, the excellence
of the photography, and the location shooting at Kronborg
Castle.[121] The intertitles for the film were taken from Shakespeare.[122]

Blom's social melodramas of 1910, and even more so of
1911, became an important part of a change taking place in
the Danish cinema that was to have profound effects both at
home and abroad. A writer in 1914 summed up this change:

> A change in the film programs, a change in the en-
> tire industry was heralded by the first modern sen-
> sational drama, The White Slave Trade. The social
> element is characteristic of this new genre. Its pop-
> ularity is, indeed, so great that "social" has become
> the most common word in the film advertisements.
> The film production appears to have found a field
> that nowadays has a large place in the sphere of
> interest of all social groups.[123]

But what is meant by "social" in this context? Ebbe Neegaard
clarifies the term as it applies to the Dnish film of this period:

> By "social" should not be understood as clear a po-
> sition towards social problem [sic] as is now implied
> in the word. What is seen in the Danish film of the
> time (particularly in those of N.F. [Nordisk Films],
> but also in those of Fotorama and Kosmorama, and
> to a certain degree in the more primitive Biorama
> (films) is the difference between life in the upper
> classes and life at the lowest levels of society, de-
> scribed, not as a social (and changeable) phenomenon,
> but as a fate which may be changeable for the indi-
> vidual, who many sink down or be saved, but which
> is based on secret unalternable laws, implied in hu-
> man nature itself.[124]

A good example of this kind of social film is Blom's
Livets Storm (The Storm of Life, 1910, 312 m.--1 reel). It
is the story of a girl who is loved by both a clerk and a marquis. Much against the wishes of her father, she chooses the
clerk. Years later the couple receives a message that the
girl's father is dying. She goes home to see him, but is too
late. Unaware that the girl is already married, the marquis

renews his offer of marriage, pledging to support the girl's
penniless mother as well. For her mother's sake the girl
marries the marquis, though a few years later he dies, and
the girl returns to her first husband.

A critic for Moving Picture World had both praise and
condemnation for this film, and his objections point to a cultural attitude that was responsible for many Nordisk films
being either cut for American release or withheld entirely as
unsuitable for American audiences.

> A picture of considerable dramatic interest, yet of-
> fering disagreeable suggestions. For a girl to leave
> her husband because he is poor and contract an il-
> legal marriage with a marquis, a former lover, is not
> the pleasantest sort of picture, even though it may
> be true.... The plot might have been worked out
> in a way to save the stigma of selling herself which
> attaches to the girl. The acting and photography
> are not to be criticized, but one does not like the
> character of the story.[125]

Another Blom film that was received with a degree of
cultural shock was Den Dødes Halsbaand (The Necklace of the
Dead, 317 m.--1 reel). In this case, it was not the moral
values of the film that caused a reaction in the reviewers,
but the horror of its subject matter. It is the story of a
girl who is buried alive. She is wearing a necklace given to
her by her lover, and the undertaker's assistant goes to the
tomb to steal it. As he touches the necklace, however, the
girl moves. Thinking she may have been buried alive, he
runs off to get the lover. When they return to the tomb,
the girl has gotten out of the coffin and is waiting inside the
crypt. After confessing his deed, they give the undertaker
the necklace which he decides to devote to the church.

> Here is a film which will make a profound impression
> upon any audience, not so much because of what they
> see as what is suggested.... There isn't much in
> the story, yet it would be difficult to devise any-
> thing which will linger longer in the memory.... It
> is not dramatic ... but it is horrifying in its sug-
> gestions, and causes the fear of something similar
> happening to one to take possession of one's faculties
> for the time.[126]

Blom directed at least one other film in 1910 in the
same genre, though it also has aspects of the social film.
Spøgelset i Gravkælderen (A Ghost in the Vaults, 242 m.--
under 1 reel) tells the story of a girl who has two admirers
and a miserly father who objects to the one she loves. The
film also has a sleepwalking and attempted theft scene that
takes place in an underground vault where the father keeps
his treasure in a coffin. No copies of Livets Storm, Den
Dødes Halsbaand, or Spøgelset i Gravkælderen are known to
exist.

Made in 1910, but not released until March 6, 1911 is
Ved Fængslets Port (At the Prison's Gate, 820 m.--circa 3
reels), which Ebbe Neergaard considers "one of the first N.F.
films of the long 'social' melodrama-type."[127] It is also the
film that marks August Blom's coming of age as a director
and Vlademar Psilander's advancement to the first rank of
Danish male stars.[128] With a sale of 246 copies, at least
18 of which were sent to the United States,[129] it was also
a great financial success.[130]

Before entering film work, Psilander had been at the
Dagmar Theater, but, according to Ebbe Neergaard, he contributed nothing of importance as an actor, "perhaps with the
exception of his performance as Bill Sykes." In 1910 he
joined Nordisk, though about the same time he made Den sorte
Drøm (The Black Dream) for Fotorama, playing opposite Asta
Nielsen. He continued with Nordisk until 1917 when he left
to form his own company, reportedly because Ole Olsen would
not pay him what he demanded. However, at the age of
thirty-three, before he could finish any films for his own
company, he died.[131]

Ved Fængslets Port is the story of a bank clerk, Aage
Hellertz (Valdemar Psilander) who leads a rather dissolute
life, spending all his money, and much that he borrows from
his mother, on his own pleasures. While partying after the
theater, he is offered a loan by a waiter who is also a moneylender. The moneylender's daughter, Anna (Clara Wieth),
works for her father, and Aage meets her one day at the
moneylender's office. He is immediately attracted to her and,
after signing a note for another loan, grabs a kiss. Failing
to receive payment on the loan, the moneylender sends the
note to Aage's mother (Augusta Blad). She confronts her son
with the note and, though angry about it, pays the loan. Not

particularly disturbed by this, Aage telephones Anna and
asks her to come to his house for an intimate supper. The
mother interrupts the supper and orders Anna to leave. Aage
leaves with her, and they get married, setting up their own
home. Both now begin to lead a partying life, which is apparently financed by further borrowing from Anna's father.
Again he asks for repayment, threatening once more to go to
Aage's mother. Aage considers suicide but instead decides
to forge his mother's name on the note. After giving the
forged note to Anna's father, he returns home in remorse and
confesses what he has done. Anna suggests he also tell his
mother. He does this, but she reluctantly refuses to help
him. He decides to steal the money from his mother, but at
the last minute cannot go through with it. His mother, who
has been watching the attempted theft, is relieved when her
son puts the money back. Anna goes to her father, wrests
the note from him, and tosses it in the fire. Her father becomes so agitated that he dies on the spot. Aage and his
mother arrive at this moment and a reconciliation of mother,
son, and daughter-in-law takes place.

As is common for Nordisk social melodramas, the action
takes place largely indoors. The sets are realistic, in design
and furnishings, and are photographed in deep focus. Many
of them include mirrors used to reflect characters who are
not directly visible in the frame and to create an expanded
playing space. There is also an effective use of double exposure in a scene that shows both Aage and Anna on the
telephone as they talk to each other.

The deep focus, combined with the careful use of mirrors and augmented by Nordisk's sophisticated lighting effects,
allowed for a mise-en-scène which, though theatrical in origin,
made a genuine contribution to the development of cinematic
forms. Minimizing action and stressing psychological and social motivation brought about a highly developed naturalistic
acting style that stands in marked contrast to much of the
film acting of the time that was so heavily influenced by stage
melodrama. The action of Ved Fængslets Port and many other
Danish films unfolds basically in real time and continuous
space, which is different, however, from the time and space
characteristic of the earliest films, whether the realistic-
oriented ones of companies like American Mutoscope and Biograph, Edison, and Lubin, or the more imaginatively oriented
films of Méliès. In those the narration is presented primarily

through the actors, as it would be on the stage, while in the
Danish films being described here, the narration comes through
a careful integration of actors with decor, including the lighting. This integration is also a direct function of the camera
placement, while in earlier films, the camera placement plays
a minimal role. Three examples from Ved Fængslets Port will
help to illustrate this point.

At the beginning of the film Aage and some friends are
at the theater watching a dance performance. The shot includes the dancer performing on stage in the background and
Aage and his friends in a box in the foreground. Both the
characters in the box and the dancer on the stage are in focus. The setup relates characters in space in a way seldom
found in earlier films, or, for that matter, in most films of
1910. The shot also creates the space of a real theater because the frame is fully articulated by the foreground and
background actions, as well as the space between them. The
result is a strong sense of the presence of spectators at a
dance performance, a sense that cross-cutting between stage
and audience achieves only by suggestion and illusion.

After Aage and Anna are married, there is a scene in
which Aage returns home and is greeted by Anna at the door.
The scene begins in darkness. Anna opens the door revealing Aage coming along a path to the house. He is seen in
normal exposure while Anna is silhouetted in the doorway.
The shot was apparently made from inside a real house since
the street behind Aage is obviously real. Both Anna and
Aage are in focus and the sense of coming home, Aage being
brought into the protection of the home, is strong. A similar effect can be found in a few other Danish films and two
years later was used by Griffith in Olaf, an Atom (1912).

The third example is the most interesting from a dramatic point of view and the most characteristic of Danish films
because it includes the use of a mirror. Aage has entered
his mother's house at night and is seen searching a drawer
for money. The room is dark, though Aage, who is at frame
left in the foreground, can be seen getting the money. At
frame right in the background is a mirror. As the scene
progresses, Aage's mother enters, though she is seen only
because she is reflected in the mirror. She is obviously
watching Aage; great tension and anguish can be clearly read
in her face. When Aage changes his mind and puts the money

back, the mother reacts with relief. At that moment a policeman and another man enter and turn on a light. They have
followed Aage thinking him to be a burglar. The turning on
of the light breaks the dramatic tension of the scene and
shifts the emphasis from the conflict between mother and son
to reconciliation as she sends the policeman away telling him
that nothing is wrong. The night effect in the apartment,
as well as the change to overall illumination, and the use of
the mirror and deep focus to give the audience both Aage's
struggle with himself and the mother's anguish over her son,
create a cinematic, rather than theatrical, narration, despite
the long, static take which presents the action as a whole,
as the theater would also have presented it. This kind of
mise-en-scène anticipates that proposed by André Bazin and
found in films such as Citizen Kane.

In the five years from 1910 to 1914 Blom made at least
eighty-eight films, most of which are long. Many of them are
in the tradition of Ved Fængslets Port, though there are a
significant number of costume dramas and literary adaptations
as well.[132] Although the distinctions among the different
kinds of films are not always clear, since the different types
have common characteristics, it is reasonable to classify eleven
of the surviving Blom films as primarily social melodramas.[133]
Among them is one from 1911 that in subject matter and plot
is very much like Ved Fængslets Port.

Kærlighedens Styrke (The Power of Love, 757 m.--2½
reels) has survived only in paper print form in the Library of
of Congress. It is more fluid in its cutting and camera placement and more rapidly paced than the typical Blom film. The
sets, however, are less solid and convincing than other Blom
films. It tells the story of Gunnar Saxild (Carlo Wieth), the
son of a wealthy businessman. Disgusted with his playboy
son, the father puts him to work in the office. There he
meets a girl, Tove (Clara Wieth). One day, on his way to
meet her, a few friends persuade him to have a drink. He
gets drunk and is late for the meeting. Having missed her,
he goes to her apartment to wait for her. When she arrives,
she finds him drunk and is disgusted by his advances. This
causes him to get even drunker. He then gets into a fight
and is put in the tank by the police. When he shows up at
work the next day, his father throws him out, though Tove
makes up with him. He gets a job in an ambulance corps
and while working in a disaster area finds Tove injured. She
convalesces, and he is reunited with his parents.

Despite the film's Library of Congress copyright, it
does not appear to have been released in the United States.
It is also more difficult to judge than Ved Fængslets Port,
since the photographic quality of the 16mm print made from
the original paper print is quite poor and the shots are not
completely in sequence. Overall, however, it seems to be at
least on a par with the earlier film.

Love affairs between members of different classes, as
seen in the two films just described, are a staple of the early
Danish cinema, and indeed, are common in the films of other
countries, as well as in literature and on the stage in that
period. A particularly good example is another Blom film
from 1911, Exspeditricen (The Shop Girl).[134] In it, a wealthy
young man, Edgar (Carlo Wieth), sees a shopgirl, Ellen (Clara
Wieth), and is immediately attracted to her. He buys her
flowers. They meet the next Sunday and, presumably, often
thereafter. Three months later Ellen is pregnant. The couple
decide to marry, and Edgar tells his mother. His father
(Thorkild Roose) convinces him not to marry Ellen and sends
him away to visit friends in the country. The daughter of
the family he visits, Lily (Zanny Petersen), gets him to write
to Ellen when she finds out about her. Edgar's father, however, has convinced Ellen's former employer, to whom the letters have been sent, to turn them over to him. When Edgar
gets no reply from Ellen, he secretly returns to the city.
The baby is born and Ellen dies shortly after. Lily visits
from the country, and Edgar sees a notice of Ellen's death in
the newspaper. Edgar and Lily go to the hospital to claim the
baby, planning also to marry.

Exspeditricen has been directed and photographed in
the same style as the other Blom films described: realistic
interiors, solidly furnished and photographed in deep focus;
basically static camera with the actors seen in medium shot,
the scenes generally covered in one setup; and naturalistic
acting. There are, however, more exterior shots than in
any of the other Blom films mentioned, and there is also more
cross-cutting.

Two scenes stand out in particular, one because of its
lighting effect and the other because of a shot transition.
The flower-buying scene was apparently shot in a real flower
shop with sunlight from the shop window being the principal,
if not only, source of illumination. The actors are seen

entirely in silhouette and the street can be clearly seen through
the window. It is a striking image, of the same type as the
scene in Ved Fængslets Port when Anna greets Aage at the
front door.

When Ellen dies in the hospital, a nurse folds Ellen's
hands over her chest and then bends over and kisses the
hands. Blom cuts to a shot of Edgar seated, hands folded,
his head resting on them and crying. The hands in both images have been placed in the same part of the frame, creating a strong link between Ellen and Edgar at a crucial moment, even though he does not know where she is or what
has happened.

Another example of the theme of class differences dis-
rupting a relationship can be found in the 1911 Ungdommens
Ret (The Right of Youth, 712 m.--2½ reels). A wealthy man,
Søtoft (Vlademar Psilander), has hired a young woman, Miss
Engelke, to take care of his teenage daughter, Else (Zanny
Petersen). Unknown to Søtoft, Miss Engelke used to be the
lover of a neighbor, von Plessen (Einar Zangenberg). Søtoft
also has a grown son, Ove (Robert Dinesen). Else sees von
Plessen kiss Miss Engelke and thinks that something is currently going on between them. Ove and Miss Engelke fall in
love and von Plessen finds out about it. In jealousy he tells
Søtoft, who refuses to believe him. Ove goes to Miss Engelke's
room one night, but is seen through the window, in silhouette,
by Else. Thinking it is von Plessen, she goes to the room
to try to spare her father's feelings. Søtoft, however, sees
the silhouette also. Von Plessen, also spying, accidentally
sets fire to some curtains with his cigarette, trapping Ove
and Else in the room. Søtoft rescues them and sends Miss
Engelke away, blaming her for everything.

Although the film is beautifully photographed, it is
ultimately less interesting than most other Blom films. The
plot is extremely contrived, and the narrative points are made
in the most obvious ways. More than other Blom films, the
story is carried by the actors' gestures and movements rather
than by an integration of these with the formal characteristics
of the medium. It does, however, use a greater variety of
camera angles to portray the action than other Blom films
and makes extensive use of compositions that play characters
in the foreground against characters in the background.

Den naadige Frøken (The Gracious Miss) reverses the
usual terms of the class relationship and has the daughter
of a count, Vibeke, in love with the gamekeeper (Vlademar
Psilander). She is engaged, however, to a man of her own
class (Thorkild Roose). He comes for a visit, but she is
cold to his advances. One night she has the gamekeeper
come to her room, but her mother knocks on the door and
the gamekeeper is forced to hide outside her second-floor
window. He is spotted by an estate guard and is apprehended
when he jumps to the ground. Thinking that he was trying
to steal a valuable necklace that Vibeke's fiance had brought
with him, the gamekeeper is put on trial. He, of course, refuses to tell the truth in order to protect Vibeke's honor.
At his trial she finally tells why he was really there, and he
is released.

Another subject of the social melodrama is the romantic
triangle, both within and without marriage. Sometimes the
triangle is related only peripherally to the main action and
theme of the film, as in Urban Gad's Afgrunden (The Abyss)
and Benjamin Christensen's Den hemmelighedsfulde X (The
Mysterious X), but more often it is central and is found particularly in relation to marriage. Three of Blom's surviving
films are probably typical.

Aviatikeren og Journalistens Hustru (The Aviator and
the Journalist's Wife, 1911, 965 m.--3 reels) pits Valdemar
Psilander, as the journalist, against Einar Zangenberg, as
the aviator, for the affections of Else Frölich, the journalist's
wife. As with many Blom films, it is clearly, if coldly, told
and illustrates most of the characteristics already ascribed to
Blom's films.

Fru Potifar (Madame Potiphar, 1911, 909 m.--3 reels)
is the story of another wayward wife, the title referring to
the Old Testament story in which the enslaved Joseph rejects
the sexual advances of his master's wife. In this modern
telling a doctor's wife makes sexual advances toward one of
her husband's friends. The friend rebuffs her and in revenge
the wife accuses the friend of improper conduct.

This film, too, is typical of Blom's style. Most scenes
are done in medium shot and in single-camera setup, though
there are a few closer shots and, in one scene, a cut from a
long shot to a close shot of the wife as she is writing at her

desk. There are also several panning shots to follow character actions in exterior scenes, even though the camera is
generally static. As might be expected there are some special lighting effects, including scenes of the doctor at a sick
child's bedside and the doctor sitting alone at his desk on the
night before a duel. Both scenes appear to use single-source
lighting from nearby lamps with the remainder of the frame in
darkness.

That same year Blom directed another film based on the
same idea and bearing almost the same title. Released nine
months before Fru Potifar and less than half its length, it is
entitled Potifars Hustru (Potiphar's Wife).[135] The earlier
film has not survived, but a review and plot synopsis in
Moving Picture World preserve the basic idea of the film and
one American reaction to it:

> The line of powerful dramatic feature pictures that
> are being released by the Great Northern Film Com-
> pany is not weakened in the least by its latest re-
> lease.... Dealing with the strongest sentiments and
> passions of mankind the Great Northern players,
> consummate artists, have the faculty of bringing
> out the full value of every situation and of making
> motives unmistakable.... Strong acting is required
> to save such scenes as are here portrayed.[136]

The third of the surviving Blom marital triangles, Af
Elskovs Naade (By Love's Mercy, 1913, 1,150 m.--3½ reels),
has an unusual plot twist involving the husband's death.
Amy (Betty Nansen), the daughter of a landowner, meets
Count von Teyn (Adam Poulsen), and they marry. Later,
she sees him with another woman and leaves him, returning
to her parents. Missing her, von Teyn gets rid of the other
woman and succeeds in bringing about a reconciliation. He
is soon injured in a horse race and crippled for life. He
asks his wife to give him a gun so he can commit suicide.
She does, is tried for her part in his death, but is acquitted.

The military man, whether as husband or lover, is a
familiar figure in Danish films. Along with the dissolute son
of a wealthy family, the circus performer, the landowner, the
count, and others, he is one of the stock characters of the
social melodrama. He has many manifestations, but two of
them, found in August Blom's work, are typical.

Hævnet (Revenge, 1911) stars Vlademar Psilander as
Hans von Bremen, an army officer who is in debt. An old
school friend, Pastor Topp (Thorkild Roose), lends him money
to pay the debt. Von Bremen falls in love with Emmy (Edith
Buemann) when he is quartered at her parent's house. After
a change in his orders which causes von Bremen to leave,
Emmy discovers she is pregnant. Her father throws her out
of the hosue, and she dies in childbirth. Twenty years pass
and von Bremen and his young wife visit Pastor Topp. With
Topp is a young man, von Bremen's son. Neither the son
nor the father know each other, and the son makes advances
to von Bremen's wife. To get even von Bremen plots to ruin
the young man by getting him into debt. He succeeds, and
the son shoots himself. Topp tells von Bremen who the boy
is and, fortunately, the son is still alive. The film is difficult to evaluate and the plot given here is incomplete, since
little more than half the original 900 m. length of the film has
survived.

Virtue is again threatened by a military man in De tre
Kammerater (The Three Comrades, 725 m.--2½ reels). The
three comrades of the title are lieutenants, one of them the
son of wealthy parents. He visits home with his two friends,
and one of them (Henry Seeman) becomes interested in his
comrade's sister. When the other two are called away on
maneuvers, he stays on and romances the girl. Returning
home after completing their duty, the girl's brother and the
other friend catch Seeman climbing out of the sister's window.
Seeman asks to marry the girl but is refused. Her brother
challenges his friend to duel, but she arrives just in time to
stop them. All are reconciled.

Moving Picture World called De tre Kammerater "a fine
military drama, embellished by Great Northern photography."
It also commented on the convincing quality of the Great
Northern actors, noting that they must have had military
training. MPW was also impressed by a cavalry scene in
which the horses plunge into and swim a stream, though they
also felt that the "story easily carries on its dramatic worth
aside from the spectacular."[137] Many Danish films from this
period have theatrical settings and revolve around characters
who are performers of some kind. Blom made two of these
in 1912.

Gøgleren (The Ham Actor, 779 m.--2½ reels) contains

several interconnected love relationships. Wilda (Clara Wieth)
and her mother go to the theater with Cordt, the manager of
a business firm. Wilda is attracted to Fritz Bohn, an actor
(Vlademar Psilander). Later Wilda rebuffs Cordt's advances
to her. In a theater café Cordt meets Bohn and his girlfriend, Lilli. Bohn is in financial need and Lilli lends him
money, though at first he rudely rejects her offer. Fritz
has dinner at Cordt's house and sees a picture of Wilda.
He tells Cordt about his problems and Cordt offers him money.
Cordt invites Wilda, her mother, and Bohn to tea one day,
and Bohn becomes interested in Wilda. Fritz asks Wilda's
mother for her daughter's hand, and they become engaged.
A half year later Fritz is again in need of money. Cordt
again lends it to him and together they attend many drunken
parties. Wilda breaks the engagement when she goes to Fritz's
apartment and finds him unconscious from drinking and a
woman's petticoat on his chair. When he regains consciousness, Fritz finds the engagement ring which Wilda has left
behind and continues his spree by going dancing. After
meeting Lilli, he realizes he has forgotten to go to the theater. He arrives too late and is thrown out of the company.
Three months later Lilli is found staggering along a street
weak from hunger. Fritz sees the police taking her to the
hospital and follows. Wilda marries Cordt, and as they are
leaving for their honeymoon, their car is stopped by a funeral
procession. They see Fritz walking behind the hearse; as he
goes by he doffs his hat.

    Like many Danish films of the period, Gøgleren has
some striking photographic and lighting effects. The most
interesting concern the opening theater performance and a
ride home from the theater. In the theater scene Wilda, her
mother, and Cordt are seen sitting in a box, obviously watching the performance. A mirror at the back of the box reflects
Fritz performing on stage. As with other mirror scenes, this
shot shows two simultaneous actions occurring in different
spaces without resorting to montage. After the theater the
three characters are riding home in Cordt's car. They are
seen in close shot with the driver in the foreground. The
lighting and the bouncing of the car, along with the tight-
ness of the space, create a strong sense of reality.

    Hans vanskeligste Rolle (His Most Difficult Part, 520 m.
--1½ reels) also begins at the theater and tells the story of
the daughter of a count who falls in love with an actor,

although she is engaged to an aristocrat. Although not a
particularly interesting film, it is typical of Blom and other
Nordisk filmmakers of the period in its lighting, use of deep
focus, single-camera setups for each scene, and its solidly
furnished sets. The opening theater scene is handled con-
ventionally by shooting past the people in the box toward the
performance on stage, deep focus relating the two planes of
action.

Blom's films are generally conservative. He had mas-
tered, and undoubtedly helped create, the Nordisk style,
part of which was the striking use of light and certain other
pictorial devices like the mirrors. Once established, however,
these shooting methods were continued, and there was little
experimentation. Blom's films, well controlled and craftsman-
like, constitute the solid middle of Nordisk production, better
than average, but lacking the spark of the best. Occasionally,
however, he achieved the unexpected. A minor example of
this capacity is seen in the 1911 erotic melodrama Dødens Brud
(The Bride of Death, 935 m.--3 reels).

Bruno (Robert Dinesen) is engaged to Henny, the
daughter of a wealthy woman.[138] Another man, Otto, has
designs on Henny. Otto gets Bruno drunk and, after leaving
his fiancé that night, Bruno is accosted by another woman on
the street. Bruno takes her to his room. Meanwhile, Henny
is in her bedroom, apparently having erotic fantasies. She is
staring at her body in the mirror. She dresses and goes to
see Bruno, sneaking into his apartment to surprise him. She
becomes aware of the other woman's presence, takes a piece of
the woman's feather boa, and leaves broken-hearted. She returns to her room, sits down before a lighted fireplace, and
proceeds to destroy Bruno's photographs and letters. Her
mother finds her crying, and Henny tells what has happened.
Later, Henny confronts Bruno with the feather boa and breaks
off the engagement.

A half year passes and Bruno reads of Henny's marriage
to Otto. Bruno sends flowers to the wedding celebration, accompanied by a note that moves Henny to go to Bruno in
anger. When she arrives, Bruno weeps and Henny, forgetting
her anger, comforts him. She stays, and they make love while
the wedding party continues. After, he suggests they commit
suicide, putting poison in their glasses. Bruno drinks, but
Henny does not. He dies and she goes back to the party and

to Otto. However, she sees an image of Bruno reaching out
to her and, returning to Bruno's apartment, she drinks the
poison. She lies down next to Bruno to die.

The unexpected quality of Dødens Brud is its passion.
In its yearning of Bruno and Henny for each other, it is one
of the most graphically erotic films of the period. This quality is strongest in the embraces between the couple and in
the scene of Henny in front of the mirror. But it can also
be seen more abstractly in Blom's handling of their lovemaking
during the wedding party. Bruno is shown taking off Henny's
wedding veil and shawl. At this point there is a cut to the
guests dancing at the party, followed by a cut back to Henny
readjusting her veil. The sequence not only implies the act
and the passage of time, but, by what it leaves out, reinforces
the strong physical bond between the characters, a bond
strong enough to cause Henny to forget about her husband
and the wedding party. As usual, the film also contains
striking lighting effects, especially in the scene in which
Henny burns Bruno's letters in the fireplace, each letter
causing a small burst of light that reflects on her anguished
face.

The sensationalism of this film is quite common in the
early Danish cinema, though not generally in August Blom's
work. He did, however, indulge this interest on more than
one occasion, as witnessed by one of his most famous films,
the 1911 Mormonens Offer (The Mormon's Victim, 1,080 m.--
3½ reels).

Moving Picture World took a stand against Mormonens
Offer and another anti-Mormon film called The Mormon, released by the American Film Manufacturing Company:

> We cannot fathom the reasons which impel the pro-
> duction of such reels after the many bitter exper-
> iences which former similar efforts have brought
> down upon their perpetrators. It is quite possible
> that ignorance and a desire to be cheaply sensa-
> tional account for these objectionable reels.... There
> are, however, two distinct kinds of ignorance: ex-
> cusable ignorance and inexcusable ignorance. In
> view of our repeated warnings against sectarian
> films, in view of the disastrous results of such sec-
> tarian films to their makers, we are constrained to

pronounce this continued ignorance as decidedly
inexcusable.[139]

Opposition to this anti-Mormon film was not universal,
however.   In England The Kinematograph and Lantern Weekly
took an entirely different stand:

> The pernicious doctrines of the Mormon faith have
> been the subject of repeated exposures by the daily
> press [my emphasis], which is to be lauded in its
> efforts to open the eyes of those foolish members of
> the gentler sex who are unlukily too easily gulled
> by the oily tongue of the deceivers when, under the
> guise of so-called religion, he disgraces the garb he
> assumes, and uses his position to sow seeds of the
> hated cult of Mormonism.

The review also called Mormonens Offer the finest of the
series of Nordisk long films and hoped that it would help
counter the growth of Mormonism in England.[140]

One way the Mormon Church responded to these attacks
and to films like Mormonens Offer was by producing its own
film on the founding and development of Mormonism.   In January 1913 the Utah Moving Picture Company of Los Angeles
released a six-reel historical drama called One Hundred Years
of Mormonism.   It was made under contract with the Church
of Jesus Christ of Latter Day Saints and with "access to
church archives."[141]   The first four reels were concerned
with Joseph Smith and the last two with Brigham Young and
the pioneers of 1847.   The New York Dramatic Mirror noted
that "in most cases" the photography was very good.[142]

Despite opposition to this three-reel film, much of which
understandably came from The Church of Jesus Christ of Latter Day Saints, Mormonens Offer sold 137 copies,[143] at least
19 of which were sold on a states' right basis in the United
States.[144]

Olaf Gram, an engineer (Henry Seeman), introduces his
school friend, Andrew Larsson (Valdemar Psilander), now a
Mormon priest, to his sister Nina (Clara Wieth) and her fiancé
Sven Berg (Carlo Wieth).   Larsson is immediately attracted to
Nina and, on their next meeting, takes her for a walk.   He
gives her an admission card to the next Mormon meeting where

he will speak. Feeling neglected by her fiancé, she accepts.
On the way to the meeting Larsson tells her of his affections,
but she shies away. At the meeting, however, she becomes
enthralled with Larsson, and later he continues his advances,
exercising an almost hypnotic power over her as he is constantly seen holding her hand and whispering in her ear.
Finally, he asks her to go to Utah with him and she agrees.

Discovering her absence and finding a note that Larsson
had written to Nina, Olaf and Sven go to the police who send
a telegram asking that the couple be stopped. Policemen
check the trains, and Larsson and Nina are forced to get off
their train and seek help from another Mormon. Nina regrets
what she has done and tries to get away, but Larsson gags
and detains her. Another woman, dressed in Nina's clothes,
is sent to the boat on which Larsson and Nina are planning
to leave. She is mistaken for Nina and grabbed by the police.
Meanwhile, Larsson and Nina board the ship in disguise. The
family receives a cable saying that Nina and Larsson have
been arrested, but soon discover the mistake that has been
made. The police send another cable to the ship. Larsson
drugs Nina to keep her quiet, and the ship's telegraph operator becomes suspicious when he notices that Larsson's mustache
is false. He tries to cable the police, but Larsson ties him up
and damages the telegraph.

Learning that they have escaped, Olaf and Sven leave
for Utah and arrive shotly after Nina and Larsson. They
follow Larsson to his house when they see him leaving the
Mormon temple. Just prior to this Nina had learned that
Larsson already had one wife. The wife tries to help Nina
escape, but Larsson catches them. Discovering the presence
of Sven and Olaf, Larsson takes Nina out of the house. The
wife sees them enter a cab, which Olaf and Sven follow. Larsson and Nina manage to get out of the cab, however, and return to the house where Larsson locks Nina in the basement.
Sven breaks in on Larsson, and they pull guns on each other.
Larsson falls through a trap door and accidentally shoots himself, while Nina is rescued.

The sectarian aspects of the film, objectionable as they
are, are largely submerged in an adventure format similar to
other Danish crime films. In keeping with this type of film,
Blom utilizes a greater variety of camera angles and more complex cutting, including cross-cutting, than in his other films.

In one case he makes a comparison common for D. W. Griffith
but unusual for him. He cuts from a shot of Nina lamenting
her position to her parents grieving; an accompanying title
reads, "sorrow at home." Also like Griffith, the chase at the
end is photographed from a moving car, though the effect of
the scene is partly ruined by the head of the driver of the
camera car appearing in the lower right of the frame, giving
the impression of a third car involved in the chase. The
scene is further hurt by city backgrounds that look like
Copenhagen rather than Salt Lake City.

Another interesting sequence is one in which the police
search the trains for the runaway couple. The first shot of
the sequence is from a moving train and shows only tracks
and other cars. Then, two policemen walk into frame peering
toward the camera as if looking into train windows. This is
followed by a medium shot of Nina and Larsson looking out a
window.

More complex in its construction is the earlier scene in
the Mormon temple where Nina has gone to listen to Larsson
preach. It begins with a long shot of the Mormon meeting
hall which fades in and out, followed by a close shot of a
sign in a window announcing services, which also fades in and
out. This is followed by a close shot of two torn and crum-
pled signs in a window, perhaps pages from the Book of Mormon, also fading in and out, a high-angle long shot of the
meeting hall from a different angle than the one which opened
the sequence, and a shot of a doorway with three signs an-
nouncing the meeting as being sponsored by the British League,
again fading in and out. All these signs are in English, indicating that the action takes place in England, which is also
the scene of the white slavery and other crime films.

In contrast to the popular sensationalism of Mormonens
Offer are Blom's more respectable costume dramas and literary
adaptations. Den sorte Kansler (The Black Chancellor) is a
three-reel costume picture which, despite a complex plot
packed with adventure, is ultimately rather dull. Moving
Picture World, however, reacted favorably to the film, calling
it "of the 'Prisoner of Zenda' type whose charm resides in its
ingenious and entertaining improbability, the author not de-
spising truth, but making it subsidiary to delightfulness."[145]

The Black Chancellor, von Rallenstein (Thorkild Roose),

rules his country with an iron hand, paying only lip service
to the authority of Princess Irene (Ebba Thomsen). He wants
to marry her to a powerful neighbor, Prince Zoba, but Irene
loves Lieutenant Pawlow (Valdemar Psilander). When von
Rallenstein presents Zoba's written proposal of marriage, Irene
declines, telling him that she loves Pawlow. Returning to his
chambers von Rallenstein sends his aid, Count Rockowitz
(Poul Reumert), to Pawlow, ordering him to carry a letter of
acceptance to Zoba. In an attempt to foil von Rallenstein's
plan, Irene arranges for a secret marriage to Pawlow, to take
place while a court ball is in progress. Aided by Pawlow's
friend, Lieutenant Groblewsky (Robert Dinesen), and Irene's
faithful handmaid, Feodora, the couple proceed to the marriage place. Rockowitz discovers the plan and informs von
Rallenstein. Too late to prevent the marriage, von Rallenstein has Rockowitz order Pawlow, at gunpoint, to commit
suicide by taking poison. After Pawlow takes the poison
Rockowitz hurries off to tell von Rallenstein, who is furious
at not being given the opportunity to witness the death.
Meanwhile, Groblewsky has seen the murder/suicide and
rushes his friend, and a physician, to his, Groblewsky's
castle. Rockowitz follows them and informs von Rallenstein,
who has Irene kidnapped and taken to Rockowitz's castle.

Groblewsky learns of the kidnapping and sets off to
rescue Irene. With the help of a peddler who knows a secret
entrance into Rockowitz's castle, he makes his way to the
room where Irene is being held. Rockowitz learns of Groblewsky's presence and a battle ensues. Groblewsky, however,
had already sent a messenger to Pawlow, now revived from his
his poisoning, and Pawlow comes to the rescue with a band
of armed men. Irene is saved and an uprising against von
Rallenstein takes place. Von Rallenstein seeks refuge with
Prince Zoba where he dies a defeated man.

As usual with Blom films the settings are realistic--the
exteriors were particularly extolled by Moving Picture World
--and the lighting effects sophisticated. Of special interest
are the deep-focus interiors and the lighting in the secret
tunnel by which Groblewsky enters the castle. There are
also several POV shots, one from Fedora's position on a balcony looking down on Pawlow after he has taken poison and
one giving what Rockowitz sees through his binoculars when
he is following Groblewsky and Pawlow, a binocular-shaped
mask emphasizing the effect.

A more interesting costume film is <u>Guvernørens Datter</u>
(<u>The Governor's Daughter</u>, 745 m.--2½ reels), made in 1912
but not released in the United States until July 1913. Once
again, a love affair interferes with a planned marriage. Sonja
(Ebba Thomsen) is secretely engaged to Lieutenant Petrowitsch
(Robert Dinesen). Her parents want her to marry General
Sabinsky (Cajus Bruun). At a banquet, Sabinsky, who has
been making his own advances to Sonja, sees her kissing
Petrowitsch. Later, Petrowitsch climbs into Sonja's room and
asks her to run away with him, but she refuses. To get his
rival out of the way, Sabinsky has Petrowitsch transferred.
While riding through the woods to his new post, he is captured by Tartars. They read his orders, discovering that
they merely ask the garrison commander to keep Petrowitsch
for a couple of months becuase his presence is inconveniencing
the general. Angered, Petrowitsch joins the Tartars. Sonja's
parents finally succeed in forcing her to become engaged to
Sabinsky. Shortly after, a peasant brings a message saying
that Petrowitsch has been captured by the Tartars. Sabinsky
is delighted, but Sonja runs away to join her lover. When
she discovers that he has joined the Tartars, she returns
home.

Four years pass and Sonja is now married to Sabinsky
and has a child. Some Tartars who have been taken prisoner
are to be executed. Sonja is relieved when she discovers
that Petrowitsch is not among them, and she asks her husband
to spare their lives, but he refuses. Later, Sonja's child
wanders into the woods and is taken by one of the Tartars.
When they discover that the child is Sabinsky's, the Tartars
offer to trade the child for the prisoners who are to be executed. It is too late, however, since the executions have
already been carried out. The Tartar general asks Petrowitsch to kill the child. He pretends to agree but instead
takes the child back to its mother, with the Tartars in pursuit. He finally arrives safely at the house, where Sonja
seems to imply that she still loves him, though the ending
of the present day print does not make this clear.

The heavy-handed seriousness of <u>Den sorte Kansler</u>,
which works against its romantic adventure plot, is largely
gone from <u>Guvernørens Datter</u>, which is much freer in its
conception and execution. Still impressive in its photographic
style, it makes good use of close shots, a panning camera,
and cross-cutting, whereas <u>Den sorte Kansler</u> is basically
static and unvaried in its choice of camera placements.

Guvernørens Datter begins with a stylized, theatrical composition not unlike those in the Sarah Bernhardt Queen Elizabeth. It shows a drawing room filled with elegantly dressed people both seated and standing in carefully pre-determined positions. The rigidity of the composition soon gives way to a more realistic style and is an effective way to represent the social structure that Sonja and Petrowitsch challenge by their secret affair. The banquet scene which soon follows is impressive in its realistic decor and startling deep focus, and is similar to the newspaper office banquet in Citizen Kane, though not as elaborately staged. André Bazin's contention that deep focus in the early cinema serves a different function than it does in Renoir or Welles is shown here, and in other early films, to be untrue. Even in this early period it allows for the development of action on several planes simultaneously, increasing the realistic effect. This is characteristic of prewar Nordisk films, which were explor-ing the possibilities of mise-en-scène, while other filmmakers, Griffith most notably, were developing an increasingly sophis-ticated montage.

In one place Blom cuts within a scene in such a way as to change our understanding of the space. After a title an-nouncing Sonja's marriage to Sabinsky, we get a medium-close shot of Sonja with her child. In the background is Sonja's maid. The emphasis is clearly on Sonja as the viewer com-pares her acceptance of a socially conventional role to her previous love for Petrowitsch. The full meaning of this change, however, is only felt in the next shot as Blom cuts to a long shot which reveals that Sabinsky is also in the room working at his desk. The personal quality of the first shot, Sonja and child, is both destroyed and reinforced by the second shot, which reveals that this intimate mother-child moment is not as intimate as it first appears because of Sa-binsky's presence. At the same time Sabinsky is not relating to his wife and child but is working, clearly marking off the social roles of the two characters, once again stressing an intimacy of mother and child that is central to the story's meaning. It is a simple but important shot juxtaposition that is uncommon in the surviving Blom films and shows an inven-tiveness lacking in Den sorte Kansler.

Although the costume films stand a step above the blatant sensationalism of Mormonens Offer, it is clear that their story lines are still melodramatic and still incorporate

what is known in stage melodrama as "sensation scenes."
This is true in some of Blom's literary adaptations as well,
including his filming of the Gerhart Hauptmann novel Atlantis.

On the sensational side is Desdemona (1911, 548 m.--2
reels), which, though not really a literary adaptation in a
strict sense, is modeled on Shakespeare's Othello. Ejnar and
Maria Lowe (Valdemar Psilander and Thyra Reiman) are actors
and are performing in the principal roles of Othello. While
rehearsing, Preben Winge (Nicolai Brechling), who plays Iago,
makes advnaces toward Maria which she rebuffs. She is,
however, having an affair with Count Brisson (Henry Knud-
sen). Winge finds out about this and tells Ejnar that he suspects Maria's faithfulness. Ejnar finds a locket that Brisson
had given to Maria. He makes himself up to look like Brisson,
a transformation that takes place before the camera, and confronts his wife. Convinced of her infidelity, he throws her
out of the house, though they continue to act together. Brisson goes to see them in Othello and takes an opportunity to
visit Maria backstage. Winge sees them together and tells
Ejnar. (These scenes are played in the characters' costumes
for Othello, thus emphasizing the comparison of stage and life
that the film portrays.) During the scene in the play where
Othello kills Desdemona, Ejnar actually kills Maria, much to
the horror of the audience. He then comes to the edge of
the stage, into medium shot, and points out Brisson as a
guilty party to the whole affair.

Desdemona is one of the most interesting of the films
with a theatrical setting because it uses the setting to examine
the relationship between art and life, a theme that is common
in all the narrative arts and that often stays in the background of other Danish films with theatrical settings.

Three scenes in particular stand out in this regard.
The first shows a meeting between Maria and Brisson in a
restaurant, the scene where Maria gets the locket. The set
is divided into sections to allow for two actions to occur simultaneously without cross-cutting, much as a theater set would
function. Maria and Brisson are seen at screen left in the
foreground, seated at a table. In the background screen
right are other diners. As the scene progresses, Winge
enters and sees the couple. In a similar scene, this time
backstage at the theater, Maria and Brisson are at screen
right and Winge at screen left hiding behind a curtain and
spying on the couple.

The most important of these three scenes comes at the
end of the film. When Ejnar kills Maria, the action is photographed in medium long shot. After the killing there is a
cut to an audience reaction shot, then to a long shot of the
stage, a traditional audience point of view. The two shots
of the stage in this brief sequence exist on two levels. The
medium long shot of the killing, which is too close for an audience point of view, portrays the action of the personal drama,
that of Ejnar and Maria. The long shot of the stage portrays
the drama of Othello and Desdemona which, at this point,
meshes with that of Ejnar and Maria. The "real life" drama
is witnessed by the Othello audience and becomes a play with
real murder, remorse, and arrest, as the police come on stage.

In 1914 Blom made Revolutionsbryllup (Wedding of the
Revolution) based on the play by the Danish author Sophus
Michaelis. Viggo Larsen had already directed an adaptation
of this play in 1909. The intervening five years had brought
in the feature film; Blom's version is over 800 m. longer than
Larsen's, as well as considerably more elaborate in its costumes, settings, and action. The players include Betty Nansen and Valdemar Psilander in the roles of Alaine and Marc
Arron.

Blom's major effort in this period, and the film for
which he is best known, is Atlantis, based on Gerhart Hauptmann's novel of the same name. Released in December 1913,
it was the longest Danish film to date and one of the longest
made anywhere in the world. Originally eight reels in length,
it reached America in a six-reel version in mid-1914. Commenting on the change in length for the American market,
Moving Picture World noted that

> ... in its original form, it was hardly adapted for
> this market. Accordingly changes have been made
> in the subject, bringing it within a length suitable
> for the demand and eliminating much material that
> lacked interest or was otherwise inconsistent.[146]

It is impossible to know exactly what was deleted from
the American version, since only the original eight-reel version has survived. Comparing the plot of the original with
a plot summary given in Moving Picture World, however, indicates that at least two scenes seem to have been deleted:
one involving a trip to Paris where the main character goes

after his stay in Berlin, and the other showing his brief relationship with a woman on board the ship to New York, a Russian Jewish immigrant to whom he is immediately attracted.[147]
The just cited review also mentions that the title of the film
"does not convey any meaning," indicating that a dream sequence involving the legendary city of Atlantis was probably
left out also.

The film begins with artfully lighted introductory portraits of the principal actors, Ida Orloff, Ebba Thomsen, and
Olaf Fønss, each turning to look at the camera. The story
then begins. Dr. Kammacher (Olaf Fønss) has a wife and
three children. His wife suffers from a hereditary strain of
insanity which at one point causes her to attack her husband
with a pair of scissors while he is sleeping. To add to his
depression over his wife's condition, Kammacher has a paper
outlining a revolutionary biological theory rejected by the
Biological Institute in Berlin. Dr. Rasmussen (Frederik Jacobsen) is called in to treat his wife. They agree to have her
put in an asylum.

Seeking a rest, Kammacher travels to Berlin where he
meets an old friend, Hans Fullenberg. They go to an invi-
tational matinee of dancer Ingegard Hahlstrøm (Ida Orloff).
Kammacher is attracted to her and receives an invitation to
tea, which he accepts. She has so many admirers, however,
that he feels superfluous. Kammacher receives another note
of rejection for his biological paper and, in disgust, leaves
Berlin for Paris.

In Paris he sees a newspaper item stating that Ingegard
will be sailing for New York on the Roland. He also books
passage and boards at Southampton. On the ship Kammacher
discovers that Ingegard operates like a reigning queen with
a host of admirers, and this once again dampens his ardor.

Kammacher meets a famous variety performer, Arthur
Stoss (Charles Unthan), who has no arms and uses his feet
for everything.[148] He also receives a cable from his mother
telling him that Dr. Rasmussen is dead. At that moment he
has a vision of his wife, mother, and himself with the children, an effect created through double exposure.

One day while Kammacher is visiting the ship's doctor,
a beautiful Russian Jewish immigrant girl, whom Kammacher

had seen earlier in steerage, comes in ill. The ship's doctor
has to leave, and Kammacher takes over. Kammacher and the
girl are immediately attracted to each other and embrace.
Later, Ingegard feigns sickness, and Kammacher goes to attend her. While there she flirts with him.

While traveling through the fog, the ship strikes a
wreck and begins taking on water. Kammacher is asleep and
dreams of taking a walk through Atlantis. He awakes to find
panic and everyone trying to leave the ship. With effort he
manages to get himself and Ingegard in a lifeboat, though
her father, with whom she has been traveling, gets left behind. They are eventually rescued by a freighter bound for
New York. While on the freighter the couple finally become
lovers.

On arrival in New York Kammacher is met by an old
friend, Willy Snyders, who invites him and Ingegard to join
a small colony of artists in the city. Kammacher and the artists go to see Arthur stoss perform, a sequence in which he
is seen playing a trumpet, playing cards, smoking, drinking,
opening a bottle with a corkscrew, and typing--all, of course,
with his feet. Later, Kammacher and his friend Dr. Schmidt
(Carl Lauritzen), visit Ritter, a sculptor. There, Kammacher
meets a pupil of Ritter's, Miss Burns (Ebba Thomsen). Returning home, Kammacher finds Ingegard flirting with an artist who is sketching her. His frustration grows when he
tries to talk with her seriously, and she will not respond.
Shortly after, he has lunch with Miss Burns.

Unable to bear all the people who always surround Ingegard, Kammacher goes to Dr. Schmidt's mountain retreat to
be alone. While there he has visions of Ingegard with her
admirers, of his dead friend, Dr. Rasmussen, and of some
card players from the ship. Schmidt receives a telegram that
Kammacher's wife has died. When he takes this news to the
mountain cabin, Kammacher collapses. Schmidt sends a letter
to their friends in New York telling them that Kammacher is
very ill, and Miss Burns goes to the house to nurse him. He
is restored to health, and she returns to Europe with him to
take over as the mother of his three children.

The American advertising and publicity for Atlantis,
put out by Great Northern Film Company, stressed four points:
the film's success in Europe, its length, its realism--by which

was primarily meant the spectacle of the ship's sinking--and
its literary origins. Of these, the literary source appears to
have been stressed the most. As part of the continuing attempt to legitimize the cinema as a serious medium, a two-page
ad in Moving Picture World mentioned Hauptmann's "name and
fame ... known the world over," claiming for him "an enviable
position in the forerank of modern authors." It also noted
that he had only agreed to a filming of his novel "after much
persuasion," but that he had "expressed gratification at the
result." The same ad proclaims Atlantis as "the last word in
film realism," calling the ship-sinking scene "one of the most
remarkable and realistic ever produced in films." The importance of the sinking to the selling of the picture is attested
to by the fact that both photographs in the ad illustrate this
sequence. 149

    Atlantis was greeted as an important film wherever it
was shown. Nordisk itself considered it an "art film,"150 and
Olaf Fønss, who plays Kammacher, wrote that with Atlantis
the cinema had become art. 151 In Germany distributors paid
15,000 marks for each of fifteen copies, making Atlantis economically important. 152 The Italian film community was given
a special screening in Turin on the release of the film there,
at which it was much admired for its realistic shipwreck
scenes. 153 In addition to English, Danish, Italian, and German versions, Atlantis was prepared for release in numerous
other countries, including France, Sweden, Portugal, and
Russia, where it was released with two endings, including one
in which Kammacher died. 154

    The inspiration for the shipwreck portion of Hauptmann's
novel was the sinking of the Titanic on April 14, 1912, an
event which also stimulated production in the movie industry.
Nordisk itself released a sea disaster film in October 1912
called Et Drama paa Havet (A Drama at Sea). Another European film, entitled The Death Ship or The Wreck of the Aurora
was advertised in Moving Picture News less than one week
after the Titanic disaster, though, given the closeness of
the dates, the timely announcement of this film may have
been a coincidence. 155 The same issue of the News carried
an ad for films from the Animated Weekly of the wreck of the
ship Ontario that had occurred recently on the Great Lakes. 156
In its next issue the News announced that Animated Weekly
had shown rescue footage from the Titanic sinking at Weber's
Theater on Broadway in New York only one week after the

disaster.157 At about the same time, Kinemacolor showed
films at the Garden Theatre in New York of the Titanic's
captain, E. J. Smith, made just before the ship's sailing.158
Scooping everyone, however, was the Eclair Company, which
announced a film called Saved from the Titanic, starring
Dorothy Gibson, who had been a passenger on that maiden
voyage. The story was to be based on her own account of
the disaster and her subsequent rescue. Eclair claimed that
she would wear the same dress in the film that she was wearing when rescued, and that the film would be released one
month after the disaster.159 Perhaps the ultimate cinematic
exploitation of the Titanic sinking was the release of films
claiming to show the Titanic, but actually showing other ships.
After the publicity and concern surrounding the real event
and the release of numerous shipwreck films, the editors of
Moving Picture News felt moved to warn the public by com-
plaining about this practice.160

With Atlantis, Nordisk Films Kompagni's movement to
the long film reached its peak in the prewar period. It is
an ambitious film, though seen in historical perspective, less
interesting than other Danish features of the period. Still,
the film has considerable merit beyond its mere length. The
narrative sticks very closely to the main character, giving a
strong sense of one man's odyssey. Everything in the film
exists to point up Kammacher's story, making Atlantis one
of the most intense character studies of the period. In comparison to more recent spectacle scenes, however, the sinking
of the ship, so highly regarded in its time, has lost much
of its impact, while the personal story still carries considerable power. In addition, the film's use of real locations,
especially the scenes at sea and those in New York and Berlin, give Atlantis an authenticity often lacking in the early
cinema.

The Berlin scenes include the main character, such as
one in which he rides in a taxicab while being photographed
from another moving vehicle. The New York scenes, made
especially for the film, are used as inserts between character
scenes, allowing the montage to suggest that Kammacher is
actually in New York. The scenes include a moving shot of
the New York skyline, a street scene with newsboys selling
papers, and a high-angle shot of Times Square. The sea
scenes include: Kammacher among a crowd of people being
transported to the ship Roland on a small boat, a distancing

effect that has documentary reality; various shipboard scenes, including a deep-focus interior of the dining room; a wreck of another ship seen through the fog;[161] well-done scenes in the lifeboats, particularly one in which a boat with survivors is seen in the foreground while a lifeboat from a rescuing freighter approaches in mid-ground and the freighter itself is seen in the background. The camera in these shots pitches with the boats because of heavy seas.

A sequence that deserves special mention, even though its existence in the narrative is more interesting than its actual execution, is Kammacher's dream of Atlantis that occurs as the ship strikes the wreck and begins to take on water. Kammacher dreams of walking through the legendary sunken city. The first shot shows him standing on the bow of a small boat heading toward a dock on which stand two men wearing broad-brimmed hats and cloaks. Kammacher and the men on the dock have their arms stretched out toward each other. The camera is behind Kammacher shooting toward the dock. The three men grasp hands as they come within range of each other, while a double-exposure image of Kammacher sleeping is seen in the lower right of the frame. The shot is quite suggestive, in the way that some of Ingmar Bergman's symbolic scenes are, and overpowers the shot that follows, the second and last one of the brief sequence. This second shot begins on a narrow cobblestone street. Kammacher and the two men enter from behind the camera and walk down the street. The double exposure of Kammacher sleeping continues. The shot has a dreamlike quality because of the camera placement and actions, but its symbolic suggestiveness is destroyed by the setting, which is obviously a Danish town. The conception of having such a sequence and its intent as to character revelation are significant even though disappointing, because the sequence does not live up to its promise.

Only three other Blom films from 1910-14 have survived. One of them, Liebelei (1913, 1,165 m.--4 reels), based on the play by Arthur Schnitzler, was codirected with Holger-Madsen, and though less than one-fourth of the film has survived, this part indicates that the whole may have been quite interesting. It is very slow-paced, so much so that even when run at sound speed the movement appears normal. The fragment begins with the arrival at the home of Fritz Lobheimer (Valdemar Psilander) of the seconds to a duel. They leave for the

duel and are seen, in a series of shots, traveling through a
beautiful wooded area in a car. The duel takes place and
Lobheimer is killed. The remaining scenes take place earlier
in the narrative and are all set in the rooms of Christine
(Christel Holch), the girl Lobheimer loves.

Den udbrudte Slave (The Escaped Convict, 1911, 625 m.
--2 reels) has also survived in fragmentary form, about half
the original length. Not classifiable as one of the types of
Blom films already described, it tells the story of two students
who are mistaken for escaped convicts and of Black Carl, a
real escaped convict who almost ruins the romantic relationship
between the students and the two daughters of a local landowner. Den udbrudte Slave has little to recommend it. The
story is poorly constructed, failing to integrate its various
strands. There is no real cross-cutting of the students' actions and Black Carl's adventures, even though the relationship between these two strands is crucial. Nor is either of
them sufficiently developed to fully engage the audience. The
only positive aspects of the film are its night, interior lighting and the use of a variety of beautiful exterior locations,
showing that even in a film as slight as this Nordisk maintained high standards of photography.

With the outbreak of World War I Nordisk launched
several big war dramas. Among these was Blom's Pro Patria
(1914, 1,358 m.--4½ reels). The film takes a pro-war stand
and seems to imply that war is just a matter of honor in which
enemies really respect each other, despite a considerable
number of corpses seen on the film's battlefields. It is not
especially good Blom and comes off as a rather stiff piece of
playacting.

The most interesting director at Nordisk during this
period was Eduard Schnedler-Sørensen. Unlike Blom and
most of his contemporaries at Nordisk, he was interested in
action melodrama and the possibilities of cross-cutting, especially as used in the chase. He was a prolific filmmaker who
worked in various genres, but his real contribution to Danish
cinema is in his action subjects, though he was adept at comedy also.[162]

Before entering film work, Schnedler-Sørensen was a
representative for an insurance company in the city of Odense,
where he met a man who was building a motion picture studio.

He became interested in this new field and gave up insurance
to become a manager for Hoffotograf Elfelt's touring motion
pictures, traveling widely around the country. The show
consisted of Elfelt's own films about the Zoological Gardens
and The Royal Ballet, as well as some dramas and comedies
bought from foreign manufacturers. On his travels he met
Frede Skaarup, who owned an electric theater in Ringkøbing.
In 1909 Schenedler-Sørensen went to Aarhus where Skaarup
had become director of Fotorama. He wrote and directed
Den ille Hornblæser and other films for Fotorama and, in
1911, when Nordisk bought out Fotorama he became a director for Olsen's company. He made his last film in 1925 and
died in 1947, at which time he was manager of the Vesterbro
Theater in Copenhagen.163

Schnedler-Sørensen's two earliest, surviving Nordisk
films are Dødsflugten (U.S. title, The Nihilist Conspiracy,
1911, 533 m.--1½ reels) and Bedraget i Døden or Gar El
Hama I (U.S. title, A Dead Man's Child or Dr. Gar El Hama I,
800 m.--2¼ reels). Both films are examples of the action melodramas that constitute the best of his work.

Dødsflugten appears to treat its subject with the kind
of ironic distancing that marks so much of cinema today. It
tells the story of Count Leo Zachochin (Einar Zangenberg)
and the woman he loves, Sonja (Karen Lund). Count Leo
gets a note from Sonja to meet her at one o'clock. Just before his arrival she gets a note summoning her to a meeting of
of a nihilist group of which she is a member. Leo finds the
note and follows Sonja and her butler to the house where the
meeting is to be held. He gets in through a window, but
while searching the house he hears someone coming and hides
in a trunk. Leo is discovered when he makes a noise, and
Sonja defends him. The group decides to spare Leo if he will
get them a copy of the secret police "wanted" list within three
days. (At this point in the print, material which would show
Leo's unsuccessful attempt to get the note appears to be miss-
ing.164) Sonja devises a plan to help Leo. She visits Chief
of Police Rechowitz (Otto Lagoni), gets the list, and throws
it out the window to Leo who is waiting below. A policeman
sees her leave with Leo and becomes suspicious. The police
follow them to the nihilist hideout. The nihilist band escapes,
with the exception of Leo and Sonja who are pursued in a
car. A running gun battle takes place, and Leo's car smashes
through a gate. (The print ends here, though in the original
version, Leo and Sonja are killed in the crash.)165

The high point of Dødsflugten is the car chase. It
has a particularly fine moving-camera shot in which the camera
looks past Leo and Sonja's car to the pursuing police. There
is also some well-planned intercutting between Leo and the
nihilists while he is searching the house. The film was quite
successful, selling 138 copies.[166]

Even more successful, selling 192 copies, was Bedraget
i Døden.[167] In addition to being more polished, it is more
significant in film history. It began a series of films concerning the exploits of a master oriental criminal, Dr. Gar El
Hama. Ultimately, five Gar El Hama films were made between
1911 and 1916. Numbers I and II were directed by Schnedler-
Sørensen and numbers III, IV, and V by Robert Dinesen. I
and II predate the famous Feuillade crime serials, Fantomas,
Judex, and Les Vampires, and, given the wide circulation of
Nordisk films, should be considered as possible influences on
them. Gar El Hama himself is certainly a precursor of Dr.
Mabuse.

Bedraget i Døden pits Gar El Hama (Aage Hertel) against
a young couple, Edith Wolfhagen (Edith Buemann) and Baron
Sternberg (Henry Seeman), and a detective named Newton
(Einar Zangenberg). Count Wolfhagen, Edith's father, has
made a will favorable to his daughter and her fiancé, Baron
Sternberg. He visits his friend James Pendleton (Otto Lagoni), a moneylender, by using a secret passage. Returning
to his own house, the count has a fatal fall. Pendleton carries the body back to the count's rooms and leaves. When
the count is found, he is still alive and sends for Pendleton,
telling him that should his daughter and her fiancé die, Pendleton would be the count's heir. The count dies, and two
months later Pendleton proposes to Edith who rejects him.
Determined to abduct her, he enlists the aid of Dr. Gar El
Hama. At Edith's wedding party Gar El Hama drugs a rose
that makes Edith unconscious when she smells it.

Edith is put to bed, and the doctor is called. Entering
her room through a secret passage, Gar El Hama slips another
drug into a glass of water at Edith's bedside. The drug
creates the illusion of death for four days, allowing Gar El
Hama and Pendleton enough time to abduct Edith from her
tomb. No sooner does Gar El Hama revive her than Pendleton
renews his advances. He also arranges for Gar El Hama to
abduct her to Constantinople. She overhears their conversation,

however, and scratches this information on the window of the
room in which she is being held.

Baron Sternberg calls on the famous detective Newton
when he discovers that Edith's body is gone. He also shows
Newton the will mentioning Pendleton. Later, Newton sees
Pendleton and Gar El Hama together and, going to the police
station, finds a photograph of Gar El Hama in the "wanted"
files. Pendleton pays Gar El Hama to kill Sternberg. Newton
sleeps in Sternberg's bed that night, and when Gar El Hama
tries to kill him, a chase ensues through the secret passage.
Gar El Hama and Pendleton flee, taking Edith with them.
Newton sees Edith's message on the mirror and, with Sternberg, rushes to the train station, just missing the train for
Constantinople. They overtake the train, and Newton jumps
on from a tressel. Putting on a conductor's jacket, Newton
enters the fugitives' compartment. A struggle ensues, and
Gar El Hama gets thrown from the train. Pendleton is apprehended and Edith and Sternberg are reunited.

Bedraget i Døden has many of the strengths of the
other Nordisk films of the period and, in addition, the virtue
of a chase involving a train, a situation more common in the
American cinema than the Danish. These final scenes probably helped give rise to the Moving Picture World comment
that the story is "pregnant with startling situations working
out a well connected and highly interesting drama...."[168]
Most of the shots in the end sequence were done on a moving
train, and, though they lack the pace of cutting that Griffith
would have given them, they are nonetheless well staged and
exciting.

Also of interest are the realistic interiors photographed
in deep focus, the numerous exits and entrances from the
bottom of the frame, made necessary by the use of trap
doors, and the expressionistic lighting in several scenes, including one showing Edith's casket illuminated by a pool of
light amidst the darkness, and one in which Gar El Hama
drugs the drink next to Edith's bed, with heavy shadows
and a small area of light defining the action. The story is
set in England, the most common setting for Danish crime
films.

Dr. Gar El Hama II (U.S. title, Dr. Gar El Hama II,
1912, 800 m.--2½ reels) continues the story of the master

criminal. Railroad workers find Gar El Hama unconscious by the side of the tracks and send for Dr. Watson (Robert Schyberg) who recognizes Hama. Watson tells the railroad man the identity of their patient, and the railroad man in turn tells his wife. Gar El Hama overhears this explanation and escapes on a handcar. The police give chase in an engine but fail to catch him. Later, he makes his way to the harbor and enters his hideout through a secret passage reached by swimming underwater.

Gar El Hama disguises himself as the president of an anticrime league. He writes Watson a letter advising him to give up the search. Watson goes to the supposed president to ask his advice and is taken prisoner and locked in a room that begins to fill with water. Worried about her husband's absence, Mrs. Watson goes to the police. An inspector accompanies her to the president's house. Watson, meanwhile, manages to escape through the door that leads to the harbor and goes to the police himself. The investigator and Mrs. Watson subdue Gar El Hama and his servant, but they escape again. Watson and the police arrive and capture them. The last scene shows Hama in jail, but ends with a mysterious close-up that implies further adventures.

Like Gar El Hama I this episode is well constructed and makes much of secret passages and sliding doors. It has the usual imaginative cinematography that can be found in other Nordisk films; in addition, it also puts an emphasis on cross-cutting.

The most interesting sequence in the film involves the chase between the engine and the handcar. In its construction, and especially in its situation, it is similar to the handcar chase in Griffith's A Girl and Her Trust, released the same year as Dr. Gar El Hama II.[169] The following shot list gives a sense of the montage.

1. Tracking shot of the handcar coming toward the camera.

2. Looking past the police in the engine to the handcar in the distance on a curve of track.

3. Handcar passes camera (a diagonal composition). Shot holds until the engine comes round a curve in the distance and rushes past camera.

4. Camera on handcar looking past Gar El Hama and railroad worker toward tracks.

5. Similar to (2). Police point ahead.

6. As (4). Gar El Hama jumps off.

7. Tracks as seen from engine. Handcar in distance and another engine approaching from opposite direction.

8. As (5).

9. As (7). Railroad worker jumps from car. Camera stops moving. Watson and police run into frame at bottom.

Like Griffith's film, the sequence is effective primarily because of the montage, although the location shooting in both films also adds to the effectiveness. Of all the Nordisk directors, this kind of scenic construction appears to have been typical only of Schnedler-Sørensen.

Two months before the release of Dr. Gar El Hama II, another sensational Schnedler-Sørensen film appeared. Entitled Shanghaied (U.S. title, Shanghaied, 718 m.--2½ reels), it is the male equivalent of the white slavery films and tells a story about a seaman who is shanghaied and finally rescued partly through the efforts of his fiancé. Like the Gar El Hama films it benefits from extensive location shooting, in this case on ships and around the harbor, and manages to overcome a loosely constructed and contrived plot by stressing action and the exotic.

In October 1912 Nordisk released one of Schnedler-Sørensen's best films, Et Drama paa Havet (U.S. title, The Great Ocean Disaster or Peril of Fire, 675 m.--2 reels). Like Atlantis, released fourteen months later, it depends on a sensational ship disaster sequence for much of its effect, a sequence which Nordisk, in its press releases, proclaims to be as thrilling as anything it had produced.170

The story begins in a music hall where Frank (Valdemar Psilander) is giving a performance. In the audience are Captain Storm (Christian Schrøder) and his daughter Oda (Ellen

Aggerholm). It is Frank's farewell performance, and he has
booked passage on Captain Storm's ship Sverige. At sea a
romance develops between Frank and Oda. One evening a
fire breaks out in the ship's bow, and Captain Storm has Oda
ask Frank to entertain the passengers to keep them from
finding out about the fire. Frank works hard at this but
finally collapses from the strain. Oda takes over and keeps
the passengers entertained until smoke begins to enter the
saloon. A panic ensues as the passengers fight to get into
the lifeboats. Everyone gets off except Frank and Oda who,
in the rush, have been forgotten. Using a line that connects
the Sverige with another ship that has come to their aid,
Frank and Oda make their way, hand over hand, to safety.

One of the interesting things about this film is that it
was prepared with more than one ending. A version for
Russian distribution has Frank and Oda drown in their attempt to get from one ship to another. Their bodies are
brought aboard the rescue ship as Captain Storm laments.
Both endings have survived and can be seen at The Danish
Film Museum.

Nordisk's willingness to make a special ending suited
to the tastes of a particular market, indicates the importance
of certain foreign markets to Nordisk's business. A company
letter from 1912 refers to the worldwide success of Et Drama
paa Havet and the special Russian ending, noting that forty
copies were earmarked for sale in Russia.[171]

In comparison with most Danish films, Et Drama paa
Havet puts an unusual emphasis on cross-cutting. In the
opening sequence of seven shots, the cutting creates a sense
of interaction between Frank and his audience.

1. Long shot of Frank on stage, seen from behind the
    box seats where Oda and her father are sitting.

2. Medium shot of Oda and Captain Storm.

3. As shot (1).

4. As shot (2).

5. As shot (1).

6. As shot (2). Oda throws flowers.

7. As shot (1). Frank catches flowers. (Cut is made
    on action of throwing the flowers.)

On board the Sverige the first contact between Frank
and Oda is presented through a carefully planned montage.

1. Frank on deck smoking. He looks to left.

2. (His point of view) Oda looks back over her shoulder
    and climbs ladder to next deck.

3. Frank walks toward camera which is placed on the
    other side of the ladder that Oda has just climbed.
    He begins to climb.

4. On the upper deck, Oda looks down the ladder.
    She coyly moves across the deck and climbs ladder
    to next higher deck. The camera pans and tilts
    up to follow her movement.

5. Begins as shot (4). Frank comes up ladder and
    looks around.

The cutting of the sequence more than the performances of
the actors establishes Oda's willingness to initiate the relationship and Frank's willingness to follow her lead.

Later, Schnedler-Sørensen intercuts shots of Frank entertaining, sailors fighting the fire, and the telegraph operator sending an SOS. In this case the cutting gives a strong
sense of the simultaneity of the actions and adds to the overall realism of the fire and panic.

Like many of his colleagues, Schnedler-Sørensen also
catered to the taste for circus films. Two examples from 1912
have survived. Both illustrate the bolder use of the camera
that sets him apart from his contemporaries.

Mellem Storbyens Artister (U.S. title, In the Den of
Lions or Life in the Circus, 620 m.--2 reels) is the weaker of the
two films because it sacrifices the story and character relationships to unnecessarily long scenes of acrobatics, lion tam-
ing, and other circus attractions. The result is that the

drama itself lacks tension. The plot revolves around Ulla
(Ella Sprange), a tightrope walker. At the beginning of the
film she, her husband Spiro, who is an acrobat, and their
son arrive at a circus to try out for a place. They are
greeted by John (Henry Seeman), Ulla's brother, who is a
jockey. They join the circus, and an animal trainer makes
advances toward Ulla, which she rejects. While performing,
Spiro falls and is killed when he breaks through the safety
net. Ulla continues with the circus, and the animal trainer
continues to pursue her. One time John fights with him.
Another time a large snake escapes while Ulla and the animal
trainer are arguing. It crawls into the tent where Ulla's
son is sleeping. She catches the snake just as it gets on
the boy's bed. The circus director asks Ulla to perform a
tightrope walk over the lion's den to attract attention to the
circus. She has no choice but to accept if she wants to keep
her job. Ulla falls into the cage, but is quickly rescued.
The animal trainer accidentally shoots himself.

Although the film uses many expressive camera angles
and has some interesting circus footage, especially the aerial
acrobatics, the narrative events are perfunctory and not well
integrated into the circus environment. Compared to the
earlier Den fire Djævle and to other Schnedler-Sørensen films,
Mellem Storbyens Artister is only of minor interest.

What I see as the principal weakness of the film, W.
Stephen Bush, writing for Moving Picture World, saw as its
great strength. The very fact that "the plot is of the slen-
derest" allows the film "to give full attention to the magnifi-
cent performances in the arena," calling up, for Bush, the
same "prickly and creeping sensations" that he got from the
circus when he was a boy. After praising a number of things
in the film, including the realistic circus audience, the photography, and Ella Sprague's acting, he concluded his review
with high praise for the entire production.

> "Life in the Circus" ... is bound to be popular with
> any and every audience. It pleases the eye from
> the first scene to the last, keeps our curiosity in
> constant questioning suspense and makes us regret
> that the "circus" does not last longer. In these
> days of spurious feature films it is refreshing to see
> a genuine feature, which keeps its promise to the
> audience by being markedly better than the average
> release. [172]

The New York Dramatic Mirror, too, praised the photography and the realistic settings of the film. In addition,
it found the story "strong ... and effectively told," predict-
ing that Mellems Storbyens Artister was "unquestionably in
line to enjoy considerable success.[173]

More interesting is Dødsspring til Hest fra Cirkuskuplen
(U.S. title, A Fatal Decision or The Great Circus Catastrophe,
805 m.--2½ reels). It is one of the many Danish social melodramas in which a nobleman falls in love with a woman of
another class.

Count Willy von Rosenørn (Valdemar Psilander) receives
news that he is bankrupt and must sell his estate. While
having lunch at a restaurant, he meets Winge (Aage Hertel),
a circus owner, and his female companion, who is also with
the circus. They invite him to a rehearsal where he shows
off his riding skill on an ornery horse. Another woman, who
has been attracted to him, congratulates him on his skill.
Later, Willy goes to a café with the first woman. Winge
comes in and, after Willy leaves, reprimands the woman out
of jealousy. A rivalry over Willy develops between the two
women. He joins the circus and begins an affair with the
first woman, which Winge soon finds out about.

One day a fire breaks out in the hotel in which they
all live. Willy and the second woman are trapped on an upper floor. They manage to get on an elevator, but because
of the burning floors below they are forced to go to the top
floor.

After being saved from the fire, the love triangle continues. To make Willy jealous, the first woman plays up to
Winge. Willy gets drunk just before he is to perform a dangerous act. The second woman convinces him not to go on,
but the first woman finally tauts him into it. The act consists
of being raised by platform to the top of the circus dome on
his horse. The guardrails are removed from the platform and
fireworks are set off. The trick is for Willy to keep his
horse from leaping off the platform. The horse leaps, however, and Willy is injured. When he regains consciousness
in the hospital, the second woman is by his side.[174]

Sales of this film may have been as high as 295 copies,
making it a great success.[175] Unlike Mellem Storbyens Arister,

nothing interferes with the central dramatic story; even the
sensational scenes, such as the hotel fire and the horse's
leap, are integrated into the plot through the involvement of
the two women. The hotel fire is realistically staged with
convincing fire and smoke and a strong sense of the characters' entrapment. In one shot the camera is mounted on the
elevator as it moves from a fiery floor to the couple on the
floor above. There is also excellent documentary-like footage
of the fire equipment in the streets below the action. The
sequence of the leap and Willy's ascension to the top of the
circus dome are just as effectively mounted and include a
dramatic cut to the empty platform after the horse has leaped,
much like the cut to the empty trapeze in <u>Den fire Djævle</u>.

A bankrupt nobleman is one of the central characters
in another Schnedler-Sørensen film from 1912. <u>Vor Tids Dame</u>
(<u>A Modern Woman</u>, 835 m.--circa 3 reels) combines social
melodrama, adventure, and comedy in an American setting.
Hans Berner (Valdemar Psilander) is the son of a noble family that has lost its fortune. Leaving his mother and sister
at home (the sister's fiancé has refused to marry her because
she no longer has money), he leaves for America to seek a
new fortune. Arriving in New York (all the American footage
was obviously shot in Copenhagen), he goes to an employment
agency but has no luck in getting a job. He finally gets a
job as a laborer by helping a foreman discover two workers
who tried to kill him. The foreman had been in a giant coal
scoop which had opened and dropped him into a river.

Later, Hans sees an ad for a chauffeur and applies for
the job. He is hired after being singled out from a group of
applicants by the millionaire employer's daughter, Anny (Clara
Wieth). Anny turns out to be quite liberated. For example,
she drives the car while Hans sits next to her. She also
pays little attention to her fiancé. Driving to the river one
day, she discovers that her speedboat is being stolen. Hans
and Anny give chase in another boat. The thief jumps overboard, and Hans grabs onto a rope attached to Anny's boat,
which drags him through the water.

Hans sends money home to his mother and sister. He
also begins to fall in love with Anny. One day the fiancé
sees them playing tennis together and, in jealousy, tells Anny's
father, who in turn fires Hans. Later Anny, her father, and
the fiancé are attacked in their car by a crowd of dissatisfied

workers. Hans saves them by convincing the workers that the town is on fire. He gets his job back, and Anny begins making advances toward him, which he tries to avoid. Hans receives a letter from home telling of his family's dire financial problems. The fiancé sends Hans a note telling him he is fired again and signs Anny's name to it. To make sure he gets rid of Hans, he also has a friend offer Hans a job on a boat. Anny discovers the forged note and forces her fiancé to tell where Hans is by imprisoning the fiancé in an empty swimming pool which she begins to fill with water. She chases after Hans in a speedboat and takes him back to her father, who objects to their marriage until Hans reveals himself to be a count. Taking Anny with him, Hans arrives home just in time to save the family estate from being auctioned.

Although Vor Tids Dame has a number of weaknesses (unconvincing backgrounds, no attempt to adjust characterizations to American types, carelessness with details, and some lack of clarity in the storytelling), it does have a bold use of the camera, especially in the boat chase scenes, and an interesting combination of generic elements which, along with the progressive image of Anny, gives the film a contemporary feeling.

Another liberated woman appears in the 1912 comedy-drama Den Stærkeste (U.S. title, Conquered or The Madcap Countess, 650 m.--2 reels). Among Schnedler-Sørensen's best films, it exhibits his talent for comedy and his highly developed sense of camera placement and cutting. In a number of instances the competition between the principal male and female characters arises directly from the montage. In other scenes, the lighting or a play upon offscreen space constitutes the film's most important expressive means.

The madcap countess of the American title is Rinette Thule (Else Frölich). Her two greatest admirers are friends, Count Frederick Ottoman (Robert Dinesen) and Charles Burns (Valdemar Psilander). While visiting Ottoman, Burns meets Countess Thule who, like Anny in Vor Tids Dame, arrives driving her own carriage, with her driver sitting beside her. She invites Burns to accompany Ottoman to a party being given at her house. A day later Ottoman and Burns are preparing to go riding when Thule arrives driving her own car. All three mount up and join a riding club on an outing. Thule

jumps her horse over a hedge and challenges Burns to do the
same. Instead he jumps a higher hedge and angers Thule.

Burns vows to marry Thule. She then throws her ring
into a pond, saying she will kiss whoever retrieves it. Burns
refuses to take part in this game. Later, they come across a
drowning child, and Burns rescues him. Just as much taken
by Burns as he is by her, Thule rejects a marriage proposal
from Ottoman and vows to marry Burns.

As part of her plan she invites Ottoman and Burns to
a garden party. Thule and Burns continue their competition
by each refusing an invitation from the other to dance. Later,
she invites Burns and Ottoman to a banquet. Following the
banquet, Thule shows a surprise to her all-male guests: a
loop-the-loop structure on which a small car can ride. She
challenges the men, telling them that the man who wins her
must ride on it. Burns takes the challenge and, although
successful, walks off. She chases after him, and they embrace.

Louis Reeves Harrison, writing in Moving Picture World,
was quite taken with the film. He called it "one of the most
beautiful comedy-dramas ever thrown on the screen." He
especially praised Else Frölich in the role of the countess,
calling her "a splendid young creature whose personality
needs no modification to carry any such part to success."[176]

More interesting than Frölich and her performance is
the formal construction of certain scenes in the film. When
the countess arrives for the day's riding, we first see Ottoman and Burns in full shot by their horses. Ottoman apparently hears a noise and walks to the right; the camera pans
to follow him. At a certain point in the pan, Thule's car is
seen driving along the road. The staging of this scene is
noteworthy because it creates an action, the approach of the
car, that is implied to exist independently of its recording by
the camera. This may seem like a small point, but such use
of space is uncommon in the early period and indicates an
unusual cinematic sense. The scene continues as the camera
pans back with Ottoman and Thule as they walk over to
Burns.

While the effect of this scene depends on a long take
and the panning camera, a later encounter between Burns and

Thule depends on a skillful montage.   The result of the montage is a clear sense of the game that the two characters play
with each other.

1. Close shot of Thule peering through bushes.

2. Long shot of Burns from an angle similar to Thule's
   point of view.

3. Close shot of Thule as in (1).

4. Long shot of Burns, as in (2).

5. Close shot of Thule, as in (1) and (3).   She with-
   draws into the bushes.

6. Two shot.   Burns in foreground, his back to Thule,
   who is in the background.   The expression on
   Burns's face indicates that he knows he is being
   watched and that he enjoys it.

Although the sequence is simple, the pacing of the alternating
shots of the two characters creates an effective comic tension.

Lesser examples of Schnedler-Sørensen's care in camera
placement and montage are seen in Burns's leap over a hedge
on his horse and his ride on the loop-the-loop.   In the first
sequence a low-angle close shot of Burns going over the hedge
is sandwiched between two long shots of the leap.   In the
second sequence, three carefully matched shots of the ride
show it in its entirety.   This caused Louis Reeves Harrison
to note that "every foot of the way is followed by the camera,
even when the car turns completely over...."[177]

Two short Schnedler-Sørensen comedies from 1912 have
survived in incomplete versions.   En urolig Vagt (U.S. title,
The Disturbed Sentry) is a slight film built on the simple situation of some soldiers looking out a window at a pretty girl.
Hardly more substantial is Badets Dronning (U.S. title, The
Queen of the Season).   As with En urolig Vagt, about one-
fourth of the film is missing, so it is impossible to make firm
judgments about it.   What remains, however, has little to
recommend it, despite the presence of Carl Alstrup and Oscar
Stribolt in the cast.   It tells the story of a married woman
who goes to the seashore by herself and is pursued by three
men.

More ambitious, but no less routine and uninspired is
Schnedler-Sørensen's 1913 comedy Naar Manden gaar paa Børsen (When the Husband Goes to the Stock Exchange).[178]
Again Oscar Stribolt and Carl Alstrup star. Stribolt plays
Consul Descombes who goes on a business trip to Paris and
takes a woman with him. Prince Louis arrives at the Descombes for a visit, and Madame Descombes has her servant
Jean (Carl Alstrup) impersonate her husband. Jean cannot
forget his status, however, and unconsciously acts like a
servant. (These misadventures are cross-cut with Descombes
partying in Paris.) Descombes reads a newspaper notice about
the prince's visit and rushes home. Meanwhile, Madame Descombes learns about the other woman. When her husband returns home, he demands an explanation. At that moment the
prince's adjutant arrives and assumes that the real Descombes
is the butler. When Descombes begins yelling at his wife,
she confronts him with her knowledge of the other woman.
The film ends with him asking forgiveness.

Of the surviving Schnedler-Sørensen films that are
purely comedies, the best is Hans Højhed (U.S. title, His
Highness, the Prince, 765 m.--2½ reels), also from 1913.
The film contains a number of interesting camera placements
and makes extensive use of certain clearly defined comic
types, most importantly small-town officials. The mayor is
fat with a large walrus moustache, the councilman is short
and fat, and others are tall and skinny. All act with a naive
provincialism that enables them to be taken advantage of by
the main character. Moving Picture World called it a "delightful comedy" and noted that "the Great Northern Film Company
have proved that it is possible to make comedy subjects of
greater length than one reel of film." The review also mentions a trial exhibition of the film at Fox's Audubon Theater
in New York, saying it "was received with unusual applause
by a large and discriminating audience."[179]

The story begins with Prince Karl Heinrich (Christian
Mølbach) feeling bored. Next, we see a journalist, Herbert
Prince (Carl Alstrup), about to leave for a three-week vacation with his friend Robert Herrick (Lauritz Olsen). Before
leaving, he shaves off his moustache, which makes him look
like the prince. On the trian a town councilman from Waldeck
mistakes Herbert for the prince and telegraphs ahead to the
mayor (Oscar Stribolt) to prepare a welcome. When Herbert
finally realizes the mistake, he decides to play the role of the

prince, with his friend pretending to be a valet. He is
greeted by the townspeople and local dignitaries and escorted
to a hotel where a banquet is given in his honor. The real
prince reads a newspaper item describing his arrival in Waldeck and decides to go there to find out who is impersonating
him. The prince forgives everyone and bestows medals on the
mayor, the councilman, and the journalist. The film ends
with a close shot of the three showing off their medals and
pointing to Herrick who does not have one.

Good location shooting, extensive use of deep focus,
and careful matching of scenes help give the film interest.
In the beginning the prince and the journalist are related
through camera placement, cutting, and movement. The
prince is playing billiards and after tiring of it, leaves the
room by the back door. Cutting directly to the newspaper
office, the journalist enters from the back of the set, giving
the immediate sense of the prince's movement being reversed
and implying, in formal terms, a connection between the two
men.

In 1914 Schnedler-Sørensen appears to have made a
film entitled Psilander, starring Valdemar Psilander, although
Marguerite Engberg makes no mention of the film either in
her three-volume catalog of Danish films, Registrant Over
dansk film, 1896-1914, or her two-volume history, Dansk Stumfilm. The Danish Film Museum, however, holds a print under
this title. Identified as directed by Schnedler-Sørensen and
written by Palle Rosenkrantz, it is made up of about 320 m.
of unassembled fragments of an evidently longer film. The
fragments show Psilander involved in some kind of melodramatic
adventure plot. He is seen taking a woman who is either dead
or unconscious out of a car, entering a room full of men and
shaking hands with them, performing on a stage, making a
rescue on horseback, and, perhaps, fencing. These fragments indicate that the complete film, if there ever was one,
might have been of real interest.

Among the other significant directors who joined Nordisk was Robert Dinesen, who had previously made his mark
as an actor in Afgrunden and as codirector of Den fire Djævle.
Although only three of his Nordisk films from 1910-14 have
survived, he made about thirty-one of them, mostly heavy
dramas and adventure films.[180] The titles of the missing films
suggest their subjects. Among them are: Scenen og Livet

(Stage and Life), Katastrofen (U.S. title, Lost Memory),
which Moving Picture World called "a splendid drama ... care-
fully directed,"[181] Satans Datter (Satan's Daughter), Naar
Nøden er størst (When Suffering Is Greatest), Dramaet i den
gamle Mølle (The Drama in the Old Mill), Kærligheds Offer
(Love's Sacrifice), En Kvindes Aere (A Woman's Honor),
Slavehandelerens sidste Bedrift (The Slave Trader's Last
Deal), and Spionen (The Spy).

Of the three surviving Dinesen films, two are of little
interest, Den glade Løjtnant (The Gay Lieutenant, 1912,
726 m.) and Amor paa Krogveje (Cupid's Devious Ways, 1914,
length unknown). The first is a conventional love drama,
unusual only in that Valdemar Psilander plays a thoroughly
unlikable character, an army lieutenant who lives only for his
own pleasures. The film has little to recommend it, whether
in story, characterization, or technique. Amor paa Krogveje
is a very slight comedy with Carl Alstrup playing a man who
must marry his cousin in order to inherit his uncle's money.

The third of the surviving Dinesen films is a major work
from the period, both in its ambitious length (2240 m.) and
its advanced technique. Entitled Under Blinkfyrets Straaler
(Under the Flashing Light's Beams), it was made in the same
year as Blom's Atlantis and Christensen's Det hemmelighedsfulde
X. It combines excellent and extensive location shooting along
the Danish coast with the Nordisk emphasis on expressive
lighting, realistic sets, the use of mirrors, naturalistic acting,
and sensational melodrama. In addition, much of the film's
dramatic effect comes from carefully executed cross-cutting
between major lines of action.

The story revolves around two brothers, Robert (Nicolai
Johannesen) and Hugo (Alf Blütecher), the sons of a wealthy
landowner. Hugo is his mother's pet and the weaker of the
two brothers, while Robert is his father's favorite. Hugo
receives a note from a girl, who has just had a child, asking
him for 15,000 kroner as a settlement. Robert advises him
to ask for their father's help. The farm's agent delivers a
large sum of money to the father from the earnings of their
dairy, and Hugo sees the money being put away. That night,
Hugo sneaks into his father's study and steals the money.
Robert hears a noise and goes to Hugo's room, where he
finds him with the money and oppressed by guilt. Robert
takes the money intending to return it to his father the next

day. The next morning Hugo is delirious. A doctor has
been called, and Robert has gone for medicine. While he is
gone, the theft is discovered. The father finds Robert's
handkerchief in the study and goes to Robert's room where
he discovers the money and the letter from the pregnant girl,
which Hugo had given to Robert. Out of love for his brother,
Robert takes the blame for the robbery, and his father sends
him away. Before leaving, Robert tells his mother about Hugo.

Four years pass, and the father dies. Robert has become a ship's captain and is transporting a cargo of nitrogly-
cerine. He writes home telling his mother he is going to pay
them a visit. During this time Hugo has become a tyrannical
master of the estate. One day Hugo meets Elly (Agnete Blom),
a lighthouse keeper's daughter. He arranges a hunting trip
on Peele Island, where the lighthouse is located, to see her
again. As Hugo and his friends approach the island, he sees
Elly through his binoculars. The men walk with Elly to the
lighthouse and meet her father (Cajus Bruun). Meanwhile,
a pilot boat arrives at Robert's ship, also bringing a letter
from Robert's mother telling of the father's death. A storm
comes up, and Hugo and his friends bed down in the lighthouse for the night. Elly's father sights Robert's ship in
distress and sets out in a small boat to help. Robert's ship
is wrecked and only Fred, the mate, and Robert, survive.
While the lighthouse keeper is gone, Hugo goes after Elly who
is tending the light. In a struggle Elly knocks Hugo down
and extinguishes the light. Robert and Fred jump overboard
just before the ship explodes. In an attempt to rescue Robert and Fred, the lighthouse keeper's boat capsizes. The
three men swim to shore. While this is happening, Elly locks
Hugo in the lighthouse, but he manages to get out by means
of a rope. Elly's father throws Hugo and his companions out
when he learns what Hugo has done. A short time later,
Robert's mother sees a newspaper story that says that the
ship Harland has exploded and the entire crew has been
killed. Robert, however, is recuperating on the island,
where he falls in love with Elly and tells her who he really
is.

One day Robert, Fred, and Elly go to the mainland.
While Fred and Elly shop, Robert goes to see his mother.
At the same time, Hugo makes plans to abduct Elly. Later,
back on the island, Hugo lures Elly out with a note saying
that her father's life is in danger. Fred follows Elly and

sees her being abducted. He gets Robert who goes after
them. Hugo's friends force Elly into a boat while Robert
chases Hugo. Elly locks her abductors into the cabin of the
boat and heads back for shore. Hugo runs into quicksand
on the beach and is killed. The next morning Robert takes
Elly to meet his mother.

The general principle of the film's construction is comparison. This occurs mostly through cross-cutting between
Robert's life at sea and Hugo's life at home, but also through
extensive use of foreground and background action: Hugo
spying on his father while the father puts the money in the
safe; Hugo in a hammock while the maid approaches from and
returns to the background; Elly and her father in the foreground while Hugo and friends go off across the hills near
the lighthouse; Elly on the beach and Hugo and his friends
arriving by boat; Robert on the deck of his ship and the
pilot's boat approaching. These elements are often cross-cut
as well, but at some point are always joined in the same frame.
This shot structure creates an overall opposition in the film
between unity and separation, reflecting the way in which
Robert and Hugo begin the film together, are separated, by
both space and moral values, and finally come together again
at Hugo's death.

The opposition is even developed in the lighting. In
the night scenes that make up Hugo's theft of the money,
the two sons are first seen in their respective rooms. Hugo
is then seen in the study and finally the sons' rooms are seen
again. All three locations are bound together by a lighting
effect, moonlight coming in through a window and illuminating
the characters' actions. The opposition between Robert and
Hugo is further drawn by having the window in Robert's room
on the right and in Hugo's room on the left. In opposition
to the carefully staged interiors, some of which use mirrors
to reflect characters and expand the playing space, are beautifully composed and impressive exteriors along the sea cliffs,
around the lighthouse, and on board real ships.

One of the most interesting yet disappointing Danish
directors is Holger-Madsen. The contradiction arises from
the unevenness of his films. His best film, Evangeliemandens
Liv (U.S. title, John Redmond, the Evangelist, 1,093 m.--3½
reels), is among the most imaginative and impressive films of
the period, while his other surviving films are uninspired,

though competent, productions. Ebbe Neergaard claims that
Holger-Madsen's contributions in the areas of lighting and
camera effects "have so far not been justly evaluated,"[182]
a contention that is primarily based on Evangeliemandens Liv.

Holger-Madsen was born on April 11, 1878. He began
an acting career in the provinces at age eighteen, working
under the direction of Albert Helsengren, Jens Walther, Odgeir
Stephensen, and William Petersen. At twenty-five he went to
the Casino Theater where he spent eight years and then to
the Dagmar Theater where he stayed for one year. In 1911
or 1912 he became a director at Nordisk where he had been
acting since 1908. In 1920 he followed the route of many of
his Danish colleagues and went to Germany where he worked
for UFA, National Film, and Joe May. Among his German
films are Am Webstuhle der Zeit, Freiwild, Die Sportschen
Jägere, and Tobias Bundtschuk, which he made for UFA and
in which he also played the title role.[183] Holger-Madsen's
career as a director essentially ended with the coming of
sound, although he did make a film as late as 1936, entitled
Sol Over Danmark. At his death in January 1943 he was
manager of the Enhave Bio.[184]

Holger-Madsen's first film as director was Under Savklingens Tænder (U.S. title, The Usurer's Son, 1913, 746 m.
--2½ reels), which Moving Picture World compared to the stage
melodrama Blue Jeans, since both contain a scene of a person
about to be cut in two in a sawmill. Although the brief review criticized the ending of the film for being drawn out, it
did admit that the sawmill scene "furnishes a thrill" and, as
usual, that "the film will carry on its excellent photography."[185]

The thrill that the MPW critic found in the sawmill
scene is not evident today, especially when compared to last-
minute rescues in other films, even in films contemporary with
Under Savklingens Tænder. The approach of the hero's body
to the saw is covered in two long adjacent takes, a medium
shot and a close shot. Although the scenes gain some suspense because they portray real time and because we actually
watch the body get closer and closer to the saw, they do not
gain enough to counter what is lost by not intercutting the
saw scenes with the heroine's attempt to effect a rescue.
The photographic qualities of the film, however, hold up.
The film contains much location work, giving a documentary
look to the sawmill scenes, though their effect is weakened

when the extras, apparently real sawmill workers, occasionally look at the camera.

The film begins as moneylender Sintram Grib (Holger-Madsen) and his son, Florian (Svend Rindom), have a falling-out over the father's miserliness. Florian leaves home, and Sintram hides his fortune in a stone grotto. He also puts a will, giving his fortune to whoever finds it, in a nearby beech tree. On his return home Sintram dies. The next day, Florian applies for a job at the sawmill but is rejected because of his father's reputation. Shortly after, however, Florian saves the mill owner's daughter, Marja (Alma Hinding), from a falling log and is rewarded with a job in the mill office. Following this he is informed that he has been left out of his father's will. A year passes, and the beech tree, in which Sintram hid the other will, is cut down. During this time Florian also gains his employer's confidence and falls in love with Marja. Marja's father (Frederick Jacobsen) finds himself in need of capital for the mill and gets an agreement from a banker (Torben Meyer) for a loan, provided Marja marries him. Meanwhile, the beech tree is brought to the mill. In comparison with the rescue at the end of the film, this sequence involves considerable cross-cutting between the main narrative line and the tree being cut, transported, and processed, giving a strong sense of the approach of an important narrative element, one that ultimately fulfills its function.

Marja sends for Florian and tells him of the marriage to the banker. In order not to be seen by her father, Florian jumps out of Marja's window and lands unconscious on top of the beech tree, which is being conveyed to the saw for cutting. Marja stops the saw at the last moment and also finds Sintram's will after the log has been cut. Her father digs up the fortune and uses it to save both his business and his daughter's future.

During 1913, his first year as a director, Holger-Madsen made thirteen films; only one other survives, however, a drama with a theater setting entitled Balletens Datter (Daughter of the Ballet). Originally 400 m. longer than his first film, it tells another type of conventional story, about a woman who gives up her career as a ballet dancer when she marries. It has the usual misunderstandings, but also slightly bizarre circumstances surrounding a duel. Although conventional in treatment and subject matter, Balletens Datter is

basically a well-crafted film, boasting the usual high standard
of photography and realistic sets.

Of Holger-Madsen's twenty-one 1914 films only three
have survived. One is a minor comedy entitled Endelig Alene
(Alone at Last, 661 m.--2 reels). Essentially, it is a one-gag
film about the inability of two newlyweds to get to bed because people will not leave them alone. The couple's frustra-
tions are communicated with much exaggeration and mugging
by the actors. In contrast to this slight comedy and the two
melodramas mentioned above, Holger-Madsen's two other surviving 1914 films are serious and interesting works.

Ned med Vaabnene (U.S. title, Lay Down your Arms,
1,509 m.--5 reels) is an antiwar film from a script that Carl
Dreyer adapted from a novel by Baroness Bertha von Suttner,
originally published in 1890. While Dreyer had not yet directed his first film and was better known as a journalist
than as a scriptwriter, Baroness von Suttner was an internationally known figure who traveled and lectured widely for
the cause of peace and had received the Nobel Peace Prize
in 1905.[186] Her fame, coupled with the war in Europe, helped
attract a great deal of attention to the Nordisk film. In addition to its regular commercial release there was a screening
at a meeting of The New York Peace Society in November
1914 along with a lecture by Dr. David Starr Jordan, chancellor of Leland Stanford Junior University.[187] It was also
screened for the inmates at Sing Sing prison on March 14,
1915 and, according to Moving Picture World, was greeted
with "a wild outburst of enthusiasm and gratitude" at the
end of the showing.[188]

Despite the attention Ned med Vaabnene received because
of its subject matter and literary source, Hanford C. Judson,
writing in Moving Picture World, admitted only that it was "a
competently made picture" and that "there are some of us who
truly need to be shown that war is what a certain general
called it." His concern was more with audience reactions to
the film and their effect on exhibitors than with the artistic
merits of the work, although he did compliment the photography, saying that the film had "some of the loveliest of
scenes and most charming of pictures."[189]

More enthusiastic was a critic for Motion Picture News,
who was impressed by the realism of the battle scenes and

touched by the sadness of the story, especially by a scene
in which one of the main characters buries his daughter ("no
more pathetic scene could be enacted"). He also noted that
Ned med Vaabnene "comes with almost prophetic timeliness at
the moment when all of Europe is plunged in war."190

    As vague as Judson's comments are, they indicate a
quality of Holger-Madsen's work that may be even more evident today. He was a competent craftsman with some good
visual ideas that were aided by one of the Nordisk's excellent
cameramen, Marius Clausen. Beyond that, he lacks the artistic personality of Eduard Schnedler-Sørensen, August Blom,
or Robert Dinesen, although in certain scenes he is more
imaginative than all of them. These special scenes, however,
are not enough to give life to the films as a whole, leaving
the viewer with a sense that the films have not really fulfilled
their promise.

    Like many Nordisk films from this period, Ned med
Vaabnene opens with cameo portraits, first of Bertha von
Suttner and then of the principal actors in the film, Augusta
Blad, Alf Blütecher, Olaf Fønss, Philip Beck, J. Fritz-Petersen,
and Cotta-Schønberg, who all appear in costume.

    The story begins as war breaks out. Arno von Dotzky
(Alf Blütecher) is called to the front. A month passes, and
his wife Martha (Augusta Blad) learns that he has been killed.
Four years later, Martha meets von Tilling (Olaf Fønss) at a
court ball. Later, they meet at the estate of her father,
Count von Althaus (Philip Beck). She agrees to see von
Tilling every Tuesday and, after some months, they marry.

    Another war is imminent and Martha is distraught at
the possibility of losing her second husband. Von Tilling is
ordered to report to his regiment and must leave his wife in
her poor physical and mental condition. At the front he receives word that the crisis in Martha's condition is past, and
he writes her that a cease fire is in effect, and that he will
leave the army as soon as he returns home. A week after he
returns, however, peace negotiations break off, and he is
immediately ordered back to the front. More time passes and,
not having heard from her husband, Martha travels to the
front to find him. Meanwhile, von Tilling is injured and taken
to the railroad station where his wife has just arrived. They
miss each other, however, though Martha eventually returns
home and finds her husband there.

Since von Tilling's wounds are not serious, the family
once again experiences a time of happiness. Then cholera,
spread from the battlefields, strikes their area. They learn
that three children have died from it, and soon their housekeeper and Martha's sister, Rosa (J. Fritz-Petersen), also
die. Count von Althaus, grieved at the loss of Rosa, collapses
and dies after Rosa's funeral. Martha and von Tilling pledge
themselves to work for peace.

Although the drama is not as powerful as it might seem
from the plot description, one scene stands out quite strongly
because of its pictorial quality. It is the scene of Rosa's
burial. Her father kneels behind Rosa's coffin which occupies
the foreground of the image. Behind him are standing black-
hooded and -robed figures, and behind them stand bare tree
trunks and branches against a white sky. The image anticipates some of the compositions of Carl Dreyer and Ingmar
Bergman. [191]

Holger-Madsen's place in film history rests principally
on Evangeliemandens Liv, which he wrote as well as directed.
Of all his films it is the most imaginative, and sustains its
dramatic effect over the entire length. In its camera work
and sets it clearly points toward developments in the German
cinema of the 1920s. Especially effective are a city set, seen
through the main character's window, and a prison set. There
are also effective and carefully worked out dolly shots that
help move the action from present to past and back again.

The film begins with a scene of Valdemar Psilander
sitting at a desk and "studying" the role of John Redmond,
the lay preacher. He makes notes in the script as he envi-
sions certain scenes.

The story begins with John Redmond, a lay preacher
popular with the poor, preaching in a public park. During
his sermon he is denounced by a man who accuses the preacher
of being a greater sinner than all of them because he spent
half his life in prison. Redmond admits this but says he was
wrongfully convicted. That night he is in his room alone,
eating. Outside his window is a city scene and an electric
sign with the letters in reverse, but which can be read as
saying "light soap." That same night Billy Sanders (Birger
von Cotta-Schønberg), the man who denounced Redmond, sits
thoughtfully in a harbor pub. His fiancée, Nelly Gray (Alma

Hinding), enters, but he sullenly pushes her away. (The
pub set is also interesting because it is constructed on two
levels, the interior of the pub and a scene outside the windows. There is action in both areas photographed in deep
focus.) Redmond enters the pub, gives Billy a leaflet, and
tells Nelly to come to see him if she ever needs help.

Shortly after, Iron Fist Charley plans a burglary and
tries to get Billy to take part, but Billy goes to Redmond for
protection. When Charley comes around, Redmond knocks
him down. Redmond then tells Billy his life story in order
to help him. The first part of the framing story ends with
a transition to Redmond's past, effected by means of a dissolve from a close shot of Redmond and Billy to a dolly-in
on Redmond as a young man dressed in evening clothes and
talking with his mother (Augusta Blad). Next, we see Redmond with a high-class prostitute who undresses in silhouette
behind a curtain in order to excite him. His parents find out
about the prostitute, and his father (Frederik Jacobsen), a
bank director, throws him out of the house. His mother
meets him secretly and gives him some money. He goes to see
the prostitute again, but she rejects him when she finds out
he no longer has an income from his parents. In anger Redmond pushes her around, but a friend of the prostitute's,
who was present, intervenes; in the struggle the friend pulls
a gun. The prostitute is accidentally shot, and the friend
runs out, dropping the gun. Redmond picks it up and the
friend returns with the police, accusing Redmond of the killing. He is tried and imprisoned.

In prison Redmond attends a church service. (This is
the most bizarre scene in the film. The seats in the chapel
are cubicles arranged in steeply banked rows so that each
prisoner is isolated from the others. In one head-on shot
the frame is filled with these cubicles, only the heads and
shoulders of the men are visible. When outside their cells,
as on the way to and from chapel, the prisoners wear masks.)
During Redmond's imprisonment his father dies. With the
help of the prison chaplain Redmond gets his case reviewed
and is released. He goes to see his mother who dies in his
arms. At this point there is a transition back to the framing
story, effected by a dissolve from the death scene to a camera
dolly forward from long shot to close shot of Redmond and
Billy sitting by the window.

Weary of life, Nelly is about to hang herself when Redmond and Billy arrive and stop her. We next see them all
in the park again. Redmond climbs on the rock he uses as
his pulpit. There is a cut to a long shot as people flock into
frame and gather around him, providing a moving end and a
meaningful contrast to the interiors and tragedy of the rest
of the film.

Another Nordisk director who deserves special mention
is Hjalmar Davidsen, who began his film career as the owner
of the Kosmorama, a Copenhagen cinema. Prior to that he
had worked in his father's wholesale codfish business. In
1910 his friend Peter Urban Gad came to him with the idea
for Afgrunden, which Davidsen then produced. From 1913
to 1917 he was a director at Nordisk, making as many as
sixty or seventy films. He received an offer from Joe May
to go to Germany but was prevented by the war from accepting it. His directing career ended soon after with a film made
for Palladium in 1919. Later, he became manager of the Alex-
andria Theater in Copenhagen. Davidsen died on February 7,
1958 at age seventy-nine.[192]

The best of his surviving films is the 1913 Ekspressens
Mysterium (U.S. title, The Monomaniac, 1,040 m.--3½ reels),
a film which presents typical Nordisk melodrama in an expressionistic mode.

The story of the film involves two rival businessmen.
Laroque (Svend Aggerholm) is the enemy of his chief manufacturing competitor, Frederic Nessieres (Valdemar Psilander).
He also holds a mysterious hypnotic power over Nessieres'
wife, Madeleine (Christel Holch). He demands that she get
him a summary of her husband's holdings on the stock exchange. She complies and takes the information to Laroque's
house that night. Nessieres recognizes the evil influence
that Laroque exercises over his home and asks his lawyer
friend Lepellier (Carl Lauritzen) for advice and help. Nessieres and Lepellier attend a dinner given by Bournet because
they know Laroque will be there. At the dinner Laroque
draws Madeleine to him. Nessieres attacks Laroque and takes
Madeleine home. To get even Laroque begins hiring workers
at a salary 50 percent higher than Nessieres is paying. Unable to match this salary, Nessieres loses his workers. In
his depressed state he considers suicide but is stopped by
Lepellier. That night Laroque once again draws Madeleine to

him by using his hypnotic power. He commands her to get
her husband's revolver. A short time later, Laroque also
demands payment of a 360,000 fr. debt that Nessieres owes
him; Lepellier lends his friend the money to pay it. Laroque
draws up a will making Madeleine his heir and then boards a
train on which Nessieres is riding. Entering Nessieres's
compartment, Laroque shoots himself with Nessieres's gun
which he had earlier obtained from Madeleine. At the moment of Laroque's death Madeleine senses a freedom from the
oppressive power that has been controlling her. Nessieres
is mistakenly arrested for murder and, while Laroque's body
is being removed from the train, a snake ring falls unob-
served from the corpse's finger. In their efforts to free
Nessieres, Madeleine and Lepellier discover marks from Laroque's ring on the revolver. They get permission to look at
Laroque's body, expecting to find the ring and so prove Nessieres's innocence. Not finding it, however, Nessieres is
sent to trial. At the last minute, a worker who found the
ring shows up and saves Nessieres from death.

     The bizarre nature of the plot attracted the attention
of an unidentified Moving Picture World critic in 1914:

>   In offering this multiple-reel photodrama the Great
>   Northern Special Feature Company gives the assur-
>   ance that it will be found to be a subject out of the
>   ordinary. The theme is so unusual and the situa-
>   tions so startling that the production is well calcu-
>   lated to hold tense interest.... Imagine a man ar-
>   ranging for his own suicide so that the circumstances
>   will warrant the arrest of his hated business rival
>   on a charge of murder. Notwithstanding the strange
>   insanity of [Laroque], the plot is worked out log-
>   ically ... and many of the scenes are startling in
>   their realism.[193]

     In subject matter and lighting Ekspressens Mysterium
is a precursor of the expressionist cinema. When Madeleine
goes to Laroque's house, she finds him sitting in the darkness, lighted only by the glow from a fireplace, which helps
create the mystery and evil surrounding the character. Later,
when Laroque uses his hypnotic power to draw Madeleine out
of the house, the night is misty and windy. This scene calls
to mind the power that later film vampires exercise over female victims. Laroque is also a Dr. Mabuse figure, a type

seen in other Danish films of the period, especially in the
Gar El Hama films and in Robert Dinesen's 1915 film <u>Dr. Volun-
tas</u> (to be discussed in the next chapter).

Not nearly as interesting, though it, too, has a compli-
cated and bizarre plot, is Davidsen's 1914 film <u>Detektivens
Barnepige</u> (U.S. title, <u>The Charlotte Street Mystery</u>, 894 m.
--3 reels). In it, an internationally known thief, Davidoff
(R. Hjort-Clausen), and his accomplice, Kate Blond (Else
Frölich), are after a necklace at an auction. It is bought by
Count and Countess Warden (Carl Schenstrøm and Helen de
Dvanenskjold). Davidoff gets their address and formulates
a plan to steal the necklace. Meanwhile, Barker, a well-known
detective (Robert Schyberg), advertises for a nurse for his
children; Kate applies for the job and is hired. Davidoff and
Kate rent a room in a building that shares a common wall with
Kate's room in the Barker house. They cut a passage between
the two rooms which they then hide by means of a wardrobe.

Posing as a dealer in antiques, Davidoff visits the
Wardens and tells the countess that he knows a woman who
wants to sell a necklace similar to the one she just bought.
He gives them Kate's address at the building next to the
Barkers' and also observes where the countess hides her
necklace.

Kate dresses in disguise and awaits the countess.
Meanwhile, we learn that Barker is in the employ of the
Wardens. During their discussion about the necklace, Kate
gets the countess to prick her finger on a drugged needle
which renders her unconscious. Kate then puts on the countess's clothes, goes to the Wardens' home, and steals the necklace. Returning to her room she revives the countess, sets
back the countess's watch by an hour, and sends her home.

The Wardens discover that the necklace is missing and
call in Barker to investigate. Barker finds a strand of red
hair on the countess's watch and goes to search Kate's room,
where he accidentally pricks his finger on the drugged needle.
Kate rolls his body onto the roof, but a railing prevents
Barker from falling to his death. After regaining consciousness Barker returns to the room and discovers the secret
passage, but Davidoff and Kate have already fled, intending
to take a boat to America. After a chase, in which Barker
uses a motorcycle and a motor boat, the couple is apprehended
aboard the steamer.

The film lacks the more original story line of Ekspressens Mysterium and the pace needed for this type of action
melodrama. Also, the final chase is too silly to be really
exciting. Moving Picture World, however, found Detektivens
Barnepige to be "replete with exciting episodes" and "thrilling
escapes."[194] Whatever its strengths or weaknesses, it illustrates that Nordisk was still exploiting one of its earliest and
most successful genres, the detective film.

In 1914 three other figures important to the Danish cinema made their first films: Dr. Karl Mantzius, an influential
theater director who held a Doctor of Philosophy degree;[195]
Lau Lauritzen, who became the principal comedy director at
Nordisk through the teens; and A. W. Sandberg.

Karl Mantzius made three films in 1914; only one of
them, Pavillonens Hemmelighed (The Secret of the Pavillion,
length unknown, 810 m. survive), has survived. Judging
from this film, Mantzius's contribution to the Danish cinema
had more to do with the prestige he brought from his theatrical work and the respectability this lent to the cinema
than it did with his films.[196] Pavillonens Hemmelighed is
quite primitive in its narrative exposition, develops no tension in its chase sequence, and is often hurt by a too distant
camera and by the excessive length of the scenes. The only
significance of the film in Danish film history is that its scenario was written by Carl Dreyer, though the material is unlike Dreyer's own later work.

A policeman meets a count and his sister on a ship.
On arriving at their destination, he is invited to visit them
at their hotel in the city and, later, at their country estate.
Being attracted to the sister, he accepts the invitation. At
the same time, he is investigating a series of jewel robberies
and on one of his encounters with the thief, is overcome by
chloroform. Later, at the count's estate, he is forbidden to
see the sister. Sneaking in one night, he is overcome by the
count who uses chloroform on him. This makes him realize
that the count is the jewel thief. The count then tells the
policeman that he can marry the sister if he helps to steal
the crown jewels. To make sure of the policeman's help, the
count drugs him. They steal the jewels, but, ironically, the
policeman is assigned to the case. While trying to capture the
count during a boat chase, the policeman is shot. The count
and his sister escape, leaving the city with the jewels.

In his first year at Nordisk, Lau (Lauritz) Lauritzen
directed at least thirty-six films, most of which were between
200 m. and 400 m. in length.[197] Before entering film work
in 1911 as a writer, he had been a lieutenant in the army
and then an actor, first in Aarhus, where he made his debut
in 1907, then at Det Ny Teater in Copenhagen. He remained
with Nordisk until 1919 at which time he became artistic director of the newly formed Palladium film company, where he
stayed until his death in 1938.[198] Just before leaving Nordisk he made a film starring a comic team which became known
as Fy (Fytrårnet) and Bi (Bivognen), Long and Short, or
literally, the Lighthouse and the Trailer. Ebbe Neergaard
describes the characters as "very shy and modest bums."
When Lauritzen went to Palladium, he took the two actors,
Carl Schenstrøm and Aage Bendixen, with him, though Bendixen was soon replaced by Harold Madsen, a circus clown.
With these two, Lauritzen made a long and successful series
of farces which increased in length from two and three reelers to features, and included a feature version of Don Quixote
in 1926.[199]

Lauritzen's only surviving film from 1914 is Flyttedagskvaler (Moving Day Troubles). It tells how Holm (Oscar
Stribolt), a wealthy gentleman, is harrassed by moving day
activities. Leaving his house because he cannot stand all
the activity, he meets a friend (Christian Schrøder) and goes
with him to the friend's house where they play cards and
drink until late. Out of habit, Holm returns to his old apartment. Thinking he is an intruder, the new tenants summon
the police. After explaining the mistake, the police let him
go, only to have him enter the wrong apartment in his building, where he is beaten by a wife waiting for her husband
who is late. Holm's wife finally locates him on the stairway;
at this point present day prints end. At 288 m. the film is
obviously incomplete, although the original length is not known.
The film is undistinguished and similar to many of the Danish
comedies of this period. Further attention will be given to
Lauritzen in the next chapter.

Anders Wilhelm Sandberg began his career as a press
photographer and, according to Marguerite Engberg, was "one
of the country's first." In 1913 he worked for Dansk Biograf-
dompagni as a still photographer and in 1914 went to Nordisk
as a cameraman and director. Although he directed throughout the period under consideration, his principal work was

done at Nordisk between 1918 and 1926 when he was the company's leading director, becoming best known for his Dickens
adaptations, including David Copperfield, Our Mutual Friend,
Great Expectations, and Little Dorrit. In 1927 he went to
Terra Films in Berlin where he made a version of A Revolutionary Wedding, The Yellow Captain (for Terra in Paris),
and three sound films. He also remade The Four Devils for
First National, in Berlin. In the early 1930s he returned to
Denmark where he continued to work until his death in 1938.[200]

Ungkarl og Aegtmand (Bachelor and Husband) is the
only surviving film of the fourteen productions that Sandberg
made in 1914, and this exists only in fragmentary form. With
half of the film's original 400 m. missing, it is difficult to
evaluate this early effort, except to say that, like the early
Lauritzen comedy, Flyttedagskvaler, it appears to be typical
of Nordisk farce in the period and without distinguishing
characteristics. It tells a story about a merchant, Marius
Meyer (Oscar Stribolt), who is out partying while his wife
Karoline (Agnes Lorentzen) stays at home. At the restaurant
a drunk takes Meyer's hat and coat by mistake. As he is
being helped into a cab, the driver picks up a card that had
fallen out of the coat and takes the drunk to the address on
the card. Meyer goes home and through a keyhole watches
the drunk making advances toward Karoline. She runs out
of the house for help, and Meyer sneaks in and exchanges
clothes with the drunk. Karoline returns with a policeman,
who is really Meyer's friend still dressed in the costume he
was wearing to the party they both had attended earlier.
The friend (Lauritz Olsen) pretends to arrest Meyer, and they
return to the party.

In addition to those already mentioned, a miscellaneous
handful of films of varying interest have survived from the
1910-14 period. The most interesting of these is Dyrekøbt
Aere (Dearly Purchased Honor) from 1911, a one-reel melodrama about infidelity directed by W. Augustinus.[201] Dr.
Thaw is being unfaithful to his wife, Rose (Nina Millung),
with the wife of a friend, Dr. Fields (Frederick Jacobsen).
Fields and his wife, Nina (Jacoba Jessen), come to dinner at
the Thaw's. During the evening Fields is called away, and
Thaw makes arrangements to meet Nina. He tells Rose that
he must go away overnight. While he is gone, Rose is murdered in her bed by a burglar. Returning home, he finds
her body and is arrested for murder. He cannot establish

his innocence, however, without telling of his affair with Nina.
He is found guilty, and Nina collapses in court. In her de-
lirium she has visions of her lover in prison. Finally, in
front of her husband, her lover, and the police, she confesses
that she was with Thaw the night Rose was murdered. Nina
then dies, and Thaw is released.

Except for one brief shot in the street, Dyreköbt Aere
is made entirely of deep-focus interior shots in high-key lighting. The sets are elaborate, realistically rendered, and photographed at an angle rather than head-on. This helps to overcome a tendency toward theatrical staging produced by the
camera almost never crossing the stage line, though it does
move closer to the actors in certain scenes. One exception
to this camera style occurs in the opening sequence, in which
there are three 180-degree cuts as Dr. Fields goes to answer
a telephone call and then returns to the dinner table. There
is also one cross-cut sequence showing Thaw with Nina and
Rose at home.

Whether this film is representative of Augustinus's work
is not known, since it is the only one of his films to have
survived. In the same year he was dismissed from Nordisk
and, in 1913, went to Germany as a director.[202]

Two minor dramas, both typical and routine examples
of Nordisk-genre films are also among this miscellaneous group.
Klovnens Hævn (U.S. title, The Clown's Revenge, 1912, 720
m.--2½ reels) is another of the many Danish circus films of
the period, containing the usual circus acts extraneous to the
plot, but, unlike the best circus films, acts that are not especially interesting or well photographed.

Manzoni, a cyclist, is part of a circus troupe. Traveling with him are his female partner, Coralie, and his wife,
Baptiste. Coralie also loves Manzoni. Pierre, a clown, makes
advances toward Baptiste but is rebuffed. One day she is
injured in a fall from a horse and must stay behind as the
troupe moves on. During this period Manzoni and Coralie
have an affair. Pierre writes to Baptiste and tells her about
it. She writes a letter to Manzoni which causes him to rush
back to her. He convinces her that there is nothing between
Coralie and him and returns to the circus. Baptiste, not
really sure, follows him and sees him together with Coralie.
While performing their act they are accidentally killed.

In his review of the film, Louis Reeves Harrison was
impressed by the circus acts and the realism of the backstage
scenes, but, citing Matthew Arnold, he found that "the 'incurable falsity' of plot in this photoplay mars what might easily have been made a story of absorbing interest and affect-
ing end." He especially complained of the film's tragic ending, noting that it "is not justified because the story is too
commonplace." In all, however, he thought that the "beautiful photography, ... a source of perpetual delight in Great
Northern films," would, along with the excellence of the
circus scenes, generate a high audience interest.[203]

Et farligt Spil (A Dangerous Play), also from 1912, is
a love story with a military background. Although copyrighted
in the United States in 1912, it was never released here.[204]
The director of the film may have been Leo Tscherning, a
minor figure at Nordisk.[205]

Just as routine as these dramas are three surviving
comedies, all one reel or less. Kærlighed og Penge (U.S.
title, Outwitted, 1912) was directed by Leo Tscherning. It
tells the story of a widow who is beseiged by three admirers
but who really loves her young son's tutor. The film has
Oscar Stribolt in the cast.

Jens brænder den af (U.S. title, John Steals a Furlough),
also from 1912, was directed by Christian Schrøder, a veteran
comic actor at Nordisk. He also plays the title role, a soldier
who gets in trouble when he leaves barracks without permission in order to see a woman.

The last, and most interesting, of the three comedies
is Billet mrk. 909 (Apply Box 909). It was made in 1913 by
another minor Nordisk director, Sophus Wolder. Its main
point of interest is a scene in which a street becomes jammed
with taxis carrying ardent suitors who have come in response
to a newspaper ad for companionship placed as a lark by two
girls.

One final, and very curious, film remains to be discussed in this section. It is not mentioned by either Marguerite Engberg or Ebbe Neergaard, nor is the production company,
director, or any of the other credits known. It is entitled
Proletardrengen og Fabrikantsønnen (The Proletarian Boy and
the Manufacturer's Son). Made in 1911, it is 258 m. long and

appears to be more a promotional film for the Boy Scouts than a commercial release. It is also primitive in its storytelling and camera work and contains extensive footage of Boy Scout activity that adds nothing to the film's narrative.

A street boy, Poul, beats up a manufacturer's son, and the assaulted boy's mother complains to Poul's mother. A Boy Scout leader invites Poul to go on an outing with the troop. There they play a kind of war game after which the victors and the defeated get together in fellowship. Shortly after, Poul sees the manufacturer's son go by on an out-of-control horse. Following, Poul finds him unconscious in a field. The scouts administer first aid and carry the boy off on a stretcher. Poul is singled out for praise by the manufacturer who, in gratitude, gives Poul a scout uniform and a bicycle.

The film is obviously out of the mainstream of Danish production and perhaps should not properly be included in this study. Even if it is a promotional film, however, it does employ a typical kind of narrative to communicate its message, showing that, even at his early period, it was recognized that one of the best ways to propagandize was through an entertainment format. Then, too, the film deserves mention for its unusual propaganda point, that scouting unites the classes, an idea not unheard of, of course, but certainly not common to the cinema.

This brief account can only give a general idea of the richness of the most important period in the early Danish cinema, a period that saw the development of the long film, the growing influence of Danish cinema in the world film industry, and the emergence of a number of important directors, writers, and actors, including Benjamin Christensen, Vilhelm Glückstadt, Peter Urban Gad, August Blom, Alfred Lind, Robert Dinesen, Eduard Schnedler-Sørensen, Asta Nielsen, Olaf Fønss, Poul Reumert, Stellan Rye, Valdemar Psilander, Holger-Madsen, A. W. Sandberg, and Carl Dreyer. It may be that the surviving films that have been used as the basis for my discussion give a distorted picture of the characteristics of this cinema, that there are lost films that might eclipse the best described here, and that directors equal to Benjamin Christensen may still be unknown. This account may have to be revised as new films and new information come to light, but the outlines of the period traced here, despite the

limitations, indicate a cinema that is interesting in its own
right and of the greatest significance to an understanding of
the worldwide development of the medium. What Ebbe Neergaard says in his study of the period, holds equally for this
one:

> ... the examples given here should have shown,
> how anxiously and competently technical-artistic
> progress was treated, and that there was really
> much genuine feeling for the film....[206]

The next chapter looks at the films made in the years
in which the great economic expansion and artistic development of the Danish cinema began to decline, years in which
"the film's adventure" took second place to the great adventure
of war.

NOTES

1. Ebbe Neergaard, The Story of Danish Film, trans.
Elsa Gress (Copenhagen: Det Danske Selskab, 1963), p. 38.
2. Neergaard called these years "financially a fairy
tale." See The Story of Danish Film, p. 38.
3. Neergaard, p. 39. He quotes Dreyer as calling one
company "The Film Company of April 12, 11 hours 49 minutes
and 28 seconds a.m."
4. Neergaard, pp. 39-46.
5. National Tidende (Copenhagen), January 23, 1921.
From an article on theater and film in Denmark.
6. Neergaard, p. 42.
7. When Afgrunden was released in the United States
in 1912, under the title Woman Always Pays, Asta Nielsen was
billed as "the German Sarah Bernhardt" in an advertisement
that appeared in Moving Picture World of April 6. A similar
ad in Moving Picture News of April 6, however, identified her
correctly as "Denmark's greatest actress." The British journal The Kinematograph and Lantern Weekly in its issue of
October 17, 1912, billed the film as "another 'Asta Nielsen'
Special," indicating that her first German films and perhaps
her second and third Danish films had been released in England before Afgrunden.
8. Edm. B. H., Masken, April 23, 1911. Quoted in
an essay by Ib Monty, "The Debate in Denmark on the Cinema
in Relation to the Theater, 1910-1914." The essay is in the
files of The Danish Film Museum.

9. Urban Gad, Filmen: Dens Midler og Maal (Copenhagen and Kristiania: Gyldendalske Boghandel, 1919). [The
Film: Its Means and Ends.]
10. Aktuelt (Copenhagen), December 29, 1969.
11. Politiken (Copenhagen), April 16, 1911.
12. Aktuelt.
13. Marine Bladet (Copenhagen), September 1966.
14. Aktuelt.
15. Asta Nielsen, Den Tiende Muse (Copenhagen:
Gyldendal, 1945), pp. 102-7.
16. Neergaard, p. 43.
17. Moving Picture World, February 1, 1913, p. 477.
18. Neergaard, p. 23.
19. Marguerite Engberg, Registrant over danske film,
1896-1914, 3 vols. (Copenhagen: Institut for Filmvidenskab,
1977), II:23. I have not seen the surviving fragment of the
Fotorama film.
20. Neergaard, p. 23.
21. Ole Olsen, Filmens Eventyr og mit eget (Copenhagen: Jespersen og Pios Forlag, 1940), p. 87.
22. Olsen, p. 87. Ebbe Neergaard quotes Olsen's
conversation with the theater manager and its results in its
entirety, as reported by Olsen in his memoirs. See pp. 24-
25.
23. Engberg, Registrant, II, p. 94.
24. In an article entitled "Exhibitor's Difficulties in
Germany," the August 31, 1911 issue of The Kinematograph
and Lantern Weekly stated that the growing use of long films
(two and three reels) in Germany was causing the sale of
shorter films to suffer. The article also announced the September release of ten to fifteen long films.
25. The Kinematograph and Lantern Weekly, April 20,
1911, p. 1653.
26. Kinematograph, January 4, 1912, p. 523.
27. Kinematograph, October 2, 1913, p. 2457.
28. Kinematograph, May 4, 1911, p. 1823.
29. The New York Dramatic Mirror, September 20,
1911, p. 28.
30. Mirror, September 13, 1911, p. 22.
31. Kinematograph, August 10, 1911, p. 751 (Outcast)
and August 17, 1911, p. 823 (Zigomar).
32. Kinematograph, September 18, 1913, pp. 2194-96.
33. Kinematograph, September 11, 1913, p. 2136.
Stellan Rye was a dramatist who began his film work in 1912
as a scenario writer and director for the Danish company Det

Skandinavisk-russike Handelshus. He went to Germany in 1913 where he made The Student of Prague, one of the most important of early feature-length films. During 1913–14 he directed sixteen films in Germany. See Engberg, Dansk Stumfilm, pp. 536, 542, 547, 556, 557, 650.

34. Kinematograph, October 2, 1913, p. 2457.

35. Kinematograph, January 15, 1914, p. 5.

36. Kinematograph, October 9, 1913, p. 2541.

37. Kinematograph, June 22, 1911, p. 333.

38. Nordisk Films shipping invoices dated August 12, 1910, March 23 and May 13, 1911, September 19 and October 3, 1912, August 20 and October 14, 1913 and January 8, 1914.

39. The New York Dramatic Mirror, December 31, 1913, p. 23.

40. Mirror, January 14, 1914, p. 57. Since All-Star Feature Company was not a film producer, the producing source of Curse of White Slavery remains a question. It is possible that the film was, in fact, Den hvide Slavehandel II, since Nordisk records list All-Star Feature Company as one of its American distributors in 1913. Also, from the Nordisk shipping invoices we know that four copies of Den hvide Slavehandel II were sent to the United States on January 8, 1914.

41. Mirror, January 21, 1914, p. 27.

42. Motion Picture News, January 17, 1914, p. 30.

43. News, February 7, 1914, p. 10.

44. Engberg, Registrant, II, pp. 11–26, 189–97, 313–15 and III, pp. 56–58, 238.

45. Neergaard, pp. 40, 68, 113.

46. Neergaard, p. 114.

47. In 1910 Nordisk and Fotorama had signed a contract whereby Nordisk would distribute Fotorama films abroad and Fotorama would distribute Nordisk films in Denmark and Norway. See Engberg, Dansk Stumfilm, pp. 225–32.

48. Neergaard, pp. 40–41. Copenhagen by Night is incorrectly included in this list since it is a comedy.

49. Filmen (Copenhagen), November 15, 1915, p. 23.

50. Neergaard, p. 40.

51. Jay Leyda, Kino: A History of the Russian and Soviet Film (London: George Allen and Unwin, 1960), pp. 47–48.

52. Arnold Hending, Herman Bang paa Film (Herman Bang on Film) (Copenhagen: Kandrup & Wunschs Forlag, 1957), p. 18.

53. Neergaard, p. 40. See also Filmen, April 15, 1916, pp. 124-25.

54. National Tidende (Copenhagen), March 26, 1949.

55. Berlingske Tidende (Copenhagen), October 17, 1954.

56. Neergaard, pp. 40-41. Marguerite Engberg does credit Lind with the codirection of the film.

57. Engberg, Registrant, II, pp. 27-29, 202-5, 325-38 and III, pp. 62-83, 239-48.

58. Engberg, Registrant, II, pp. 10, 186-88, 312 and III, p. 55.

59. John Ernst, Benjamin Christensen (Copenhagen: Det Danske Filmmuseum, 1967), p. 3.

60. The biographical data given here comes from an article in Jyllands Posten, April 4, 1959, by Ib Monty and from the monograph by John Ernst.

61. Filmen, January 1, 1917, pp. 67, 69.

62. In interviews about his Hollywood period, Christensen claims to have been the first person to introduce a mobile microphone while shooting scenes for The Haunted House. He says they simply hung the microphone from a bamboo pole held by an assistant. See Ernst, pp. 28-30. The awarding of a cinema management post to film personalities is a custom in Denmark. Christensen spent the last fifteen years of his life in this capacity. In some cases, such as Dreyer's, who became manager of a Copenhagen cinema, these jobs were the person's only source of income. Among others, these posts went to August Blom, Olaf Fønss, Urban Gad, Holger-Madsen, Eduard Schnedler-Sørensen, Else Frølich, and Johan Ankerstjerne.

63. Benjamin Christensen, "Barnet som lär sig att gå," Filmrevyen (Sweden), 1921, quoted in John Ernst, Benjamin Christensen, p. 45.

64. Carl Dreyer, "New Ideas About the Film: Benjamin Christensen and His Ideas," Politiken (Copenhagen), January 1, 1922, included in Donald Skoller, ed., Dreyer in Double Reflection (New York: E. P. Dutton & Co., 1973), p. 31.

65. W. Stephen Bush, "Sealed Orders," Moving Picture World, March 1914, p. 1654.

66. The New York Dramatic Mirror, March 18, 1914, p. 34.

67. Motion Picture News, March 28, 1914, p. 47.

68. Ernst, pp. 8-9.

69. The success of Benjamin Christensen's structuring of this sequence is attested to by a remark made in the March 18, 1914 New York Dramatic Mirror review already referred to. Commenting on Spinelli's entrapment, the writer notes that the viewer is "not told this by a sub-title, you actually see for yourself that it is impossible for the count to get out."

70. Neergaard, pp. 44-46.

71. Det Skandinavisk-russike Handelshus was also sole distributor of films and motion picture apparatus made by The Hepworth Manufacturing Company of London. See Nordisk Biograf Tidende (Copenhagen), October 1909.

72. Compiled from unidentified biographical material in the files of the Danish Film Museum.

73. Aftenposten (Copenhagen), May 30, 1920.

74. Ove Brusendorff, Filmen I-III (Copenhagen: Universal-Forlaget, 1939-41), cited Neergaard, p. 45.

75. Engberg, Registrant, II, pp. 301-307, 503-522, and III, pp. 22-35, 219-237.

76. Marguerite Engberg, Den Danske Stumfilm (Copenhagen: Det Danske Filmmuseum, 1968), p. 29.

77. Engberg, Registrant, II, pp. 301-307, 503-522, and III, pp. 22-34, 219-237.

78. Neergaard, p. 46.

79. Neergaard, p. 46.

80. The character names used in this description come from the Dutch intertitles of the surviving version. The only name change made is that of the wife, called Carla in the Dutch titles, changed to conform to Marguerite Engberg's cast list. See Engberg, Registrant, III, p. 221.

81. Neergaard, p. 45.

82. Engberg, Registrant, II, p. 505.

83. Engberg, Registrant, II, pp. 505, 507.

84. Moving Picture World, July 5, 1913.

85. The print I saw at The Danish Film Museum measures 620 m. Marguerite Engberg, Registrant, II, p. 8, gives the length of the surviving material at 200 m. Her figure is either incorrect or footage has been lost or removed since my 1975 viewing of the film. The original length is not known.

86. Engberg, Registrant, II, pp. 163-72.

87. Neergaard, p. 41.

88. Engberg, Registrant, II, pp. 317-22.

89. Engberg, Registrant, II, pp. 339-42.

90. Neergaard, p. 41. Philipsen claimed that his theater was the largest in Northern Europe. It included an elegant promenade, a restaurant, waiting rooms, a tea room, and

boasted a concert orchestra to provide music for the films.
Ads for the theater show a drawing of an audience dressed
in elegant formal attire in front of the theater. For an example of one of these ads see Filmen, I, October 15, 1912.
    91. Engberg, Registrant, III, pp. 40-54.
    92. Engberg, Registrant, III, pp. 3-21, 201-18.
    93. Engberg, Registrant, III, p. 3.
    94. Engberg, Registrant, III, p. 9.
    95. Engberg, Registrant, III, p. 11.
    96. Engberg, Registrant, III, p. 13.
    97. Engberg, Registrant, III, p. 15.
    98. Engberg, Registrant, III, p. 16.
    99. Engberg, Registrant, III, p. 207.
    100. Engberg, Registrant, III, pp. 3, 4, 13, 14, 207-9.
    101. Engberg, Registrant, III, p. 201.
    102. Engberg, Registrant, II, pp. 31-162, 208-99, 345-
469 and III, pp. 84-177, 250-419.
    103. Engberg, Registrant, II, pp. 42-45, 47, 48, 52,
82, 84. Although I have found no record of Fabian paa
Kærlighedsstien or Fabian henter Jordemoder (see Appendix
B) being shown in the United States, Nordisk records indicate that copies of both were sent to Great Northern in New
York. Otherwise the films without U.S. titles do not appear
to have been distributed in the United States, though a film
fitting the description of Fabian som Musiklærer under the
title The New Teacher (see Moving Picture World, June 8,
1912) was released in June 1912.
    104. Moving Picture World, September 3, 1910, p. 633.
    105. Moving Picture World, September 17, 1910, p.
749.
    106. Engberg, Registrant, II, pp. 80, 94. Dobbelt-
gængeren has negative number 671 and Den hvide Slavehandel
I number 689.
    107. Marguerite Engberg gives the original length of
the film as 217 m. (Registrant, II, p. 80), but the version
held by The Danish Film Museum measures 268 m.
    108. Although I have found no record of this film be-
ing released in the United States, Nordisk records indicate
that eighteen copies were sent to Great Northern on June 15,
1911. Marguerite Engberg gives the original length as 261 m.
and the surviving material as 236 m. See Registrant II, p. 75.
The print I saw at the Danish Film Museum measures 430 m.
(circa 1½ reels).
    109. Engberg, Registrant, II, pp. 93, 116, 119. Each
film was about one reel.

110. Moving Picture World, April 8, 1911, p. 903.

111. Trial of Hawley Harvey Crippen, ed. Filson Young, Notable British Trials Series (London: William Hodge & Co., 1920).

112. Engberg, Registrant, II, p. 114.

113. This film was part of a series of Christian Schrø-der (a leading Danish comic actor) films made from 1910 to 1912. In all there were five films, all with titles bearing the actor's name. In addition to this one there were Christian Schrøder som Soldat (... as Soldier), ... som Don Juan (... as Don Juan), ... som Lejetjener (... as Occasional Waiter), and ... i Panoptiken (... in the Waxworks).

114. La Femme is based on the play entitled Madam X by Alexander Bisson which had had a successful run in New York at the time of the film's opening. Moving Picture World preferred the film to the stage production, saying that it had "eliminated much that is not required and ... kept the salient features, emphasizing them in a way that makes them stand out clearer and ... more real." It also commended the acting and called the film "well worth seeing." See Moving Picture World, October 29, 1910, p. 118.

115. Diamantbedrageren received a mixed reception in the United States. Comparing it favorably to the other Nordisk detective films, Moving Picture World (November 19, 1910, p. 1299) noted that Nordisk has "an established reputation for detective stories and this picture will help in maintaining the reputation." MPW also commended the film for its excellent acting. The New York Dramatic Mirror (November 23, 1910, p. 5176), however, gave Diamantbedrageren a backhanded compliment. After praising the film as "a detective story of considerable ingenuity" which had received "an admirable mounting," it rather snobbishly suggested that whether the story is worth telling occasions "diversity of opinion." Overall, the Mirror's review has a patronizing tone.

116. All the films in this list were one reel or less, with the exception of Den Livegne which was a little over one reel; none of them seem to have survived.

117. Neergaard, p. 29.

118. Biographical information is from an article in an unidentified provincial newspaper story written on Blom's seventieth birthday. In the files of the Danish Film Museum.

119. Moving Picture World, September 10, 1910, p. 576.

120. Moving Picture World, April 15, 1911, p. 765.

121. The Kinematograph and Lantern Weekly, March 16, 1911, p. 1375.

122. Kinematograph, January 19, 1911, p. 677. Shake-
speare adaptations were common in other countries as well.
In a selection devoted to authors who had been filmed, the
July 17, 1915 issue of Moving Picture World listed the follow-
ing Shakespeare films: Twelfth Night (Vitagraph, 1910),
Hamlet (Lux, 1910), A Winter's Tale (Thanhouser, 1910),
The Merry Wives of Windsor (Selig, 1910, and Eclipse, 1911),
Julius Cæser (Cines, 1912, and Kleine, 1914, 6 reels), Romeo
and Juliet (Selig, 1910, and Pathe 1913, 2 reels), As You Like
It (Vitagraph, 1912), The Merchant of Venice (Eclipse, 1913,
2 reels, and Universal, 1914, 4 reels), Antony and Cleopatra
(Kleine, 1913, 3 reels, and Pathe, 1914, 2 reels), The Tempest
(Union Features, 1913), Othello (Pathe, 1910, and Cines,
1914, 5 reels), Richard III (Shakespeare Film Company, 1913,
4 reels), Cymbeline (Thanhouser, 1913, 2 reels). Unless
otherwise noted the films were probably 1 reel in length.
    123. Emilie Altenloh, Zur Soziologie des Kino (Jena,
1914), cited by Ebbe Neergaard, p. 27.
    124. Neergaard, pp. 27-28.
    125. Moving Picture World, October 8, 1910, p. 938.
    126. Moving Picture World, December 24, 1910, p. 35.
    127. Neergaard, p. 29.
    128. Neergaard, p. 29. One Danish trade paper cited
Valdemar Psilander and Maurice Costello as the world's most
famous actors. See Biografteaterbladet (Aarhus), January
1913.
    129. Nordisk's shipping invoices dated March 23 and
24, 1911, May 8, 1911, and June 1, 1911.
    130. Engberg, Registrant over danske film, 1896-1914,
vol. II (Copenhagen: Institut for Filmvidenskab, 1977), p.
215.
    131. Neergaard, pp. 29-30.
    132. Engberg, Registrant, I and II.
    133. About twenty-two Blom films from 1910-14 have
survived.
    134. Nordisk's shipping invoices indicate that two
prints of this film were sent to New York in September 1911
under the title In the Prime of Life, but there is no indication that the film was ever distributed in the United States.
It was common practice for Nordisk to send sample copies to
its New York office for evaluation by Ingvald Oes, the manager of Great Northern Film Company.
    135. Engberg, Registrant, II, pp. 219, 267.
    136. Moving Picture World, January 6, 1912, pp. 68,
127.

137. Moving Picture World, May 17, 1913, pp. 920-21.
138. The character names come from Dutch titles for
the film and may not be the names used in the original Danish
prints.
139. "The Sectarian Film Once More," Moving Picture
World, January 27, 1912, p. 282.
140. The Kinematograph and Lantern Weekly, September
7, 1911, pp. 993, 995. The March 3, 1917 issue of Motion
Picture World contains a review of an American film called
A Mormon Maid, starring Mae Murray and Hobart Bosworth.
Billed in an advertisement as "a stupendous, thrilling exposé
of a hidden chapter of American life" (Motion Picture World,
February 28, 1917), it tells the story of an attempt by a Mormon leader to get a pioneer girl to become one of his wives.
The review of the film called it "anti-Mormon propaganda."
141. The New York Dramatic Mirror, January 15, 1913,
p. 62.
142. Mirror, February 12, 1913, p. 31.
143. Engberg, Registrant, II, p. 273.
144. Nordisk's shipping invoices, dated October 4 and
23, 1911, and January 1, March 14, and April 4 and 13, 1912.
See also Moving Picture World, February 10, 1912, p. 470.
145. Moving Picture World, September 21, 1912, pp.
1158-59.
146. Moving Picture World, June 13, 1914, p. 1520.
147. Moving Picture World, June 20, 1914, p. 1744.
148. Charles Unthan was a real-life variety performer
on whom Hauptmann based the character of Arthur Stoss.
Ida Orloff of Vienna's Burgtheater was the model for the
dancer Ingegard. See Engberg, Dansk Stumfilm, p. 488.
In 1914 Unthan appeared in a German film released in England
as The Tragedy of the Three M's. He played a circus performer who saves an equestrienne and her acrobat lover from
the machinations of the head of the circus troupe. In a review of the film Unthan was identified as "the armless man of
Atlantis." See The Kinematograph and Lantern Weekly, April
16, 1914, p. 97.
149. Moving Picture World, June 6, 1914, pp. 1358-59.
Ole Olsen's own account of Hauptmann's initial resistance to
having his novel filmed, as well as other recollections of the
production, can be found on pp. 111-13 of Olsen's autobiography, Filmens Eventyr og mit eget.
150. Engberg, Dansk Stumfilm, p. 482.
151. Olaf Fønss, "Omkring Atlantis," Filmen, October
15, 1913, pp. 5-11.

152. The Kinematograph and Lantern Weekly, August
21, 1913, p. 1767. See also Engberg, Dansk Stumfilm, p.
496.
    153. Kinematograph, January 22, 1914, p. 7.
    154. Engberg, Dansk Stumfilm, p. 499.
    155. Moving Picture News, April 20, 1912, p. 29.
    156. News, April 20, 1912, p. 33. Animated Weekly
was produced and distributed by the Sales Company, an organization founded by a group of independent producers in
April 1910 and headed by Carl Laemmle.
    157. News, April 27, 1912, p. 24.
    158. News, April 20, 1912, p. 9.
    159. News, May 4, 1912, p. 27.
    160. News, May 11, 1912, p. 6.
    161. This shot of the wreck seen in the fog appears
to come from the same footage used in another 1913 Nordisk
feature, Under Blinkfyrets Straaler, which premiered on the
same day as Atlantis.
    162. In a letter dated August 24, 1939, included in
the files of The Danish Film Museum, Schnedler-Sørensen
claims to have directed about 200 films and to have written,
either alone or in collaboration, about fifty scenarios.
    163. Biographical information comes from articles and
interviews in two Copenhagen newspapers, Berlingske Tidende,
January 30, 1933, and Politiken, September 22, 1946.
    164. See the plot description in Moving Picture World,
February 27, 1912.
    165. Moving Picture World, February 27, 1912.
    166. Engberg, Registrant, II, p. 242.
    167. Engberg, Registrant, II, p. 282.
    168. Moving Picture World, April 22, 1912.
    169. In 1974 I tried to establish a link between the
two films in "Influences between National Cinemas: Denmark
and the United States," Cinema Journal (Winter 1974-75). I
speculated that the Griffith film, which had been released in
the United States on March 12, 1912, may have been seen by
Schnedler-Sørensen before he made Dr. Gar El Hama II, which
was premiered in Denmark on September 16, 1912. Given the
large number of American Biograph films shown in Denmark
(see ch. 2, n. 18), it seemed very possible that this influence existed. In 1975, however, I had a conversation with
Marguerite Engberg about this speculation and she informed
me that according to Nordisk production records, Dr. Gar
El Hama II had been completed prior to the release of Griffith's
film in America. It seems, therefore, that the existence of

these sequences in the two films is coincidental. Marguerite
Engberg comes to the same conclusion in Dansk Stumfilm, p.
270.

170. Moving Picture World, December 14, 1912, p. 1090.

171. Cited in Engberg, Dansk Stumfilm, p. 458.

172. Moving Picture World, January 25, 1913.

173. The New York Dramatic Mirror, January 8, 1913,
p. 27.

174. The gaps in the story as outlined here are probably due to missing footage. Only 670 m. of the original
805 m. have survived. See Engberg, Registrant, II, p. 361.

175. Engberg, Registrant, II, p. 361.

176. Moving Picture World, January 4, 1913, p. 31.

177. Moving Picture World, January 4, 1913.

178. At 800 m. Naar Manden gaar paa Børsen attempts
a more complex story than either En urolig Vagt (110 m.) or
Badets Dronning (309 m.). See Engberg, Registrant, II, pp.
352, 398, and III, p. 170.

179. Moving Picture World, April 18, 1914, p. 367.

180. Engberg, Registrant, II, pp. 356-467, and III,
pp. 99-391.

181. Moving Picture World, February 15, 1913.

182. Neergaard, pp. 28-29.

183. From a Holger-Madsen letter dated July 7, 1939
in the files of The Danish Film Museum.

184. Ektrabladet (Copenhagen), April 7, 1938, and
January 12, 1943.

185. Moving Picture World, June 7, 1913.

186. Moving Picture World, July 18, 1914, p. 448.

187. Moving Picture World, November 28, 1914, p.
1238.

188. Moving Picture World, March 27, 1915.

189. Moving Picture World, August 22, 1914, p. 1078.

190. Motion Picture News, August 22, 1914, p. 57.

191. A still from this scene can be found on p. 275 of
Marguerite Engberg's Dansk Stumfilm.

192. Politiken (Copenhagen), January 31, 1954.

193. Moving Picture World, May 16, 1914, p. 984.

194. Moving Picture World, November 21, 1914, p.
1094.

195. Because of Dr. Mantzius's reputation his entering
filmwork was significant enough to receive attention outside
Denmark. See The Kinematograph and Lantern Weekly, April
23, 1914, p. 37.

196. Mantzius was born on February 2, 1860 and made

his theater debut as an actor in 1883. In 1889-90 he was a director at the Dagmarteatret and was at Det Kongelige Teater from 1890-1913, serving as a director from 1909-13. He received his Ph.D. in 1901 and died May 17, 1921.

197. Marguerite Engberg, Registrant, III, pp. 318-418.

198. Biographical information comes from an unidentified newspaper article written at the time of his death, contained in the files of The Danish Film Museum and from Marguerite Engberg's Dansk Stumfilm, pp. 643-44.

199. Neergaard, p. 57.

200. Biographical information comes from unidentified material in the files of The Danish Film Museum, Marguerite Engberg's Dansk Stumfilm, p. 651, and Neergaard, pp. 67-72.

201. Nordisk records indicate that eighteen prints of Dyrekøbt Aere were sent to the United States in September 1911 and March 1912. I have not, however, found any record of the film being released here.

202. Engberg, Dansk Stumfilm, p. 631.

203. Moving Picture World, May 29, 1913, p. 1317.

204. The Library of Congress paper print is the only surviving version of the film. Original length: 775 m.

205. Engberg, Registrant, II, p. 350.

206. Neergaard, p. 37.

CHAPTER THREE:

1915-1917

World War I had a profound effect on the world film
industry, on belligerent and nonbelligerent nations alike.
And for those nations most dependent on the foreign sales
of their films, the effect was the greatest. As the war continued, production was curtailed and markets were lost. As
early as August 1914, at the outbreak of the war, The New
York Dramatic Mirror expressed a concern that foreign producers, especially in France, Germany, and Russia, were
likely to close down entirely because of the conscription of
their workers. Pathé and Eclair already had curtailed the
operations of their American plants in Jersey City and Fort
Lee, and fear was expressed that the American Vitagraph
Company plant in Paris would soon be affected.[1] One month
later, Moving Picture World confirmed these fears on a broad
front:

> The first shrill blast of the war trumpet sounded
> the doom of the continental film business.... Euro-
> pean trade outside the British Isles has been
> throttled and completely strangled in the grip of
> war.... In Germany, Russia, France, Austria,
> Belgium, and the Balkans business was shut down
> in a moment. The workers were called to the serv-
> ice of their country; the people were in too serious
> mood for entertainment.[2]

Fighting in continental Europe also interrupted distribution and exhibition of films. The normal channels of commerce were closed, as were the theaters themselves in many
places. Although the situation presented an opportunity for
film producers in the neutral countries to step up production
to compensate for the curtailment of production among the

combatants, it tended to have the opposite effect. In the
United States, for example, Moving Picture World reported that
"every domestic company which had any foreign trade has
adopted a policy of retrenchment." Fearing that their productions might not reach their intended markets, the producers waited and watched developments in Europe. This policy
underscored the importance of foreign trade even to so large
a domestic industry as that of the United States. MPW went
so far as to claim that "companies operating in this country
and having a big foreign business reap a greater profit from
that business than they do from the home trade."[3]

     The opportunities and dangers that the war presented
for the film industries of the neutral countries raised both
ethical and economic questions. How should a neutral country
use this potential economic advantage? One answer given for
the United States probably expresses the attitude taken by
most countries, not only for their film industries, but for all
their foreign trade:

> Despite the stupendous and sanguinary conflict which
> is rending the nations of Europe and demoralising
> the business machinery of the world at large, the
> motion picture industry of the United States, just
> now, at least, seems to be particularly favored of
> fortune. Although cut off from much of the world's
> market, the loss thus sustained is compensated, for
> the time being, by the cessation of picture production
> in the principal centers of the industry abroad, and
> the general report concerning conditions here is con-
> sequently encouraging. Not only are our manufac-
> turers called upon to supply the great demands of
> our own country, but those countries interrupted
> by the European war must look to us for their sup-
> ply of pictures. This presents a rare opportunity to
> American manufacturers which, however much we may
> deplore the circumstances that make the opportunity,
> should not be permitted to pass unheeded. This
> would seem to be the psychological moment for every
> branch of industry in America and not the least of
> these is the motion picture.[4]

     Not all observers of the events were as optimistic about
the ability of American manufacturers to successfully take advantage of this "rare opportunity." One prominent domestic

manufacturer expressed the opinion that as long as the war
continued, American films could not be supplied to the foreign
exhibitors. He also expressed the opinion that the loss of
foreign markets would bring an end to the production of
feature-length films and force producers to go back to one
and two reelers. The expense involved in making long films,
he believed, could not be justified from the profits of the
domestic market alone.[5]

Another effect of the war on the neutral countries came
from the shortage of chemicals and other motion picture supplies. Germany and France, the major suppliers of photographic materials to the world market, suspended production
of these materials.[6] This resulted first, and immediately, in
an increase in the cost of the supplies in stock and still available. Metol, a chemical used in film developing, for example,
soared in cost from three to ten dollars a pound.[7] Second,
the shortages threatened production itself should supplies
become unobtainable or the costs too high. The best carbons
and condensing lenses, which were produced in Germany,
were no longer available, except for the supplies that American distributors had in stock when the war began. Some
companies, such as The Raw Film Supply Company, stopped
soliciting new business so that it could continue supplying
its old customers.[8]

Although there was initial panic in the film communities
of the noncombatant countries, their domestic production and
export operations continued. Even in Denmark, the neutral
country probably most dependent on foreign trade for the
health of its film industry, it took more than two years for
the war to have a deadening impact. As late as mid-1916
Nordisk Films Kompagni continued to exercise a major economic influence on the German film industry, which itself,
despite earlier shutdowns, continued to make films. The
German industry was, however, in a weakened position. In
an attempt to protect domestic manufacturers against foreign
competition, the Interior Ministry had issued an edict on February 25, 1916 prohibiting the importation of films, though
the edict allowed for exceptions. Nordisk took advantage of
the exception clause and was granted the right to import about
1,700,000 feet of film up to September 1. Since this figure
included negatives from which copies that did not come under
the quota could be made, the actual number of feet of film
that Nordisk could sell was many times the initial figure.

Nordisk also was able to distribute films that it had imported
from other countries, and so was in a position to offer a
great variety of films to German exhibitors.[9] In February
1912, Nordisk also purchased the largest Bavarian film distributor, Carl Gabriel, in Munich, which included a chain of
theaters. Since Carl Gabriel had been Nordisk's biggest competitor in Bavaria, this gave Nordisk almost complete dominance of the South German market.[10]

The strength of Nordisk production during this same
period is attested to by figures cited by Ebbe Neergaard.
In 1913 Nordisk produced 87 films, a third of which were
more than two reels in length. In 1914 this figure jumped to
125, two-thirds of which were two reels or longer, and 1915
and 1916 saw 143 and 123 films respectively, most of them
three reels and longer.[11]

Despite these apparent signs of vitality, however, it
is indisputable that Nordisk had entered a period of decline
that began at least with the outbreak of war, if not earlier.
Ebbe Neergaard tends to put emphasis on the war as the
principal cause of Nordisk's decline,[12] while Marguerite Engberg sees the economic problems brought on by the war as
merely accelerating "a decline of which the roots had been
manifested earlier in the golden age."[13]

One early economic indicator of this decline can be seen
in a shrinking of Nordisk's profits during 1913-14. In 1913
the company declared a 65 percent dividend for its stockhold-
ers; in 1914 the dividend dropped to 33 percent. Engberg
ascribes this profit loss to two factors: increased competition
on the international market, partly due to companies also making longer films, and rising production costs at home. Accompanying these changes was a growing stock of unsold films
which doubled in 1914.[14]

In addition to the economic causes for Nordisk's decline,
there were also artistic causes. "Something must have gone
wrong with the movies themselves," suggested Ebbe Neergaard:

> Maybe the public had changed while N.F. had not.
> N.F. mastered almost to perfection a certain genre,
> the one hour melodrama..., the story of passion and
> licentiousness that takes the hero down into exciting
> immoral strata.... That was what the company was

equipped for and could do faultlessly. If they ven-
tured beyond that, things were apt to go wrong.

As an example of this problem he cited the prestigious production of Atlantis which, despite "many fine ideas and attempts on Blom's behalf, seemed loosely constructed, preten-
tious and stilted."[15] Marguerite Engberg refers to "the Danish producers' lack of ability to create an artistic milieu" in
this later period, and notes that the "films were made as
though they had just left an assembly belt."[16]

     The surviving Nordisk films of the war period are evi-
dence that the criticisms voiced by Neergaard and Engberg
are fundamentally correct. This is not to say the films are
without merit but that they lack the "genuine feeling for the
film" that Neergaard cited as characteristic of the golden age.
Admittedly, this is a vague criticism, and it should also be
considered a highly tentative one since very few Nordisk
films have survived from the 1915-17 period. Yet, it does
seem that the excitement of the previous five years had died
out and with it the experimentation. The lighting effects,
the stories, the realism of interior settings, the extraordinary
use of natural and urban locations, the intensity of the naturalistic acting style, the emphasis on fate and the passions
--all those things which made up the Nordisk style began to
solidify into mere formulas.

     But why should this have happened? Why was Nordisk
unable to maintain its energy beyond the short span of four
or five years? The economic problems brought on by the
war, the strain on Nordisk's resources as film production
costs rose, and the competition--all of these, of course, were
contributing factors. But more important, perhaps, was the
constant erosion of Nordisk's artistic base, its human resources. As Danish films became more important in the international film world and as Nordisk assumed a position of lead-
ership in the Danish industry, other film producers, both domestic and foreign, tried to capitalize on the Nordisk success
by hiring its film artists. Among the first was Urban Gad,
who left Nordisk for Germany in 1912. A lesser director,
William Augustinus, followed in 1913. Robert Dinesen and
Eduard Schnedler-Sørensen, two of Nordisk's best directors,
left in 1917, Dinesen to Sweden, then in 1917 to Germany,
and Schnedler-Sørensen to Fotorama. In 1920 Holger-Madsen
left for Germany. Lau Lauritzen, Nordisk's most important

comedy director, left Nordisk in 1919 to become artistic director of Palladium, taking with him two of Nordisk's best comic actors, Oscar Stribolt and Carl Schenstrøm. The cameramen Axel Sørensen and Johan Ankerstjerne left in 1913 and 1915 respectively, Sørensen to work in Germany and Ankerstjerne to work for Dansk Biografkompagni where he photographed Benjamin Christensen's second film, Hævnens Nat. In 1919 another great Nordisk cameraman, Sophus Wangøe, followed in Robert Dinesen's footsteps and went to work for Svensk Palladium. Among the actors who left were the popular comic Frederick Buch (1914), Betty Nansen (1914, to work for Fox in America), Clara Pontoppidan (1913, for Sweden), Ebba Thomsen (1918, to Astra Films), Carlo Wieth (1913, for Sweden) and Valdemar Psilander (1916, to form his own company).[17]

These defections may be part of a larger problem that Marguerite Engberg attributed directly to Ole Olsen:

> Ole Olsen was a great man of business, but unfortunately he lacked the sense of assembling the best talents in his company. He let Asta Nielsen go, did not persuade Alfred Lind and Benjamin Christensen to work for him, just to mention some of the gravest errors he made.[18]

Without a stable company of experienced artists revitalized by the regular introduction of new talent with innovative ideas, Nordisk could not maintain its artistic health. When this artistic crisis was joined with a disruption of Nordisk's regular trade network, the company's decline from a position of international influence became inevitable.

The extent of the economic crisis that Nordisk, and Danish producers in general, faced, needs to be understood within the larger framework of Danish trade and international relations at the beginning of World War I. "It is a proof of the importance of trade and commerce," writes Viggo Starcke, "that up to the outbreak of World War I the Danes had the lowest tariffs, and the highest standard of living in Europe, and a larger import and export per head than any other country."[19]

As it had been for centuries, Denmark was dependent on the sea for its economic health, and the importance of the

sea increased as Denmark entered the twentieth century.
Between 1870 and 1914 Danish shipping tonnage tripled and,
after 1900, consisted principally of steamships.[20] Among
other goods, this large and modern merchant fleet carried
Danish films which "constituted a valuable item of export."[21]
Along with that of the Royal Porcelain Factory, Bing and
Grøndal, and Georg Jensen, these ships carried the fame of
Nordisk Films Kompagni. Before the first decade of the new
century was over, the Nordisk trademark of a polar bear
astride a globe was known throughout the film world.

When war came in the summer of 1914, Denmark was
officially on good terms with all the combatant nations, even
though there was much anti-German sentiment left from the
disastrous defeat Denmark had suffered at the hands of Germany in the 1864 war and from subsequent conflicts with
Prussia. Because of these sentiments the Danes had to be
especially careful that their position of neutrality be convincing to Germany. Complicating Denmark's problems was the
extensive trade it carried on with both sides in the conflict.
Of Denmark's agricultural trade 60 percent was with England
and 30 percent with Germany. Denmark was also dependent
on other countries, especially England, for raw materials.
In addition, now that the war had started, Germany needed
Danish ports to carry on its trade with America. It was,
therefore, in the interest of all the parties concerned that
these conflicting interests be kept in balance. Despite this
need, however, Danish shipping came to a standstill almost
immediately in 1914 because of the fear of submarine attacks
and minefields and because insurance companies would not
insure Danish shipping against war-related loses. Only an
assumption of insurance responsibilities by the government
got Danish shipping going again.[22]

The favorable, though dangerous, trade position that
Denmark found itself in rapidly caused an increase in the
demand for Danish products. Germany, especially, became a
good customer and, at one time, was buying 50 percent of all
Danish exports. As the war continued, however, the trade
situation became increasingly entangled with military consid-
erations. In January 1917 Germany specified a number of
areas as dangerous for shipping and declared unrestricted
submarine warfare. To make matters worse, Great Britain
declared a new policy relating to neutral ships carrying coal
from British ports. Henceforth, a percentage of this shipping

was to support the Allied cause.   Two hundred thousand tons
of Danish shipping went to this purpose, making Danish trade
with Britain even more dangerous.   During April 1917 alone
33 Danish ships were sunk.   (For the whole war the number
reached 274 ships, 236 from submarine attacks and 38 from
mines.)   When the United States entered the war, it restricted
trade with Denmark out of fear that certain products would
be reexported to the enemy.   This forced Denmark, despite
its losses from German submarines, to strengthen its trade
ties with Germany.[23]

The conditions that restricted Danish trade in other
goods also restricted trade in motion pictures.   Transporta-
tion of goods across the continent was difficult because of
the fighting and consequent disruption of the normal trade
routes, and transport on the seas became increasingly subject
to submarine attack.   Conditions became so difficult that the
New York office of Nordisk Films Kompagni was forced to close
in October 1916.   A notice of the closing appeared in the
October 28, 1916 issue of Moving Picture World:

> The Great Northern Film Company, which was estab-
> lished as the American office of the Nordisk Films
> Company, Copenhagen, has decided to temporarily
> discontinue its office in the United States for rea-
> sons which may be laid down to the conditions cre-
> ated by the European conflict.... The regular re-
> leasing schedule has been affected more or less dur-
> ing the past year or more, and until these conditions
> subside, the company has decided to discontinue
> releasing its product regularly as heretofore.[24]

Although the announcement called the closing temporary,
Great Northern did not open its doors again.   A few films,
apparently those already on hand, were released even after
the closing, and notices of these releases can be found in
Motion Picture News as late as the December 23, 1916 issue.
Shortly after, Ingvald Oes, the manager of Great Northern,
became the general agent for Scandinavia, Russia, Finland,
and Holland of Famous Players Lasky Corporation, with his
office located in Copenhagen.[25]

The inability of Great Northern to get sufficient film
shipments from Copenhagen became the general situation for
the Nordisk branches.   A report on a Nordisk general business

meeting held in June 1917 declared that the company had
been almost completely prevented from exporting films since
January of that year, and that this loss of foreign markets
had had a profound effect on the company's economic standing.[26] The final blow to the Nordisk export business, however, came when the German government moved to consolidate
the Germany film industry in the formation of Universum Film,
Inc. (UFA).

Germany had always been Nordisk's most important market. The company had five branch offices in Germany, owned
sixty movie theaters, held shares in at least four German film
companies (Licht-Spielhaus, Continental Projection, Kammer
Lichtspiele, and Oliver Film), and owned a small production
company. Nordisk interests were so widespread that by 1916
it was, as Marguerite Engberg has noted, "a powerful force
in the German film industry." Its interests were so important that when UFA was formed, Nordisk was offered, in return for its German holdings, one-third of all UFA stock,
worth about 30 million marks to Nordisk. According to Ole
Olsen, however, this forced sale of Nordisk holdings cost
his company a fortune because he was forbidden by his contract with UFA to convert the stock to cash until two years
had passed. By that time, said Olsen, inflation had eroded
the original 30 million marks to the value of about 900,000
Danish kroner, resulting in a loss to Nordisk of 5 million
Danish kroner.[27]

The various factors involved in Nordisk's decline finally
led to the temporary cessation of production. The August 1,
1917 issue of Filmen carried a notice of the closing, ascribing
it directly to "international conditions."[28] In all, Nordisk
produced 61 films in 1917;[29] in 1918 the number dwindled to
only a handful.[30] In 1919, with the end of the war, Nordisk
production climbed to 39 films (although most of them were
one reelers), but then fell off to only eight films in 1920.
The time of international importance of the Danish cinema had
clearly passed.

NORDISK

Only a small number of the films made in 1915-17 have
survived. Yet they are so consistently similar to the films
made during the preceding four years that they can probably

be taken as representative of Nordisk production during the
period of decline. Included are films directed by Holger-
Madsen, Robert Dinesen, Eduard Schnedler-Sørensen, Hjalmar
Davidsen, A. W. Sandberg, and Lau Lauritzen.

Holger-Madsen

Neither of the two surviving Holger-Madsen films from
this period measures up to Evangeliemandens Liv, or even to
the sincere, though somewhat dull, Ned med Vaabene. Both,
however, are examples of the craftsmanship that characterizes
Holger-Madsen's work. What they are missing is the inventive-
ness in camera treatment and set design that make Evangeliemandens Liv his best film.

Hvor Sorgerne Glemmes (Where Sorrows Are Forgotten
1915) is a four-reel melodrama set among the aristocracy.[31]
The film stars Rita Sacchetto as Cecilie, the oldest daughter
of the impoverished and seriously ill Countess Schack (Henny
Lauritzen). Because of her mother's illness, Cecilie has taken
over most of the family duties. Ernst (Anton de Verdier), a
composer and Cecilie's lover, visits the family and the couple
swear eternal faithfulness to each other. The countess is
forced to sell her estate, and Ernst promises to buy it back
when he becomes successful. Princess Sara von Staffenfeldt
(Gerda Christophersen) offers Cecilie a position as lady-in-
waiting and governess for her son's two small children. At
a party in honor of Princess Sara's son, Prince Robert (Alf
Blütecher), Cecilie and her brother and sisters appear in a
series of tableaux. The prince falls in love with Cecilie and
asks to marry her. Just before Countess Schack dies, Cecilie
promises to marry the prince even though she loves Ernst.
Meanwhile, Ernst, though sick, continues to work on his
opera, inspired by the thought of Cecilie. Cecilie writes to
Ernst telling him of her impending marriage to the prince,
and Ernst tries to stop the wedding. Failing to do this,
Ernst wanders off into the country seeking solitude. He
collapses and is taken in by the blind organist who played
at Cecilie's wedding. Knowing that he has only a few days
to live, Ernst asks to see Cecilie. While out riding with her
husband and friends, Cecilie leaves the group and goes to
Ernst. Realizing that she is not with the group, the prince
rides off to find Cecilie. He falls off his horse, however,
and is killed. His body is brought to the organist's house

just after Ernst dies. Having lost everything, Cecilie becomes a nun.

Hvor Sorgerne Glemmes is superbly photographed by
Marius Clausen who was the cameraman on all of Holger-
Madsen's films. It also boasts well-executed and convincing
sets and the usual expressive Nordisk lighting. But, like
most Holger-Madsen's films, the drama carries little conviction
and generates little interest in the viewer.

In 1917 Holger-Madsen once again turned to a war theme
and made the pacifist film Pax Aeterna. At six reels and
written in collaboration with the novelist and dramatist Otto
Rung, it is one of Holger-Madsen's longest and most ambitious
films. It continues the traditional Nordisk style but with the
camera generally closer to the action than in most Nordisk
dramas. It also has excellent battle footage used to point
up the pacifist theme. The film was released in February
1917 shortly after Germany had declared unrestricted submarine warfare; however, as Ebbe Neergaard has commented,
it "does not seem to have left any impression on the war or
the course of power politics."[32]

Neergaard's comment is relevant to a discussion of Pax
Aeterna because the film calls for the establishment of a congress of European nations to end the war. It begins with a
series of close-shot portraits of the main characters accompanied by titles explaining their backgrounds. King Elin XII
(Frederick Jacobsen) has worked all his life to maintain peace.
Professor Claudius (Philip Bech) teaches at the university and
is an ardent pacifist. Gregor (Marius Egeskov), Claudius's
son, and Malcus (Anton de Verdier) are both students and
good friends. Crown prince Alexis (Carlo Wieth) and Bianca,
Claudius's daughter, are in love, and Alexis vows to marry
her even if it costs him the throne. Alexis is also inspired
by Claudius's pacifist views. Wilmer (Carl Lauritzen), minister of war, is working in opposition to Claudius and is trying
to convince King Elin of the need to be militarily prepared.
Malcus is also in love with Bianca but realizes that she is in
love with Alexis.

King Elin dies and war breaks out. The country mobi-
lizes and Malcus, who is a citizen of the enemy country, returns home. Claudius's house is evacuated as the enemy approaches, but Claudius and Bianca are captured. Also seized

is the manuscript of Claudius's life-long work "Pax Aeterna."
Malcus, who is now the leader of a horse patrol, sees them
and convinces his comrades to let them go. Now free, Claudius and Bianca join the Red Cross. Malcus kills Gregor in
battle and is in turn killed. As a nurse, Bianca finds the
bodies of Malcus and Gregor. Seeing Bianca's grief, Alexis
vows to work for peace. Having driven the enemy back
across the border, Alexis decides not to enter their country.
Instead, he suggests to Claudius the creation of a congress
of nations to settle controversies peacefully. Claudius voices
scepticism that peace can be obtained, but Bianca asks him to
take on the task. With the backing of the Red Cross, Claudius and Bianca set out on a peace mission. A half year later,
representatives from all the European nations convene in a
congress, and Bianca delivers a passionate plea for peace.
(Her talk is illustrated by cutaways to scenes of death and
suffering.) The delegates sign a document drafted by Alexis
pledging to submit future controversies to arbitration under
the auspices of the Red Cross. Having succeeded in their
peace effort, Alexis and Bianca announce their intention to
marry.

Robert Dinesen

        In the tradition of the Gar El Hama films and of Ekpres-
sens Mysterium, Dinesen made a 1915 four-reel melodrama with
a Dr. Mabuse-like figure who destroys a competitor through
an almost hypnotic manipulation of the competitor's actions.
Entitled Dr. Voluntas or Dr. X, it tells the story of two doctors who are both searching for a cancer cure. Dr. Felix
(Carlo Wieth) is called a genius, and Dr. Voluntas (Gunnar
Tolnæs) reacts with jealousy and annoyance. Voluntas reads
a newspaper account telling how Felix is ahead in his research
and has great expectations for success. Despite his success
in medicine, however, Felix is dissatisfied with the cheerless
life he leads and seeks advice from Voluntas, whose romantic
success Felix secretly admires. Voluntas points out Margaret
(Johanne Fritz-Petersen) to Felix while she is swimming, and
tells Felix she can be his if he wills it. Felix agrees to follow
Voluntas's advice exactly. He begins by dressing more fash-
ionably. Voluntas takes Felix to a gambling casino, and they
win a fortune. They also encounter Margaret at the casino,
where Felix begins romancing her. Vincent (Henry Seeman),
Margaret's brother and a lieutenant, is transferred to another

city thus leaving his sister alone (Margaret and Vincent are
orphans) and more vulnerable to Felix's advances. With Voluntas's help Felix finally succeeds in seducing Margaret. By
now Felix has become the prisoner of his passions and has
forsaken his research, allowing Voluntas to take the lead in
the search for the cure.

Seidel (Arne Weel) sees Felix and Margaret together at
a place in the country. Three months later Seidel tells Vincent about Felix and Margaret. Meanwhile, Margaret has become pregnant. Felix tries to buy off Margaret with a check
for 5,000 kroner, but she returns it. Vincent challenges
Felix to a duel. Margaret shows up just after Felix has
scored and Vincent dies damning his sister as a whore. Felix turns himself in to the police and is given a one-month
jail sentence for dueling.

After Felix's release from jail, he goes to a dress ball
with Voluntas who, significantly, is dressed as the devil.
While chasing another woman, Felix has a vision of Margaret
that causes him to regain his senses. He goes to Margaret
who is in the hospital with her baby only to find out that
both have died. Voluntas finally develops the cancer serum
and Felix, on reading of Voluntas's success, poisons himself.
As he is dying, he has visions of Margaret reaching out to
him and of Voluntas in his devil costume standing over him
in triumph.

Dr. Voluntas has stunning deep-focus photography by
Sophus Wangøe. The camera treatment and settings are typical of the Nordisk style, though like Pax Aeterna, and in
keeping with general trends in the cinema, the camera positions are more varied and closer to the actors than in earlier
Nordisk films. The demonic nature of Dr. Voluntas and the
expressive lighting, especially in Voluntas's house and at the
costume ball, point toward later expressionist films and suggest a direct influence on the German cinema which may have
been carried by the Danish filmmakers who went to work in
Berlin.[33]

In 1916 Dinesen made Maharadjahens Yndlingshustru
(The Maharaja's Favorite Wife, 4½ reels), an exercise in
exotica quite typical of Nordisk, except for a twist in the
story's ending that is unusual for its time.

Kuno Falkenborg (Carlo Wieth) is in love with his
cousin, Elly (Lilly Jacobsen). While walking by the sea they
meet the maharaja (Gunnar Tolnæs). That evening the maharaja sends his servants to put roses all around Elly's hotel
room while she is out. They also leave a copy of 1001 Nights,
a necklace, and a note to meet the maharaja at ten that evening. This quickly leads to a proposal of marriage and Elly's
acceptance of it. She does not tell Kuno of this and secretly
meets the maharaja by using a rowboat to get to the meeting
place. The next day Kuno finds Elly's empty rowboat and
thinks she has drowned.

Next we see Elly in India wearing harem dress. The
maharaja keeps Elly's European clothes in a box locked in a
cabinet. Meanwhile, Kuno, who is a naval officer, receives
sailing orders for India. When Elly discovers she is part of
a harem she is horrified, and when the maharaja next calls
for her, she spurns him. She asks for her freedom, but in
anger he sends her back to the harem. By coincidence, Kuno
and his fellow officers are invited to a party by the maharaja.
While there Elly contacts Kuno, and Kuno meets with the maharaja, telling him that a European woman cannot be satisfied
with part of a man's love. The maharaja, deciding to give
Elly a choice, puts two boxes, one containing her European
clothes and one containing his jewels, in Elly's bedroom while
she is asleep. Elly understands the choice that has been
given her and puts on her old clothes. The maharaja tells
his guards to allow Elly to leave but to kill whoever might
follow her. She leaves followed by a robed figure. The
guards disrobe the figure only to discover it is the maharaja
who, obviously, was trying to commit suicide. He grabs a
knife and is about to use it on himself when Elly stops him.
Seeing this, Kuno realizes that she really loves the maharaja.
The film ends as Elly and the maharaja return to the palace.

The ending is unusual because the conventions of this
type of film make us expect that Elly wants to leave and must
be rescued from an evil fate. In fact, the film fulfills this
expectation right up to the end and until then belongs in the
same category as the 1909 Kærlighed i Orienten (U.S. title,
Saved from the Sultan's Judgment) and the 1911 Mormonens
Offer (U.S. title, A Victim of the Mormons). The end, on
the other hand, gives the film an unexpected moral perspective
that violates our expectations and makes the story more interesting. Despite the ending, however, and the usual brilliant

photography by Sophus Wangøe, including some extraordinary
evening interiors, the film is not as noteworthy as Dr. Voluntas, or much of Dinesen's earlier work.

Eduard Schnedler-Sørensen

        In his last year at Nordisk, before going to Fotorama
as a director, Schnedler-Sørensen made a serial-like adventure
called Pigen fra Palls (The Girl from Palls). In the multitude
and the type of its incidents this four-reel feature resembles
the American serial The Perils of Pauline. It includes adventure, romance, riots, escapes, and a big fire by some oil
tanks--all aided by Johann Ankerstjerne's exciting location
photography, much of it involving seascapes. And among
Pigen fra Palls's best assets is its star, Karen Caspersen,
perhaps the most attractive of all Danish heroines. Unfortunately, the only print available when I saw the film, was
one without titles and in which the shots were almost completely out of sequence. Despite the condition of the print,
however, the film is apparently of great interest and might
possibly be among Schnedler-Sørensen's best films.

Hjalmar Davidsen

        Except for the unusual and striking Ekpressens Myster-
ium, made in 1913, none of Hjalmar Davidsen's surviving films
are of particular interest. They are handsomely mounted and
well photographed, like most Nordisk films from 1911 on, but
they lack both the intensity of feeling that characterizes the
best of the social melodramas and the vitality and imagination
of the best action films. His two surviving films from the
1915-17 period are no exception.

        Hans store Chance (His Big Chance, 1915, 932 m.--
525 m. survive) tells another story, so common in the early
Danish cinema, of a young man who must go away to seek his
fortune so that he may rescue those he loves from financial
troubles. Arendt's (Valdemar Psilander) fiancée and her
mother are in great need of money. He gives them his life
savings and goes to Australia seeking work. At first he gets
a job for a railroad company as an attendant at a crossing
post. One day he saves the life of a wealthy man, John Roch,
and is rewarded with a job as Roch's assistant. Shortly after,

Roch leaves on a business trip, and Arendt must contact him
quickly to save an important stock transaction. Using a
stolen locomotive to catch Roch's express train, Arendt succeeds and is made a partner in Roch's business. This enables
Arendt to send for his fiancée.

In 1916, Davidsen's last year at Nordisk, he made
Pjerrot (Pierrot, 1,549 m.--5 reels). Obviously intended as
a heart-rending drama of misunderstanding, separation, and
reunion, Pjerrot fails to capture the feelings inherent in the
situations it portrays. It continues the tradition of Nordisk
films with a theatrical setting.

Jean and Gabrielle Riot (Gunnar Tolnæs and Zanny
Petersen) are to be married. Old Layette, who it later turns
out is Gabrielle's father, works in the office of the theater
where Jean is employed as an actor. Layette has been gambling company money and must replace it before the books are
audited. Jean borrows from a moneylender and gives 18,000
kroner to Layette to cover his debt. To avoid further temp-
tation Layette leaves the theater and travels. Meanwhile,
Jean works hard to pay off the loan, but Gabrielle, who
knows nothing of the whole matter, just thinks Jean is being
tight with his money. Garoche (Erik Holberg), the manager
of the theater, takes advantage of Gabrielle's dissatisfaction
and takes her to a ball while Jean is working. Jean finds
out, however, and leaves Gabrielle and the country. Four
years later he returns and gets a job as Pierrot in the pantomime troupe for which Layette works. Jean's daughter attends a performance and later goes backstage to meet Pierrot.
A fire breaks out in the theater and both the child and Layette are overcome with smoke. Jean rescues the child and
gives her to Gabrielle, who does not recognize Jean because
of his costume. Later, the child asks to see Pierrot and
Jean goes to the house. Layette sends a letter to Gabrielle
explaining everything and then dies. Jean and Gabrielle are
reunited.

A. W. Sandberg

More interesting than Pjerrot, though similar in plot and
feeling, is A. W. Sandberg's Klovnen (The Clown, 1916,
1,375 m.--4½ reels). It continues the Danish tradition of circus films, though unlike most of them, it becomes a serious

study of the personal tragedy of one character and minimizes
the circus setting itself. In its concern for the tragedy of
the main character, it has been compared to Joseph von Sternberg's The Blue Angel.[34] Sandberg remade the film under
the same title in 1925.

Kovnen succeeds better than Pjerrot for two reasons:
Sandberg's direction (he handles the slow pacing of the story
without losing the dramatic intensity) and Valdemar Psilander's
performance in the main role. Psilander's sensitivity as an
actor allows the viewer to feel the character's sufferings[35]
while Gunnar Tolnæs in Pjerrot is wooden and merely mourn-
ful, and the viewer soon loses interest in him. Generally,
Klovnen is similar in style to other Nordisk films, though the
interiors are bigger and there are more close-ups.

Joe Higgins (Valdemar Psilander), a circus clown, and
Daisy Bunding (Gudrun Houlberg) are good friends. Mr.
Wilson, a theater impresario, visits the circus, is impressed
with Joe, and offers him a contract. Joe accepts on the condition that Daisy and her parents (Peter Fjelstrup and Amanda
Lund) go with him. Two years pass; Joe and Daisy are now
married and affluent. Daisy has become unfaithful to Joe and
is seeing Count Henri (Robert Schmidt). Joe sees them kissing one day and is deeply hurt. Daisy leaves Joe for the
count, though the count is not exactly delighted to have her
full time. One year passes. Count Henri's feelings for Daisy
have cooled, and she begins to regret having left Joe. One
day, Joe and Daisy accidentally meet at a nightclub. On seeing her, Joe runs out, but Daisy follows him. She goes to
his home, where Joe lives with Daisy's parents, but her father
throws her out. Daisy tries to drown herself and ends up
unconscious in a hospital. Joe goes to see her, and she asks
his forgiveness. Daisy dies, and Joe swears to kill Henri if
he ever sees him again. Many years pass. The Bundings are
dead, and Joe is once again with a traveling circus; he is
now an old man living on memories. One day he sees Henri
at a circus performance and shoots him. Joe then dies himself.

Lau Lauritzen

Six of Lau Lauritzen's films have survived from this
period, though two exist only in fragmentary form. All are

one reel or less, and taken together give a good sense of
Lauritzen's comic perspective and the type of material he
used. Throughout the teens his farces were an important
part of Nordisk's production.[36]

Less than one-fourth of Den bedrøvelige Ridder (The
Sad Knight) or Ridderen af den bedrøvelige Skikkelse (The
Knight of the Rueful Countenance, 1916) remains. The fragment tells the story of Hannibal, who takes flowers to his
beloved. He is wearing a funny striped shirt with his evening clothes and tries to hide the shirt behind the flowers.
He goes through various other contortions, such as hiding
behind a chair and tucking a napkin under his chin when
they go to the dinner table. The situations themselves are
similar to those used in the Fabian films of 1910, though the
film style is in keeping with the cinematic developments of the
time in which it was made.

Because of extensive location shooting Jeg skû tale med
Jør'nsen (I Want to Talk to Jør'nsen, 1916) is among the most
interesting of Lauritzen's films. The way in which the title
is written indicates a speaker with a working-class accent,
and the story itself involves characters and setting which
are meant to appeal to a working-class audience. It is essentially a slapstick comedy and provides a vivid contrast to
the more subtle comedies with middle- and upper-class settings,
such as Schnedler-Sørensen's Den Stærkeste and Vor Tids
Dame. The rapid pace of this and other Lauritzen comedies
also provides a contrast to the usual slow pace of the dramas
of the period.

Jeg skû tale med Jør'nsen treats comically what in reality was a serious social problem for the Danish working
class--alcoholism.[37] It tells the story of Nokke and Jørgensen,
street car track maintenance men and the best of friends.
Nokke constantly tells Jørgensen what to do, and Jørgensen
meekly submits. When Jørgensen does not show up for work
one morning, Nokke goes to his house, only to discover that
Jørgensen has been taken to the hospital because heavy drinking had been causing him to see elephants. Earlier in the
film he was seen swatting at imaginary flies. Nokke goes to
the hospital, and, after several misadventures, is mistaken
for a mental patient. A chase ensues as hospital personnel
try to subdue Nokke with a straightjacket. In his attempt
to escape, Nokke breaks through a floor only to fall into
Jørgensen's padded cell.

The best of Lauritzen's surviving films is the 1916 <u>De</u>
<u>tossede Kvindfolk</u> (<u>The Foolish Female</u>). It has a more com-
plicated plot and better pacing than any of the others. Storch
and Søndergaard are partners in a wholesale business. It is
Storch's birthday, and his wife gives him a watch. It is
Søndergaard's anniversary, but he has forgotten it and his
wife is angry. Reminded by Storch of the anniversary,
Søndergaard sends flowers to his wife. When she receives
them, she sends a note to her husband asking him to meet
her for lunch. By mistake she puts one of her name cards
in the envelope (intended to accompany some flowers she was
sending to Storch for his birthday). When Søndergaard receives the card, he assumes it is his wife's way of telling
him that she is still angry. The note gets sent along with
the flowers. Meanwhile, Storch's wife shows up at the office
and asks her husband to have lunch with her, but he tells
her he is too busy. Just then the flowers arrive and, seeing
the lunch invitation, Storch's wife thinks her husband is
planning to meet another woman. She goes home and begins
packing. While this has been occurring, Mrs. Søndergaard
has been waiting at the restaurant. Thinking she has been
neglected, she returns home in anger. When he learns that
his wife is leaving him, Storch shows the mysterious lunch
invitation to Søndergaard. They rush home to their wives
and explain everything.

The last three surviving Lauritzen farces were made
in 1917. <u>Frøken Theodor</u> (<u>Miss Theodor</u>) appears to be a
parody of a situation that might easily have been treated as
drama. The film even employs editing and camera placement
techniques--extensive use of close-ups and cross-cutting--
that are more common to the dramatic film. It tells the story
of Baron Dandy (Lauritz Olsen) who is fond of young women
and frequents a girls' housekeeping school. He has for weeks
been following Grete (Ulla Poulsen) who complains to Theodor
(Arne Weel), asking him to stop Dandy. Theodor dresses up
as a woman and gets Dandy to follow him home. There he
reveals himself as a man, beats Dandy, and throws him out.

<u>En uheldig Danser</u> (<u>An Unsuccessful Dancer</u>) stars Oscar
Stribolt as a husband who has secretly been taking dancing
lessons from Miss Nelson. He takes his wife dancing and
makes a fool of himself. She leaves, thinking he has been
seeing another woman, but he follows her home trying to explain everything. The film is incomplete so that the resolution
of the misunderstanding is not known.

Another of the more interesting Lauritzen comedies is
Ægtemand for en Time (Husband for an Hour). It has a
matter-of-fact kind of cruelty in its plot situations similar
to that often found in American comedies of the period. In
one scene the Nordisk comedy lot appears in the background.
The story involves two friends, one of whom must pretend to
be married when his Aunt Nicotine comes to visit. While preparing to fool the aunt, they steal furniture from a neighbor
who is moving, take food from a store without paying, and
find a girl to play the wife. The neighbor and two moving
men come after them with guns, but the friends knock them
out.

THE OTHER COMPANIES

Some of the best work from 1915-17 came from Nordisk's
competitors. Although never an economic match for Nordisk,
they were often artistically more interesting. This is especially true during the war years. The few films that have
survived from other companies indicate a continuing vitality
in the Danish cinema that deserves special mention and contrasts with the general decline at Nordisk.

Dansk Biografkompagni

In 1915 Benjamin Christensen released his second film,
Hævnens Nat (U.S. title, Blind Justice), one of the best Danish films of the period. It has all the strengths of Det hemmelighedsflude X but is more carefully edited, better paced,
and more moving. In addition, the principal chracter, Strong
John, played brilliantly by Christensen himself, is more interesting than Lt. van Hauen of the earlier film, and as such
engages the viewer's attention and emotions more fully.[38]

Hævnens Nat (Night of Revenge) costars Karen Caspersen, who played the wife in Det hemmelighedsflude X, and was
photographed by Johan Ankerstjerne. It was released in the
United States by the American Vitagraph Company.[39] Present day prints of the film are made from an original tinted
British release version also titled Blind Justice, and are 1956
m. in length (6½ reels). The credits list Christensen as Benjamin Christie and refer to "his last sensational international
success," Sealed Orders.[40] The opening shot is a rotating

model of Dr. West's house where the main action takes place.
Following is a shot of Christensen explaining to Karen Caspersen (billed as Miss Katherine Sanders) the location of the
rooms in the house; he takes the roof off the model. As this
action is occurring, the camera dollies away to show the whole
scene. The story then begins.

A New Year's Eve celebration is going on at Ranton
Manor. A ragged man carrying a child secretly enters the
house from the snowy night. The owner of the house receives a message that Strong John, who has been accused of
a murder at the circus, has escaped and taken his child from
the poorhouse. That night John breaks into Ann's (Karen
Caspersen) room and begs her to help him get milk for the
baby. He also tells her he is innocent of the murder. (Christensen uses an extraordinary dolly shot for Strong John's
entrance into the house. The scene begins on a close shot
of Ann who is looking at the camera. She screams, and the
camera dollies back through the window pane to a position
outside the house. John enters the frame and climbs in the
window.) Ann agrees to help him but is caught by her uncle.
She is persuaded to help capture John, though against her
instincts. John vows to get even with Ann for betraying
him.

Fourteen years pass. Ann is married to Dr. West and
has a little girl. She is happy, but she still fears John's
threat. The circus has opened and Professor Wilken, an
elephant trainer, reads of John's release from prison. The
authorities are now convinced that John is innocent, especially since a new piece of evidence has come to light. The
news of new evidence worries Wilken.

John, now an old and borken man, is freed. He gets
the right to have custody of his son, but when he goes to
the orphanage to claim him, he learns that the boy was
adopted when six months old. John meets an old prison
friend and goes home with him. There he encounters "Slim"
Sam Morton and another man who have just stolen a dog.
(The scene opens with a close shot of Morton combing his
hair and holding a mirror. The camera dollies back slowly
to reveal the others who are present.) They are in the
business of stealing dogs, then selling them. One of the
gang takes a dog to Dr. West's house where he sees a note
and two keys. The note reveals that Dr. West has an adopted

son and that the keys are for West's town house which he is
closing because he is going to his country house. The thief
steals the keys, and West buys the dog. That night, in a
semiconscious way, John joins in a burglary of Dr. West's
town house. (The ransacking of the town house is intercut
with happy family scenes at the country house.) Meanwhile
at the circus, Wilken goes mad from worry and falls down
some stairs. On his death bed he reveals a note which confesses to the murder for which John had originally been jailed.
As the burglary continues, John finally realizes what he is
doing. Going through the bag of loot, he comes across a
box that he had seen in Ann's room fifteen years before.
Suddenly, everything comes back to him. In the box he
finds one of Ann's letters to her husband mentioning John's
threat.

A short time later, John phones Dr. West and pretends
there has been an accident. West says he will come right
away. When he arrives at the address given him, he finds
his wife's letter and is subdued by John. West had left home
in such a hurry, however, that he forgot the key to his med-
ical case. Ann sends their adopted son (really John's son)
after West to give him the key. The boy arrives, and John
locks him in a closet. The boy cuts a hole in the closet
with his knife, reaches through, and cuts the gag over Dr.
West's mouth. Meanwhile, John has set off for the country
house. With West giving directions, the boy is able to reach
the telephone and call the police. The police arrive at West's
house and shoot John, though before dying he is reunited
with his son and cleared of guilt. (This is presented by a
title and a final tableau.)

Filmfabrikken Danmark (formerly Det Skandinavisk-Russike Handelshus)

Second only to Hævnen's Nat in this period is Vilhelm
Glückstadt's Det gamle Spil om Enhver (That Old Play About
Everyman). Made in 1915 and 1056 m. in length (3½ reels),
it utilizes an elliptical narrative, flashbacks that are not immediately identifiable as such, metaphoric sequences, and
parallel lines of action. This unusual narrative structure
marks the film as an important link in an avant-garde tradition in the cinema that found its first major flowering in
France, Germany, and Russia in the 1920s. Of the three

surviving Glückstadt films, it is his most advanced and important work.

The film begins with a shot of a dark forest that gets progressively lighter. This image dissolves to a pan across the clouds which in turn dissolves to a shot of trees blowing in the wind against a sky background. Finally, this dissolves to a long shot of a town in bright sunlight seen through silhouetted trees. A silhouetted figure enters the frame. Cut to a title (a poem). Return to the image of the town seen through the silhouetted trees. Cut to a room which appears to be empty. Theobold (Rasmus Ottesen) enters from behind a column that is fully visible in the center of the room. After this unusual and poetic opening, the story begins.[41]

Theobold paces around the room and is seen from several different camera positions. Sylvia (Gudrun Houlberg), a minister's daughter, enters. They talk. This sequence is intercut with shots of clanging bells and people entering a church. As Theobold sits at his desk, there is a dissolve to a shot of him (without the beard he is wearing in the opening scene) sitting at a table which occupies the same position in the frame as his desk did. His mother (Jonna Neyendam) is in the background sewing. The minister (Valdemar Møller) enters, and there is a dissolve to a scene of the minister apparently teaching Theobold something. Then follows a sequence between Theobold and Sylvia as lovers. Apparently disowned by everyone, they go off together on a ship. Theobold gambles and wins. Sylvia is seen standing on a bridge; a train goes by below. Theobold enters frame (now wearing his beard). Cut back to Theobold at his desk. (All the scenes that come between the two shots of Theobold at his desk are connected by dissolves and constitute a recapitulation of Theobold's past relationship with Sylvia.)

Martha (Elze Schube) tells Theobold's mother that she loves Kurt (Peter Malberg). They stand together with the mother. Cut to a short which excludes Martha and Kurt but maintains the mother in same position in her chair but now at the extreme left of the frame. In the previous shot she was at the right of the frame. The right position of the frame is now occupied by a double-exposure shot of Theobold and Sylvia, apparently indicating that the mother is making a comparison between the two couples. Cut back to the previous shot of Martha, Kurt, and Theobold's mother.

In the next sequence Theobold takes Martha away from
Kurt. He takes her to his house where he dresses her in
fine clothes. Sylvia returns to Theobold and he, in turn,
sends Martha back to Kurt. Theobold gives a large banquet
at which he has visions of himself with Death standing behind
him. Sylvia takes Theobold to their bedroom. This scene
dissolves to one in the woods where Theobold (without beard)
is flanked by a satanic figure (male) and an angelic figure
(female). The satanic figure wins out in a struggle for Theobold, and the shot dissolves back to Theobold and Sylvia in
the bedroom. This dissolves to a scene of Theobold (without
beard) at home with his mother. The satanic figure rises up
behind Theobold's chair. This is followed by a sequence re-
capitulating earlier scenes, but with the satanic figure playing
a part in conflict with the angelic figure. The minister enters
and gets Theobold to pray just before dying.

Less adventurous than either Det gamle Spil om Enhver
or the earlier Den Fremmede, though still very well done, is
another 1915 Glückstadt film, I Storm og Stille (In Storm and
Calm, 743 m.--2½ reels; the end of the film appears to be
missing some scenes). Like Den Fremmede, it tells a conventional story but with a freedom of execution and a rapid
pacing that allows the film to transcend the scenario. Throughout the film, the camera is generally in close shot, and the
actors move freely within the frame.

I Storm og Stille begins with the camera tracking Alice
Kirschner (Gudrun Houlberg) and Heinz Falck (Emanuel Gregers) as they ride horses.[42] Alice and Heinz are about to be
married, even though Heinz owes Grauer (P. Andersen), a
moneylender, 6,000 marks. Alice's father informs Heinz that
Alice will receive 10,000 marks when she marries and another
50,000 in three years. Bayer, Heinz's friend, throws a bachelor party for him. Trying to contact Heinz, Alice's father
goes to the Metropol Hotel where the party is being held.
The future father-in-law is angered when he sees Heinz but
allows the wedding to take place.

Heinz continues to borrow money during the next three
years. Finally, he goes to Grauer to tell him he cannot pay
his debt. Alice, meanwhile, goes to a music gathering with
Bayer, at which she sings and gets an offer to perform at
a theater. Alice discovers an accounting sheet of Heinz's
debts. Grauer shows up at Alice's parents' house while Alice

and Heinz are there, but gets no money from Alice's father.
Because of their need for money, Alice secretly takes on the
singing job she had been offered and signs a contract for
10,000 marks. On her opening night she tells Heinz that
she is going out with her parents. While she is gone, their
child gets sick and must have an emergency operation. Heinz
tries to locate Alice only to learn that she is not with her
parents. He immediately suspects her of having an affair with
Bayer who had come to pick her up that night. Finally, he
locates her at the theater. Meanwhile, the child has been
operated on successfully. The next day Alice's parents show
up. At this point, present day prints end, but it appears
that Heinz and Alice will be reconciled.

A fragment of one other production of Filmfabrikken
Danmark has survived. Titled Telegramtyvene (The Telegram
Thieves, 904 m.--3 reels--286 m. survive), it tells the story
of three men and a woman who intercept racing results before
they are announced and then quickly bet and win. They do
this by means of a secret telegraph key installed in the basement of a racetrack betting office. In the course of the action one man becomes dissatisfied with his share and tries to
get revenge on the rest of the gang by going to the police.
Meanwhile, the female member of the gang causes dissension
by forsaking one member of the gang for another. The film
stars Valdemar Møller, Emanuel Gregers, and Agnes Rehni.

The fragment suggests that the film in its entirety must
have been quite interesting, especially in its brisk pacing and
varied and imaginative camera placements. One sequence, for
example, contains striking, angled mirror shots that show
the stairway in the thieves' hideout. The fragment is another
example of the originality of this Danish production company
and further suggests an aesthetic in marked contrast to the
predominant Nordisk style.

Filmfabrikken Skandinavien (formerly Biorama)

Aage Brandt began his film career as an actor for
Nordisk and Biorama and joined the directoral staff of Bio-
rama in 1912, the year the company changed its name to
Filmfabrikken Skandinavien. In 1915 he made a film called
Skæbnens Dom (Fate's Judgment, 1,100 m.--3½ reels--83 m.
survive), only a small fragment of which has survived. This

is unfortunate since the fragment, apparently an epilogue to
the main story of the film, is of interest. It is beautifully
photographed, having back lighting, a firelight effect, and an
effective interior that opens out onto a garden, with the interior and exterior light perfectly balanced. From the epilogue
we learn that Jean Stonne has become a famous author and
has settled in a small provincial town (with his wife and
daughter?). A woman--a shadow from the past, according
to a title--shows up at their home while Jean is away. The
wife implores the woman not to disrupt their happiness, but it
it is the sweetness of the daughter that convinces the woman
to leave.

Kinografen

        A 1915 Kinografen film, Det Indiske Gudebillede (The
Indian Idol), combines exoticism and crime in a British setting,
and is interesting more for the popular entertainment quality
of its cloak-and-dagger melodrama than for its execution.
The film contains some cross-cutting between parallel lines
of action but develops little suspense. Most scenes are done
in one take, and there is no cutting within the scenes. The
film stars Anton de Verdier, Alfi Zangenberg, and Tronier
Funder, and tells an ill-defined story about a secret Indian
society that tries to gain possession of a small idol given to
a doctor by a dying old Hindu. The ending of present day
prints seems to go against the logic of the story, but this
may be due to some missing material. The film was originally
100 m. longer than its present 2½ reels (see Appendix A).

                        *   *   *

        The years that have been covered in this study were
the most important in the history of the Danish cinema. They
were years in which Denmark played a significant role in the
international film market, both artistically and economically.
After a late start with the fiction film, compared with other
important film-producing countries, Denmark soon developed
its film industry into one of the four or five most important
in the world. This development was largely due to the outward-looking energies of Ole Olsen and the company he founded,
Nordisk Films Kompagni. Not content with the small economic
base provided by the Danish home market, Olsen expanded
his business and firmly established it on an international basis,

setting up distribution offices throughout Europe and in the
United States. The success of this worldwide operation was
dependent not only on Olsen's business sense but on the high
quality of the films his company produced. Because of the
success of Nordisk, numerous other production companies were
formed. Most were of little significance, but a few (Kosmorama, Det Skandinavisk-russike Handelshus, Kinografen, Biorama, Dansk Biografkompagni) were influential. With the outbreak of World War I the Danish cinema began a period of
economic and artistic decline from which it never recovered.
The loss of international markets especially contributed to this
decline, though other factors, including a large-scale exodus
of Danish film artists to work in other countries, were also
important.

During the golden age of the Danish cinema, however,
Danish films often set the standard for certain kinds of productions in other countries. I have cited the comments on
this influence in Russia, Germany, and Italy made by other
film historians, as well as the high praise given to Danish
films in trade journals of the period. Germany, in particular,
seems to have come under the influence of Danish films. For
Nordisk Films Germany was, from the beginning, its most important market, and it continued to be until the formation of
UFA in 1917.

The golden age also saw the emergence of the most important Danish film artists, including Benjamin Christensen,
Vilhelm Glückstadt, August Blom, Eduard Schnedler-Sørensen,
Asta Nielsen, Urban Gad, Valdemar Psilander, Alfred Lind,
and Robert Dinesen. Although these artists have been largely
forgotten or neglected, their work remains to be rediscovered
and given its rightful place in film history. In many cases
their contributions to the development of the medium are as
important as those of their more famous contemporaries in
other countries. The reinstatement of these individuals'
reputations has been one of the major tasks of this study.

Probably no development in Denmark in the years 1910-
14 was more significant than the growth of the long film, the
international distribution of which helped stimulate the production of long films in other countries. Although there was
initial resistance to longer films on the part of the more conservative producers, distributors, and exhibitors, the public
responded favorably, and perhaps no more so than in Denmark,

where lines formed to see the very first Danish long film, the Fotorama production Den hvide Slavehandel (The White Slave Trade). Much of the worldwide reputation of the Danish cinema in this period was built on this move to longer films which allowed a more complex development of action and character. Whatever the hesitations on the part of other producers, the Danish companies proved to be in touch with the future of the medium. A number of Danish films from this period are seminal works of the feature-length cinema. Among them are Det hemmlighedsflude X, Hævnens Nat, Atlantis, Under Blinkfyrets Straaler, and Evangliemandens Liv.

The type of film that most characterizes the golden age is the melodrama of strong passions and sensational incidents in which subjects such as murder, infidelity, jealousy, and greed are dominant. At Nordisk these characteristics are linked to a consistent film style. This Nordisk style is best defined in terms of highly expressive lighting, realism of interior settings, naturalistic acting, deep-focus photography, and extensive use of location shooting. The subjects often raised censorship problems outside Denmark, especially in the United States. In some cases films were completely forbidden by censoring authorities or were cut to conform to local standards.

There was not much preparation for this remarkable flowering of the Danish cinema. The beginning of the fictional film in Denmark dates only from 1906, and although the films made between 1906 and 1909 contain indications of the types of films to come, they hardly predict the rapid development of of the dramatic film from 1910 on. Prior to 1906 the Danish cinema was entirely dominated by the nonfiction film, even though taste for the fiction film was being developed through the importation of foreign-made films.

The rapid development of the Danish fiction film is paralleled by its rapid decline. After 1914 the artistic innovations of the golden age began to harden into conventions. At least this is true of Nordisk productions; other companies, especially Filmfabrikken Danmark, continued to be innovative. In addition, the war in Europe severely limited the ability of the Danish cinema to maintain its foreign markets. In 1917 Nordisk was forced to shut down most of its operation, signaling the end of the period of Danish influence.

The principal aim of this history has been the critical restoration of the early Danish cinema. Important in its own time, it has since been neglected by film history, partly from ignorance and partly from the unavailability of the films themselves. Much remains to be done, both in researching the period and in linking the Danish cinema to that of other countries. This work cannot go ahead easily until Danish films become more accessible. When they do, judgments about the early cinema will become that much more accurate and complete.

NOTES

1. The New York Dramatic Mirror, August 5, 1914, p. 24. The August 15, 1914 issue of Moving Picture World reported that the Vitagraph Paris plant was already closed, "as the entire force had been drawn to the colors." (p. 963).

2. Evan Strong, "War's Black Mark," Moving Picture World, September 12, 1914, p. 1515.

3. MPW, August 22, 1914, p. 1090.

4. MPW, September 5, 1914, p. 1343.

5. MPW, August 22, 1914, p. 1090. The article does not identify the domestic manufacturer it cites.

6. The Kinematograph and Lantern Weekly, August 20, 1914, p. 32.

7. The New York Dramatic Mirror, August 12, 1914, p. 24.

8. Moving Picture World, August 15, 1914, p. 964.

9. MPW, July 29, 1916, p. 782.

10. MPW, February 12, 1916, p. 937.

11. Ebbe Neergaard, The Story of the Danish Film, trans. Elsa Gress (Copenhagen: Det Danske Selskab, 1963), p. 47.

12. Neergaard, pp. 47-56.

13. Marguerite Engberg, Dansk Stumfilm, 2 vols. (Copenhagen: Rhodos Internationalt Forlag for Videnskab, Kunst og Debat, 1977), p. 619.

14. Engberg, Dansk Stumfilm, pp. 628-29.

15. Neergaard, p. 49.

16. Engberg, Dansk Stumfilm, p. 619.

17. Engberg, Dansk Stumfilm, pp. 630-54.

18. Engberg, Dansk Stumfilm, pp. 628-29.

19. Viggo Starcke, Denmark in World History (Philadelphia: University of Pennsylvania Press, 1962), p. 324.

20. Steward Oakley, A Short History of Denmark (New York and Washington: Praeger Publishers, 1972), p. 204.

21. Oakley, p. 218.

22. W. Glyn Jones, Denmark (New York and Washington: Praeger Publishers, 1970), pp. 114-18.

23. Jones, pp. 118-23.

24. Moving Picture World, October 28, 1916, p. 529. The office had already closed temporarily in 1914.

25. Filmen, March 1, 1917, p. 122.

26. Filmen, July 1, 1917, pp. 184-85.

27. Neergaard, pp. 48, 49; and Engberg, Dansk Stumfilm, p. 593. In a letter to its branch office in New York, dated February 28, 1911, Nordisk cited its German branch as the one that really kept the business going. As proof the letter claims that 130 copies of Den hvide Slavehandel were sold in Germany alone.

28. Filmen, August 1, 1917, pp. 214, 216.

29. Neergaard, p. 47.

30. Marguerite Engberg, Dansk Stumfilm, 1903-1930 (Copenhagen: Det Dansek Filmmuseum, 1968), pp. 40-42.

31. In Dansk Stumfilm (p. 620) Marguerite Engberg outlines an administrative policy concerning story content established at Nordisk in 1910 and maintained through the period under discussion. She notes that after 1912 the typical love intrigues and love triangles that constituted the basic story material "as a rule took place among the upper classes, the aristocracy, and among royalty." Previous to 1912 the characteristic setting was middle-class.

32. Neergaard, p. 51.

33. Marguerite Engberg raises this question in her discussion of Vilhelm Glückstadt's De Dødes Ø, based on the paintings of Böcklin and concerning the struggle between light and dark, good and evil. The script was written by Stellan Rye who, in 1913, went to Germany where he directed The Student of Prague, often considered a forerunner of the expressionist film. Engberg also regrets that De Dødes Ø has not survived, since it might make an interesting comparison with Fritz Lang's Der müde Tod. Might Rye have taken an aesthetic that he acquired at Filmfabrikken Danmark, the producer of De Dødes Ø, to Germany and applied it on his own The Student of Prague? See Dansk Stumfilm, p. 556.

34. Harold Engberg, A. W. Sandberg og hans Film (Copenhagen: Aschehoug Dansk Forlag, 1944), p. 17.

35. Harold Engberg suggests that Psilander felt a special affinity for the character of Joe Higgins.

36. Neergaard, p. 52.

37. Robert T. Anderson, Denmark: Success of a Developing Nation (Cambridge, Mass.: Schenkman Publishing
Co., 1975), p. 72. As part of a discussion of working-class
social and health problems, Anderson makes the following observation: "Perhaps the most serious, when all of its social
and cultural implications are taken into account, was alcoholism. Around 1900 men drank, and drank heavily throughout
their lives, knowing that it caused disability and death. A
common saying around 1900 was that every seventh man died
of drink. One study of adult male deaths found that nearly
one in four came from alcoholism as either a primary or contributing cause."

38. The best example of Christensen's considerable
acting talents is the performance he gives as the painter
Claude Zoret in Carl Dreyer's 1924 German production Mikaël.

39. John Ernst, Benjamin Christensen (Copenhagen:
Det Danske Filmmuseum, 1967), p. 11.

40. An article in Moving Picture World refers to Christensen as Ben Cristy and describes his current visit to the
United States to sell Blind Justice. It also comments on a
"unique feature" of the film: "An absolutely unique feature
of this production is that it presents a unity and homogeneity
not possessed by any other; for it is the work of Mr. Cristy
alone. He wrote the story, he directed the picture, enacted
the leading role, edited and did all else in connection with
the finishing touches, thus making a perfect whole which
proclaims it to be the creation of one sole master mind."
September 2, 1916, p. 1554.

41. The only surviving version of the film has Dutch
intertitles and credits. The character names, therefore, may
not be the same as in the original Danish version.

42. The only surviving version has German intertitles
and credits. The characters' names, therefore, may not be
the same as in the original Danish version.

APPENDIX A:

FILMOGRAPHY

This appendix contains basic credit information and plot synopses not already given in the text on selected fiction films made in Denmark from 1903 to 1917.

AF ELSKOVS NAADE (By Love's Grace, 1913)
U.S. title: Acquitted
    Production: Nordisk Films Kompagni
    Direction: August Blom
    Script: Albert Varner (pseudonym for Sven Lange)
    Camera: Johan Ankerstjerne
    Cast: Adam Poulsen, Carl Lauritzen, Henry Lauritzen,
      Betty Nansen, Torben Meyer, Johannes Meyer
    Length: 1,150 m.

AFGRUNDEN (The Abyss) (1910)
    Production: Kosmorama
    Direction: Peter Urban Gad
    Script: Peter Urban Gad
    Camera: Alfred Lind
    Cast: Asta Nielsen, Robert Dinesen, Poul Reumert, Hans
      Neergaard, Arne Weel, Oscar Stribolt, Emilie Sannom
    Length: 750 m.

AMBROSIUS (Ambrose) (1910)
    Production: Fotorama
    Direction: Gunnar Helsengreen
    Literary Source: Play by Christian Mølbech
    Camera: Thomas Hermansen
    Cast: Aage Fønss, Marie Niedermann, Aage Schmidt, Alfred Cohn
    Length: 139 m. (surviving material)

AMOR PAA KROGVEJE (Cupid's Devious Ways) (1914)
    Production: Nordisk Films Kompagni
    Direction: Robert Dinesen
    Cast: Carl Alstrup, Ebba Thomsen

    Bing, one of the partners in the firm of Bing and Bang,
must marry his cousin Ingeborg (Ebba Thomsen) to inherit
his uncle's money. Ingeborg is a friend of Mrs. Bang and
is coming to visit her. Bing sees Ingeborg without knowing who she is. Attracted, he tries to follow her but is
unsuccessful. Several days later he sees her again, this
time riding a bicycle. When she is not looking, he lets
the air out of her tires by using his stick pin, which he
accidentally leaves in the tire valve and which she keeps.
He then offers to help her, though, unbeknownst to him,
she knows what he has done. Later, Ingeborg sees a picture of him at the Bang's house and discovers who he is.
Bing is invited to dinner at the Bangs and, of course,
sees her again, still not knowing she is his cousin. He
wants to marry her, but tells her he has no money at
present. He then shows her the letter from his uncle
and the truth of who she is comes out.

ANARKISTENS SVIGERMODER (The Anarchist's Mother-in-Law)
(1906)
    Production: Nordisk Films Kompagni
    Direction: Viggo Larsen
    Camera: Alex Sørensen
    Cast: Viggo Larsen, Margrethe Jespersen
    Length: 90 m.

ANSIGTSTYVEN (The Face Thief) (1910)
    Production: Fotorama
    Direction: Gunnar Helsengreen
    Script: Aage Garde
    Cast: Aage Garde, Philip Bech, Peter Malberg, Alfred
        Cohn, Aage Schmidt, Aage Fønss, Marie Niedermann,
        Aage Bjørnbak, Axel Garde, Jenny Roelsgaard
    Length: 100 m. (surviving material)

ATLANTIS (1913)
    Production: Nordisk Films Kompagni
    Direction: August Blom
    Script: Karl Ludwig Schröder and Axel Garde
    Literary Source: novel by Gerhart Hauptmann

Camera: Johann Ankerstjerne
Cast: Olaf Fønss, Frederik Jacobsen, Carl Lauritzen, Ida
  Orloff, Ebba Thomsen, Charles Unthan
Length: 2,280 m.

AVIATIKEREN OG JOURNALISTENS HUSTRU (The Aviator and
the Journalist's Wife) (1911)
Production: Nordisk Films Kompagni
Direction: August Blom
Script: Christian Nobel
Camera: Alex Graatkjær (Sørensen)
Cast: Valdemar Psilander, Else Frölich, Einar Zangenberg
Length: 965 m.

A journalist and his wife go to an airfield to interview
an aviator. The wife flirts with the aviator, arranging to
meet him later. (It is common in Danish films to have the
infidelity spring from the wife's actions.) The journalist
becomes suspicious and sees them together. He plans to
get revenge by sabotaging the aviator's plane, but the
aviator sees him and repairs the damage. The journalist
learns that his wife has gone up with the aviator and re-
morsefully thinks both will be killed. After landing safely,
the aviator calls off the affair and the journalist and his
wife are reunited.

AEGTEMAND FOR EN TIME (Husband for an Hour) (1917)
Production: Nordisk Films Kompagni
Direction: Lau Lauritzen
Length: circa 1 reel

BADETS DRONNING (The Queen of the Baths) (1912)
U.S. title: The Queen of the Season
Production: Nordisk Films Kompagni
Direction: Eduard Schnedler-Sørensen
Script: G. Hetsch
Cast: Else Frölich, Carl Alstrup, Oscar Stribolt, Torben
  Meyer
Length: 309 m.

A woman is sent by her husband to the seashore while
he stays at home with their child. While there, she is
pursued by three men who compete with each other for
her attentions. When she leaves for home, they follow her
on board the train. At the station, she is greeted by her
husband and child. She introduces the three men and
leaves them standing in amazement on the platform.

BADHOTELLET (The Baths Hotel) (1914)
 Production: Kinografen
 Camera: Poul Eibye
 Cast: Mitzi Mathé, William Brewer, Edith Psilander, Einar
   Zangenberg
 Length: 1,240 m.

   Gregoire, a manufacturer, and his wife, Lola, decide
to go to a health spa for a vacation. Lola meets an old
love, Baron Plessen, and tells him that she is now married,
though unhappily. When she announces her plans to go
to the health spa, the baron decides that he will go too.
While Gregoire smokes cigars in bed, Lola looks lovingly
at a photo of the baron. Aboard a steamer, apparently
on their way to the hotel, the baron makes Gregoire's
acquaintance.

BALLETDANSERIDEN (The Ballet Dancer) (1911)
 Production: Nordisk Films Kompagni
 Direction: August Blom
 Script: Alfred Kjerulf
 Camera: Axel Sørensen (Graatkjær)
 Cast: Asta Nielsen, Valdemar Psilander, Johannes Poulsen,
   Valdemar Møller, Karen Lund
 Length: 800 m.

BALLETENS DATTER (Daughter of the Ballet) (1913)
 Production: Nordisk Films Kompagni
 Direction: Holger-Madsen
 Script: P. Nielsen
 Camera: Marius Clausen
 Cast: Svend Aggerholm, Oluf Billesborg, Rita Sacchetto,
   Torben Meyer, Christian Schrøder
 Length: 1,160 m.

   Count de Croissel (Svend Aggerholm) falls in love with
a dancer, Odette Blant (Rita Sacchetto), returning often
to see her at the theater. He sends her flowers, dines
her, and takes her for speedboat rides. He marries her,
but only when she promises to give up the theater. A year
passes, and she becomes bored with her new life. One
day she visits the theater with a friend. When she returns
home, she tries on her old ballet costume, and dances in
front of the mirror. Her husband enters and reprimands
her.
   Later, de Lange, the theater director (Torben Meyer),

needs a replacement for an injured dancer and asks Odette
to fill in for one night. She agrees on the condition that
no one will find out. She tells her husband that she must
visit her sick aunt and goes off to perform. That night,
de Croissel goes to the ballet and sees Odette performing.
At home, he confronts her and decides to leave, thinking
Odette has been having an affair with de Lange. He also
challenges de Lange to a duel, but de Lange gets three
pills from his uncle, a druggist, two pills that will anes-
thetize a man for an hour and a third pill which will revive him. (The actual use of the pills is missing from
contemporary prints.) The film ends with a reconciliation
between de Croissel and Odette.

BARNET SOM VELGØRER (The Child as Benefactor) (1909)
U.S. title: Child as Benefactor
  Production: Nordisk Films Kompagni
  Direction: Viggo Larsen
  Camera: Aage Brandt
  Cast: Aage Brandt
  Length: 275 m.

BEDRAGET I DØDEN (The Illusion of Death) (1911)
(Dr. Gar El Hama I)
U.S. title: A Dead Man's Child
  Production: Nordisk Films Kompagni
  Direction: Eduard Schnedler-Sørensen
  Script: Ludvig Landmann
  Cast: Aage Hertel, Carl Johan Lundquist, Edith Beumann,
    Henry Seeman, Otto Lagoni, Einar Zangenberg
  Length: 800 m.

DEN BEDRØVELIGE RIDDER (The Sad Knight) (1916)
  Production: Nordisk Films Kompagni
  Direction: Lau Lauritzen
  Length: circa 1 reel

BILLET MRK 909 (Apply Box 909) (1913)
  Production: Nordisk Films Kompagni
  Direction: Sofus Wolder
  Script: Viggo Kleisby
  Camera: Marius Clausen and Johan Ankerstjerne
  Cast: Frederik Jacobsen, Alma Hinding, Johannes Henrik-
    sen, Lizzi Thaler, Holger Syndergaard, Frederik Buch,
    Birger von Cotta-Schønberg
  Length: circa 320 m.

Two old business friends, each acting unbeknownst to
the other, answer a newspaper ad for companionship that
had been placed by two girls as a lark. The girls answer
every letter of response, telling the men to meet them at
a particular place. Soon, the whole street is filled with
waiting taxis and arguing men. The girls watch the chaos
from a window. The two businessmen pull out guns and,
after chasing away all the others, catch the girls. They
demand kisses from the girls, after which they let them
go.

BJØRNETAEMMEREN (The Bear Tamer) (1912)
    Production: Det Skandinavisk-russike Handelshus
    Direction: Alfred Lind
    Script: Alfred Lind
    Camera: Alfred Lind
    Cast: Lili Bech, Peter Fjelstrup, Ahnfeldt-Rønne, Alfred
        Lind, Rasmus Ottesen
    Length: 1,103 m.

BRUDEKJOLEN (The Wedding Dress) (1911)
    Production: Biorama
    Script: Johanne Madsen
    Cast: Ilse Nathansen, Ludvig Nathansen, Alma Lagoni,
        Olga Svendsen, Bertha Lindgreen, Mette Andersen,
        Jørgen Lund, Martha Olsen, Erik Winther
    Length: 450 m.

The film tells a Cinderella-like story of a poor girl who
is invited by a society woman to the homecoming celebration
for her childhood playmate, the son of a rich family. She
has no appropriate dress, so her mother makes over her
own wedding dress for the girl to wear. At the party the
son pays attention only to her, completely disregarding the
state consul's daughter, who leaves the party in anger.
He proposes to the poor girl and is accepted, to the delight of the woman who had invited her to the party.

EN BRYLLUPSAFTEN (A Wedding Night) (1911)
    Production: Kinografen
    Direction: Einar Zangenberg
    Script: Peter Nansen
    Cast: Olivia Norrie, Robert Dinesen, Mathilde Nielsen
    Length: 290 m.

ET BUDSKAB TIL NAPOLEON PAA ELBA (A Message to Napoleon on Elba) (1909)
U.S. title: A Message to Napoleon or An Episode in the Life
of the Great Prisoner of Elba
    Production: Nordisk Films Kompagni
    Direction: Viggo Larsen
    Camera: Axel Sørensen
    Cast: Viggo Larsen, Sofus Wolder, August Blom, Hertha
        Strandvold, Axel Schultz
    Length: 204 m.

BUKSESKØRTET (A Pair of Trousers) (1911)
    Production: Biorama
    Cast: Amelie Kierkegaard, Anna Møller, Carl Alstrup

    A husband laughs at his wife's friend who visits them
    wearing pants. The wife, however, likes the pants and
    without telling her husband, orders a pair for herself.
    The next day, the friends go for a walk wearing their
    pants and are chased by a crowd. The wife has her pants
    pulled off before the husband arrives and he takes the two
    women home where they all laugh about the experience.

CAPRICIOSA (1908)
U.S. title: The Magic Purse
    Production: Nordisk Films Kompagni
    Direction: Viggo Larsen
    Literary Source: Thomas Overskou
    Camera: Axel Sørensen
    Cast: Jørgen Lund, Petrine Stone, Mauritz Olsen, Mathilde
        Nielsen
    Length: 184 m.

DER VAR ENGANG (Once Upon a Time) (1907)
    Production: Nordisk Films Kompagni
    Direction: Viggo Larsen
    Literary Source: a play by Holger Drachmann
    Camera: Axel Sørensen
    Cast: Viggo Larsen, Robert Storm Petersen, Gustav Lund,
        Clara Nebelong
    Length: 265 m.

DESDEMONA (1911)
    Production: Nordisk Films Kompagni
    Direction: August Blom

Script: Ludvig Jensen
Camera: Johan Ankerstjerne
Cast: Anton Gambetta-Salmson, Ebba Thomsen, Cajus
    Bruun, Robert Dinesen, Augusta Blad, Svend Bille,
    Lilly Frederiksen
Length: 745 m.

DETEKTIVENS BARNEPIGE (The Detective's Nanny) (1914)
U.S. title: The Charlotte Street Mystery
    Production: Nordisk Films Kompagni
    Direction: Hjalmar Davidsen
    Script: A. Lumbye
    Camera: Louis Larsen
    Cast: R. Hjort-Clausen, Else Frölich, Robert Schyberg,
        Carl Schenstrøm, Helene de Dvanenskjold
    Length: 894 m.

DOBBELTGAENGEREN (A Victim of his Double) (1910)
    Production: Nordisk Films Kompagni
    Cast: Aage Hertel, Otto Lagoni
    Length: 217 m.

DR. GAR EL HAMA II (1912)
U.S. title: Dr. Gar El Hama II
    Production: Nordisk Films Kompagni
    Direction: Eduard Schnedler-Sørensen
    Script: Eduard Schnedler-Sørensen
    Camera: Alex Graatkjær (Sørensen)
    Cast: Aage Hertel, Robert Schyberg, Christian Schrøder,
        Ella Sprange, Carl Lauritzen, Amanda Lund, Lauritz
        Olsen, Gerda Christoffersen
    Length: 800 m.

DR. THÜRMERS MOTIONSKUR (Dr. Thürmer's Exercise Treatment) (1913)
    Production: Selandia
    Cast: Astrid Krygell, Alf Nielsen, Susanne Felumb-Friis,
        Jørgen Lund
    Length: 297 m. (surviving material)

    A woman goes to Dr. Thürmer for a treatment that will
give her more energy. The doctor has her inhale a vapor,
and she finds that she can move with tremendous speed.
She buys some to use on her husband in order to cure
him of laziness. After using it, he turns around at fast

speed, falls into a death-like sleep, and dreams he is being
chased by a giant bottle of Dr. Thürmer's vapor. In the
dream the vapor affects all who come into contact with it.
About three-quarters of the way through the film another story is introduced concerning a young man named
Paul Müller who is the friend of some school girls. The
girls' teacher tries to keep Paul away from them, but he
plays some tricks on the teacher that enable him to see
the girls. Just as it is beginning to seem as if this material is from another film entirely, the husband runs by
with the vapor bottle chasing him and sets them all into
motion. The film ends with a shot that appears to come
from earlier in the film when the husband fell asleep.

DR. VOLUNTAS (1915)
    Production: Nordisk Films Kompagni
    Direction: Robert Dinesen
    Camera: Sophus Wangøe
    Cast: Carlo Wieth, Gunnar Tolnæs, Johanne Fritz-Petersen,
        Henry Seeman, Arne Weel
    Length: 4 reels

ET DRAMA FRA RIDDERTIDEN (A Drama from the Age of
Chivalry) (1907)
    Production: Nordisk Films Kompagni
    Direction: Viggo Larsen
    Camera: Alex Sørensen
    Cast: Clara Nebelong, Viggo Larsen, Gustav Lund
    Length: 152 m.

ET DRAMA PAA HAVET (A Drama at Sea) (1912)
U.S. title: The Great Ocean Disaster or Peril of Fire
    Production: Nordisk Films Kompagni
    Direction: Eduard Schnedler-Sørensen
    Script: Alfred Kjerulf
    Camera: Axel Graatkjær (Sørensen)
    Cast: Valdemar Psilander, Christian Schrøder, Ellen Ag-
        gerholm, Otto Lagoni
    Length: 675 m.

DYREKØBT ÆRE (Dearly Purchased Honor) (1911)
    Production: Nordisk Films Kompagni
    Direction: William Augustinus
    Script: Alfred Kjerulf

248 The Danish Cinema

Cast: Gerhard Jessen, Nina Millung, Frederik Jacobsen, Jacoba Jessen, Axel Boesen, Otto Lagoni, Julie Henriksen
Length: 310 m.

DØDENS BRUD (The Bride of Death) (1911)
Production: Nordisk Films Kompagni
Direction: August Blom
Script: Otto Gulman
Cast: Aage Hertel, Robert Dinesen, Augusta Blad, Svend Bille, Jenny Roelsgaard, Johanne Krum-Hunderup, Otto Lagoni, Agnete Blom
Length: 935 m.

DØDSFLUGTEN (The Flight from Death) (1911)
U.S. title: The Nihilist Conspiracy
Production: Nordisk Films Kompagni
Direction: Eduard Schnedler-Sørensen
Script: A. Holch
Cast: Karen Lund, Einar Zangenberg, Otto Lagoni, Carl Alstrup, Franz Skondrup, Carl Lauritzen
Length: 533 m.

DØDSSPRING TIL HEST FRA CIRKUSKUPLEN (Death Jump on Horse from the Circus Dome) (1912)
U.S. title: A Fatal Decision or The Great Circus Catastrophe
Production: Nordisk Films Kompagni
Direction: Eduard Schnedler-Sørensen
Script: Alfred Kjerulf
Cast: Valdemar Psilander, Jenny Roelsgaard, Aage Hertel, Frederik Jacobsen, Frederik Christensen, Fru Ræder
Length: 805 m.

DØDSVARSLET (A Death Warning) (1912)
Production: Filmfabrikken Skandinavien (Biorama)
Direction: Aage Brandt
Script: Aage Brandt
Cast: Fritz Lamprecht, Vera Brechling, Knud Rassow, Tronier Funder
Length: 700 m.

EKSPRESSENS MYSTERIUM (The Mystery of the Express) (1913)
U.S. title: The Monomaniac
Production: Nordisk Films Kompagni

Direction: Hjalmar Davidsen
Script: Carl Gandrup
Camera: Louis Larsen
Cast: Valdemar Psilander, Christel Holck, Carl Lauritzen,
   Svend Aggerholm, Birger von Cotta-Schönberg, Holger
   Syndergaard
Length: 1,040 m.

ELVERHØJ (Elf Hill) (1910)
Production: Biorama
Direction: Jørgen Lund
Literary source: play by Johan Ludvig Heiberg
Cast: Jørgen Lund, Carl Petersen, Agnes Lorentzen,
   Frans Skondrup, Ludvig Nathansen, Hr. Nobel, Victoria
   Petersen, Karen Caspersen, Oscar Stribolt, Hr. Peder-
   strup
Length: 340 m. (surviving material)

ELVERHØJ (Elf Hill) (1910)
Production: Fotorama
Direction: Gunnar Helsengreen
Literary source: play by Johan Ludvig Heiberg
Cast: Philip Bech, Martha Helsengreen, Jenny Roelsgaard,
   Peter Malberg, Aage Fønss, Marie Niedermann, Johannes
   Rich, Aage Bjørnbak, Alfred Cohn
Length: 250 m.

ENDELIG ALENE (Alone at Last)
Production: Nordisk Films Kompagni
Direction: Holger-Madsen
Script: P. H. Nielsen
Camera: Marius Clausen
Cast: Rasmus Christiansen, Luzzy Werren, Carl Schen-
   strøm, Torben Meyer, P. Jørgensen, Frederik Jacobsen
Length: 661 m.

Newlyweds Adolf (Rasmus Christiansen) and Charlotte
(Luzzy Werren) want to be alone but are continually interrupted by other people, by a man on a train who will not
leave their compartment, by Charlotte's parents who come
for a visit, and by Charlotte's aunt who even sleeps in the
bed with Charlotte, forcing Adolf to sleep elsewhere. In
desperation Adolf rents an apartment and slips his wife a
note telling her to meet him there. The aunt finds the
note, however, and, thinking Adolf is to meet another

woman, goes to the apartment along with Charlotte's parents. With the help of a doctor friend Adolf concocts a plan whereby he pretends to be crazy, chasing everyone around with a knife. The doctor arrives and puts Adolf in a straightjacket, telling all the relatives that he must be left alone. That night Adolf and Charlotte finally get to bed together, but both are so tired that they just fall asleep.

EVANGELIEMANDENS LIV (The Evangelist's Life) (1914)
U.S. title: John Redmond, the Evangelist
  Production: Nordisk Films Kompagni
  Direction: Holger-Madsen
  Script: Holger-Madsen
  Camera: Marius Clausen
  Cast: Valdemar Psilander, Frederik Jacobsen, Augusta
    Bald, Birger von Cotta-Schønberg, Alma Hinding, Else
    Frölich, J. Ring, R. Schyberg, P. Bech
  Length: 1,093 m.

EXSPEDITRICEN (The Shop Girl) (1911)
  Production: Nordisk Films Kompagni
  Direction: August Blom
  Script: Lauritz Lauritzen
  Camera: Axel Graatkjær (Sørensen)
  Cast: Carlo Wieth, Clara Wieth, Thorkild Roose, Ella la
    Cour, Zanny Petersen, Lauritz Olsen, Henny Lauritzen,
    Elna From
  Length: 980 m.

FABIAN PAA KAERLIGHEDSSTIEN (Fabian on Lovemaking)
(1910)
  Production: Nordisk Films Kompagni
  Camera: Axel Sørensen
  Cast: Victor Fabian, Ingeborg Rasmussen, Axel Boesen
  Length: 100 m.

FABIAN PAA ROTTEJAGT (Fabian on Rat Hunting) (1910)
U.S. title: Fabian Hunting Rats
  Production: Nordisk Films Kompagni
  Camera: Axel Sørensen
  Cast: Victor Fabian
  Length: 90 m.

ET FARLIGT SPIL (A Dangerous Play) (1912)
  Production: Nordisk Films Kompagni

Direction: Leo Tschering (?)
Script: Langkjær
Cast: Dagny Schyberg, Aage Hertel, Jenny Roelsgaard,
    Frederik Christensen, Robert Dinesen, Hilmar Clausen,
    Frederik Jacobsen
Length: 775 m.

A girl's father is trying to marry her to an army officer. She tells this to the man she loves (Robert Dinesen).
Realizing that Dinesen looks like the officer, they decide
to pretend that he is the officer, and, with the help of a
friend disguised as a minister, they get married. The
real officer reads about the marriage in the newspaper and
rushes to the girl's house, arriving just after the couple
has left. A chase in horse-drawn sleighs ensues, and
Dinesen and his friend fall out of their sleigh. The girl
is taken back to her father. With the help of his friend
Dinesen once again gets the girl and once again is pursued. The father and the officer catch up to them, but
only after a marriage has been performed by a real minister. Dishonored, the officer commits suicide.

DE FIRE DJAEVLE (The Four Devils) (1911)
Production: Kinografen
Direction: Robert Dinesen and Alfred Lind
Script: Carl Rosenbaum
Literary source: Herman Bang
Camera: Alfred Lind
Cast: Edith Buemann, Robert Dinesen, Carl Rosenbaum,
    Tilley Christiansen, Einar Rosenbaum, Aage Hertel,
    Antoinette Winding
Length: 880 m.

FLYTTEDAGSKVALER (Moving Day Troubles) (1914)
Production: Nordisk Films Kompagni
Direction: Lau Lauritzen
Script: Johannes Baack
Cast: Oscar Stribolt, Phillippa Frederiksen, Christian
    Schrøder
Length: 288 m. (surviving material)

DEN FLYVENDE CIRKUS (The Flying Circus) (1912)
U.S. title: The Flying Circus
Production: Det Skandinavisk-russike Handelshus
Direction: Alfred Lind

Script: Carl O. Dummreicher
Camera: Alfred Lind
Cast: Lili Bech, Richard Jensen, Rasmus Ottesen, Emilie
    Otterdahl
Length: 975 m.

DEN FREMMEDE (The Stranger) (1914)
    Production: Filmfabrikken Danmark (Det Skandinavisk-
      russike Handelshus)
    Direction: Vilhelm Glückstadt
    Cast: Emanuel Gregers, Gudrun Houlberg, Rasmus Otte-
      sen
    Length: 651 m.

FRU POTIFAR (Madame Potiphar) (1911)
    Production: Nordisk Films Kompagni
    Direction: August Blom
    Script: Bertel Krause
    Camera: Johan Ankerstjerne
    Cast: Valdemar Psilander, Gerda Krum Juncker, Henry
      Seeman, Alma Hinding
    Length: 909 m.

    During a garden party, a doctor (Valdemar Psilander)
is called away to attend a sick child. His wife leaves the
party with a mutual friend, a military officer (Henry Seeman). She makes advances to the officer, but he rejects
them. She writes a note to her husband, who has stayed
with the child all night, accusing the officer of improper
conduct. The doctor confronts his friend with this accu-
sation and challenges him to a duel. The wife tries to
stop the duel but is too late. The officer gets shot just
before the wife arrives. She confesses her lie, and the
doctor quickly goes to the aid of his friend who, it turns
out, is only wounded. From his recovery bed the officer
convinces the doctor to forgive his wife. He does, and
a reconciliation takes place.

FRØKEN THEODOR (Miss Theodor) (1917)
    Production: Nordisk Films Kompagni
    Direction: Lau Lauritzen
    Cast: Lauritz Olsen, Ulla Poulsen, Arne Weel
    Length: circa 1 reel

FYRTØJET (The Tinder Box) 1907)
    Production: Nordisk Films Kompagni

Direction: Viggo Larsen
Literary source: story of the same name by Hans Christian Andersen
Camera: Axel Sørensen
Cast: Oda Alstrup, Robert Storm Petersen, Viggo Larsen, Petrine Stone, Gustav Lund, Valdemar Petersen
Length: 223 m.

DET GAMLE SPIL OM ENHVER (The Old Play About Everyman) (1915)
Production: Filmfabrikken Danmark (formerly Det Skandinavisk-russike Handelshus)
Direction: Vilhelm Glückstadt
Cast: Gudrun Houlberg, Rasmus Ottesen, Jonna Neyendam, Valdemar Møller, Else Schube, Peter Malberg
Length: 1,056 m.

GENNEM KAMP TIL SEJR (Through Trials to Victory) (1911)
U.S. Title: Through Trials to Victory
Production: Nordisk Films Kompagni
Direction: Peter Urban Gad
Script: Harriet Bloch
Cast: Thorkild Roose, Augusta Blad, Edith Buemann, Poul Reumert, Henry Seemann, Svend Bille, Otto Lagoni
Length: 770 m.

DEN GLADE LØJTNANT (The Gay Lieutenant) (1912)
Production: Nordisk Films Kompagni
Direction: Robert Dinesen
Script: Thomas Krag
Cast: Valdemar Psilander, Ebba Thomsen, Cajus Bruun, Marie Ring, H. Clausen, A. G. Salmson
Length: 726 m.

An army lieutenant, Victor (Valdemar Psilander), becomes engaged to a girl named Lucca (Ebba Thomsen). At their engagement party Victor gets drunk and insults a guest, pushing his face into the cake. Later, we see Victor with some fellow officers at a feast. Again, he is drunk and Lucca sees him that way. She breaks off their engagement. After leaving the army, Victor sails for South America. Three years later Lucca is married to a manufacturer. Victor returns from South America and meets Lucca and her husband on the street. They invite him to a party, at which he makes advances toward Lucca.

She agrees to visit him at his place but once again rejects
his advances. He visits her at home while her husband is
present. Later, the husband sees her tear up a letter and
throw it into the fireplace. Suspicious, he gets out the
fragments of the letter and discovers that it is from Victor.
The three of them go riding in a chauffeur-driven car at
high speed and crash into a tree, apparently by design.

GUVERNØRENS DATTER (The Governor's Daughter) (1912)
U.S. title: The Governor's Daughter
    Production: Nordisk Films Kompagni
    Direction: August Blom
    Script: Ludvig Jensen
    Camera: Johan Ankerstjerne
    Cast: Anton Gambetta Salmson, Ebba Thomsen, Cajus
      Bruun, Robert Dinesen, Augusta Blad, Svend Bille,
      Lilly Frederiksen
    Length: 745 m.

GØGLEREN (The Ham Actor) (1912)
    Production: Nordisk Films Kompagni
    Direction: August Blom
    Script: Poul Knudsen
    Cast: Augusta Blad, Valdemar Psilander, Ferdinand Bonn,
      Clara Wieth, Holger Madsen, Jenny Roelsgaard
    Length: 779 m.

GAARDMANSDATTEREN (The Farmer's Daughter) (1912)
    Production: Filmfabrikken Skandinavien (Biorama)
    Length: 475 m.

A poor farm hand, Hans, is in love with Anna, the
farmer's daughter. Her brother finds out and tells their
father, who dismisses Hans. Hans then leaves for America to make his fortune. Later, Anna's father is in debt
and wants her to marry a wealthy suitor. She refuses,
but fortunately Hans returns, having struck it rich in the
West. He is now welcomed by the father.

HANS HØJHED (His Highness) (1913)
U.S. title: His Highness, the Prince
    Production: Nordisk Films Kompagni
    Direction: Eduard Schnedler-Sørensen
    Script: Marius Wulff
    Camera: Carl Fischer

Cast: Mølbach, Carl Alstrup, Lauritz Olsen, Oscar Stribolt, Olga Svendsen, Zanny Peterson
Length: 765 m.

HANS STORE CHANCE (His Big Chance) (1915)
Production: Nordisk Films Kompagni
Direction: Hjalmar Davidsen
Cast: Valdemar Psilander
Length: 932 m.

HANS VANSKELIGSTE ROLLE (His Most Difficult Part) (1912)
Production: Nordisk Films Kompagni
Direction: August Blom
Camera: Johan Ankerstjerne
Cast: Carl Lauritzen, Augusta Blad, Else Frölich, Ferdin-
and Bonn, Robert Dinesen, Frederik Buch
Length: 520 m.

Linda (Else Frölich), the daughter of Count Bernberg,
and her mother (Augusta Blad) are sitting in a theater
box watching Kurt Barner play Hamlet. Linda cannot stop
thinking about Barner. Her father owes money and wants
Linda to marry the wealthy Count von Pfalz (Robert Dinesen). Barner and Linda meet at a party and again while
riding. One night, at the theater, Linda gives him a locket inscribed with the words "I Love You." Pfalz sees
her do this and, getting a look at the inscription, breaks
off the engagement. Linda's mother goes to see Barner
and asks him to break off his relationship with her daughter. He agrees to do so even though he is in love with
her. He does this by pretending to be a drunkard and
debauchee.

HEKSEN OG CYKLISTEN (The Witch and the Cyclist) (1909)
U.S. title: The Witch and the Cycle
Production: Nordisk Films Kompagni
Direction: Viggo Larsen
Camera: Axel Sørensen
Cast: Petrine Stone, Arvid Ringheim
Length: 65 m.

DET HEMMELIGHEDSFLUDE X (The Mysterious X) (1913)
U.S. title: Sealed Orders
Production: Dansk Biografkompagni
Direction: Benjamin Christensen

Script: Benjamin Christensen
Camera: Emil Dinesen
Cast: Benjamin Christensen, Karen Caspersen, Otto Rein-
    wald, Bjørn Spiro, Fritz Lamprecht, Hermann Spiro,
    Amanda Lund, Svend Rindom, Robert Schmidt, Holger
    Rasmussen, Charles Løvaas
Length: 1,977 m.

HENRETTELSEN (The Execution) (1903)
    Production: Peter Elfelt
    Direction: Peter Elfelt
    Script: Christian Lundsgaard and Scheel Vandel
    Cast: Francesca Nathansen, Victor Betzonich
    Length: circa 40 m.

EN HJEMLØS FUGL (A Homeless Bird) (1911)
U.S. title: Homeless
    Production: Fotorama (Danafilm)
    Script: Erling and Ljut Steensgaard
    Cast: Marie Niedermann, Aage Schmidt, Peter Nielsen,
        Philip Bech, Jamma Creutz Nathansen, Ljut Steensgaard
    Length: 962 m.

HOLGER DANSKE (Ogier the Dane) (1910)
    Production: Fotorama
    Direction: Eduard Schnedler-Sørensen
    Camera: Thomas Hermansen
    Cast: Gunnar Helsengreen, Aage Schmidt, Aage Fønss,
        Aage Bjørnbak
    Length: 15 m. (surviving material)

HULDA RASMUSSEN or DYREKØBT GLIMMER (Dearly-Bought
Tinsel) (1911)
    Production: Nordisk Films Kompagni
    Direction: Peter Urban Gad
    Script: Otto Gulmann and Palle Rosenkrantz
    Cast: Frederik Jacobsen, Elna From, Emilie Sannom,
        Johannes Poulsen, Axel Strøm, Ellen Kornbeck
    Length: 855 m.

DEN HVIDE SLAVEHANDEL (The White Slave Trade) (1910)
    Production: Fotorama
    Direction: Alfred Lind
    Script: Louis Schmidt
    Camera: Alfred Lind

Cast: Christel Holch, Kaj Lund, Alfred Cohn, Peter Niel-
sen, Gunnar Helsengreen, Maja Bjerre-Lind, Aage
Schmidt, Kai Lind, Philip Bech, Frederik Buch
Length: 706 m.

DEN HVIDE SLAVEHANDEL I (The White Slave Trade I) (1910)
Production: Nordisk Films Kompagni
Direction: August Blom
Camera: Axel Sørensen
Cast: Ellen Rindom, Svend Billie, Ella la Cour, Einar
Zangenberg, Lauritz Olsen, Doris Langkilde, Otto
Lagoni, Julie Henriksen
Length: 603 m.

DEN HVIDE SLAVEHANDEL III (The White Slave Trade III)
(1912)
Production: Nordisk Films Kompagni
Direction: Peter Urban Gad
Script: A. Schmidt
Cast: Augusta Blad, Lilly Lamprecht, Richard Christensen,
Amanda Lund, Viggo Lindstrøm, Frantz Skondrup
Length: 665 m.

DEN HVIDE SLAVINDE (The White Slave Girl) (1906)
Production: Nordisk Films Kompagni
Direction: Viggo Larsen
Script: Arnold Richard Nielsen
Camera: Axel Sørensen
Cast: Gerda Jensen, Viggo Larsen, Gustav Lund
Length: 155 m.

HVOR SORGERNE GLEMMES (Where Sorrows Are Forgotten)
(1915)
Production: Nordisk Films Kompagni
Direction: Holger-Madsen
Camera: Marius Clausen
Cast: Rita Sacchetto, Henry Lauritzen, Anton de Verdier,
Gerda Christophersen, Alf Blütecher
Length: 4 reels

HAEVNENS NAT (Night of Revenge) (1915)
U.S. title: Blind Justice
Production: Dansk Biografkompagni
Direction: Benjamin Christensen
Script: Benjamin Christensen

Camera: Johan Ankerstjerne
Cast: Benjamin Christensen, Karen Sandberg (Caspersen),
     Peter Fjelstrup, Charles Wilken, Ulla Johansen, Jon
     Iversen, Aage Schmidt, Grete Brandes, Elith Pio, Fritz
     Lamprecht, Osvald Helmuth, Otto Reinwald, Jørgen
     Lund, W. Jordan
Length: 1,956 m.

HAEVNET (Revenge) (1911)
     Production: Nordisk Films Kompagni
     Direction: August Blom
     Script: Valdemar Hansen
     Cast: Valdemar Hansen, Ella la Cour, Edith Beumann,
        Thorkild Roose, Henry Seeman, Valdeman Psilander
     Length: 900 m.

I BONDEFANGERKLØR (In the Claws of Confidence Men)
(1910)
     Production: Fotorama
     Script: Johannes Pedersen
     Cast: Marie Niedermann, Gunnar Helsengreen, Aage Fønss
        Aage Schmidt, Alfred Arnbak, Philip Bech
     Length: 50 m. (surviving material)

I SIDSTE SEKUND (At the Last Second) (1913)
     Production: Selandia
     Script: Alf Nielsen
     Camera: Leo Hansen
     Cast: Alf Nielsen, Hjalmar Løve, Elisabeth Christensen,
        Frederik Christensen, Fru Lomholt, Oluf Billesborg
     Length: circa 600 m.

     A young hunter, Leo, rescues Countess Paulola from a
runaway horse. The lady's husband, Count Zarowsky,
gives Leo a cigarette case as a token of his gratitude.
Zarowsky, who is the director of the army's gunpowder
factory, and his assistant, Simakz, make an important discovery in their lab. Zarowsky is called away and, while
he is gone, Simakz makes advances to the countess. She
rebuffs him, as earlier she had also rebuffed the advances
of Lieutenant Zarkoff. She did, however, give Zarkoff a
necklace which she must get back. Her sister, Jennea,
asks Leo, who has just been called to military service, to
deliver a note to Zarkoff. Leo gets the necklace, but
Simakz, who has followed Leo, tries to prevent him from

getting it back on time. After much chasing around, the
countess gets the necklace just in time to wear at a party
at which Zarowsky wants her to show it off. Having failed
in one plan, Simakz steals the explosive discovery. Leo,
however, follows him until Simakz falls and the chemical
explodes, killing him. As a reward for his services Leo
gets Jennea.

I STORM OG STILLE (In Storm and Calm) (1915)
  Production: Filmfabrikken Danmark (formerly, Det
    Skandinavisk-russike Handelshus)
  Direction: Vilhelm Glückstadt
  Cast: Emanuel Gregers, Gudrun Houlberg, P. Andersen
  Length: 743 m.

ILDFLUEN (The Firefly) (1913)
  Production: Kinografen
  Direction: Einar Zangenberg
  Cast: Alfi Zangenberg, Einar Zangenberg, Johanne Fritz-
    Petersen, William Brewer, Sophus Erhardt, Ella la Cour,
    Richard Christensen, Emma Wiehe
  Length: 1,325 m.

  Lillian and Ralph (Einar Zangenberg) are the children
of Countess Barri. One day Michael, a gypsy, asks the
countess to see his sick child. Seeing the child mistreated
by his parents, the countess orders the gypsies to leave
her estate. That night, Lillian, without telling her mother,
goes to the gypsy camp to see their monkeys. The gypsy
child dies while Lillian is there, and they decide to kidnap
Lillian. Ralph follows the gypsies and, to protect Lillian,
asks to become a member of the family. Twelve years pass
and the gypsies are back in the vicinity of the countess's
estate. A circus agent offers Michael and Lillian a job.
Ralph overhears, tells Lillian, and leaves for the time being
since he cannot accompany them to the city anyway. On
the road Ralph meets Baron Silber and fixes his car for
him. The baron offers Ralph a job as chauffeur. Baron
Silber sees Lillian at the circus and falls in love with her,
returning every evening to see the performance. Michael
loses all his money gambling, and, when he finds out about
the Baron's love for Lillian, he agrees to a match if the
baron will pay him. The baron picks up Lillian in his car
and begins making advances. Ralph stops the car, fools
the baron into getting out, and drives off with Lillian.

Michael finds out about Ralph and vows revenge. Ralph
and Lillian go to the countess and reveal who they are,
but Michael shows up, traps the three of them in an old
tower, and sets a bomb. Ralph gets the bomb and, just
in time, throws it away. It lands near Michael and kills
him.

DET INDISKE GULEBILLEDE (The Indian Idol) (1915)
    Production: Kinografen
    Cast: Anton de Verdier, Alfi Zangenberg, Tronier Funder
    Length: 2½ reels

Doctor Schmidt (Anton de Verdier) receives a note asking him to treat a man in St. James Street. The note tells
him it will be to his advantage. On arrival he finds a rich
old Hindu who gives him a small idol and warns him to be-
ware of a secret Indian society. The old man dies; two
members of the society enter the room and look for the
idol. The doctor leaves taking it with him. The society
swears to find the idol which the doctor has put on his
mantle at home. Schmidt is visited by his friend Dick
Jackson (Tronier Funder). A member of the society gains
entrance to the house under pretense of being sick. While
the doctor is getting medicine, the Indian finds the idol
and is about to take it when Jackson stops him. The
doctor hides the idol, and Jackson follows the Indian whom
they have allowed to leave. The next evening, while the
doctor and his wife Alma (Alfi Zangenberg) are out, the
Indian and two companions return to the house. The butler hears noises and investigates, but the Indians manage
to drug him. As Schmidt and Alma are arriving home, one
of the Indians hands him a note falsely saying that Dick
Jackson's wife has been taken ill. Schmidt leaves with the
Indian and Alma finds the butler unconscious. When she
sees a hand coming through the curtains, she gets a gun.
She then calls the Jacksons and tells them she is holding
one of the Indians at gunpoint. Dick Jackson and Dr.
Schmidt rush off to help her, but she is not there when
they arrive. The Indians take Alma to their hiding place,
but Dick surprises them there. They get away, however,
and leave a note for Schmidt telling him he can have his
wife in exchange for the idol. He meets with the Indians,
and the exchange is made. Dick Jackson, who has been
hiding at the meeting place, hands the Indians a deporta-
tion order. They seem to thank Jackson and later Alma

receives a necklace from the secret society. (The apparent incongruity of the ending may be due to missing footage. The print on which this description is based is probably 100 m. shorter than the original.)

JEG SKU TALE MED JØR'NSEN (I Want to Talk to Jørgensen) (1916)
Production: Nordisk Films Kompagni
Direction: Lau Lauritzen
Length: circa 1 reel

JENS BRAEDNER DEN AF (Jens Takes Off)
U.S. title: John Steals a Furlough
Production: Nordisk Films Kompagni
Direction: Christian Schrøder
Script: Christian Schrøder
Camera: Axel Graatkjær (Sørensen)
Cast: Christian Schrøder, Jutta Lund

Jens, an enlisted soldier, leaves his barracks without permission when he receives a note from a woman asking him to meet her. An officer sees him leave and follows him to the meeting. When Jens sees the officer approaching, he hides under the table where he is forced to listen to the officer's lovemaking. As Jens is returning to the barracks, the officer cuts the rope Jens is using to climb the barracks' wall and Jens falls into a moat. When Jens finally gets back, the officer is waiting for him and has Jens put in the guardhouse. The woman goes to the officer and threatens to tell his wife about the previous night if he does not release Jens. He agrees, and Jens is given a pass to see the woman.

KAMELIADAMEN (The Lady with the Camellias) (1907)
U.S. title: The Lady with the Camellias
Production: Nordisk Films Kompagni
Direction: Viggo Larsen
Literary Source: Alexander Dumas
Camera: Axel Sørensen
Cast: Oda Alstrup, Robert Storm Petersen, Viggo Larsen, Gustav Lund, Lauritz Olsen
Length: 266 m.

KLOVNEN (The Clown) (1916)
Production: Nordisk Films Kompagni

Direction: A. W. Sandberg
Cast: Valdemar Psilander, Gudrun Houlberg, Peter Fjel-
    strup, Amanda Lund, Robert Schmidt
Length: 1,375 m.

KLOVNENS HAEVN (The Clown's Revenge) (1912)
U.S. title: The Clown's Revenge
Production: Nordisk Films Kompagni
Script: Valdemar Hansen
Cast: Agnete von Prangen, Henry Seeman, Aage Hertel,
    Abba Thomsen, Otto Lagoni, Christian Schrøder, Ella
    Sprange
Length: 720 m.

KORNSPEKULANTEN (The Grain Speculator) (1912)
Production: Det Skandinavisk-russike Handelshus
Cast: Gudrun Houlberg, Valdemar Møller, Ove Jarne,
    Hildur Møller, Hugo Bendix
Length: 756 m.

KAERLIGHED OG PENGE (Love and Money) (1912)
U.S. title: Outwitted
Production: Nordisk Films Kompagni
Direction: Leo Tscherning
Script: Harriet Bloch
Camera: Jørgen Hansen
Cast: Else Frolich, Oscar Stribolt
Length: 324 m.

A widow (Else Frolich) is beseiged by three admirers,
a lieutenant, a poet, and a rich man, though she herself
is in love with her young son's tutor. She is visited by
a friend from America and gives a party in her friend's
honor. The friend meets the widow's cousin, an army
officer, and falls in love with him. At the end the widow
and the tutor and the friend and the cousin announce their
engagements. The three suitors wish them well.

KAERLIGHEDENS STYRKE (The Power of Love) (1911)
U.S. title: The Power of Love
Production: Nordisk Films Kompagni
Direction: August Blom
Script: Alfred Kjerulf
Camera: Axel Graatkjær (Sørensen)
Cast: Axel Strøm, Carlo Wieth, Clara Wieth, Ella la Cour,

Carl Lauritzen, Julie Henriksen, Ella Sprange, Aage
Lorentzen, Otto Lagoni, Zanny Petersen
Length: 757 m.

KØBENHAVN VED NAT (Copenhagen by Night) (1910)
Production: Biorama
Direction: Carl Alstrup
Camera: Ma. A. Madsen and A. J. Gee
Cast: Frederik Jensen, Oscar Stribolt, Lauritz Olsen,
Madna Redhøl, Susanne Felumb-Friis, Victoria Petersen,
Carl Petersen, Emilie Sannom, Agnes Lorentzen, Carl
Alstrup
Length: circa 400 m.

Some gentlemen go out on the town for the night and
get arrested. They are released and continue their partying. Eventually, their wives go looking for them and find
them with some women. One man spends a lot of time trying to get undressed, constantly falling over himself and
the furniture. Another man dances around drunk as his
wife tries to help him. A third sheepishly tries to make
up to his wife and succeeds, giving her a ring.

KØRSEL MED GRØNLANDSKE HUNDE (Driving with Greenland
Dogs) (1896-97)
Production: Peter Elfelt
Direction: Peter Elfelt
Camera: Peter Elfelt
Length: 10 m.

LEJLA (1913)
Production: Dania Biofilm Kompagni
Direction: O. E. Nathanson
Script: Palle Rosenkrantz
Cast: Nathalie Krause, Arne Weel, August Liebmann, Peter
Malberg
Length: 1,019 m.

LIEBELEI (1913)
Production: Nordisk Films Kompagni
Direction: August Blom and Holger-Madsen
Literary source: play by Arthur Schnitzler
Camera: Marius Clausen and Johan Ankerstjerne
Cast: Valdemar Psilander, Augusta Blad, Christel Holch,
Frederik Jacobsen, Carl Lauritzen, Holger Reenberg
Length: 1,165 m.

DEN LILLE HORNBLÆSER (The Little Bugler) (1909)
Production: Thomas S. Hermansen (Fotorama)
Direction: Eduard Schnedler-Sørensen
Script: Eduard Schnedler-Sørensen
Literary source: poem of the same name by H. P. Holst
Camera: Alfred Lind
Cast: Cristel Holch, Frede Skaarup, Gunnar Helsengreen,
Aage Bjørnbak, Aage Schmidt, E. Schnedler-Sørensen
Length: 380 m.

LUMPACIVAGABUNDUS or HAANDVÆRKERSVENDENS ÆVENTYR
(The Journeymen's Adventure) (1912)
Production: Filmfabrikken Skandinavien (Biorama)
Cast: Olga Svendsen, Oscar Stribolt, Gerhard Jessen,
Jørgen Lund, Alma Lagoni, Holger Pedersen, Fru Løns-
mann, Alfred Arnbak, Johan Nielsen, Aage Brandt,
Charles Løvaas, Hr. Wennerwald, Vilhelm Møller, Arnold
Jensen
Length: 750 m.

LØVEJAGTEN (The Lion Hunt) (1907)
U.S. title: Lion Hunting
Production: Nordisk Films Kompagni
Direction: Viggo Larsen
Script: From an idea by Ole Olsen
Camera: Axel Sørensen
Cast: Viggo Larsen, Knud Lumbye, Thomsen
Length: 215 m.

MAHARADJAHENS YNDLINGSHUSTRU (The Maharaja's Favorite
Wife) (1916)
Production: Nordisk Films Kompagni
Direction: Robert Dinesen
Cast: Carlo Wieth, Lilly Jacobsen, Gunnar Tolnæs
Length: 4½ reels

MELLEM STORBYENS ARTISTER (Among the Big City's
Artistes) (1912)
U.S. title: In the Den of Lions or Life in a Circus
Production: Nordisk Films Kompagni
Direction: Eduard Schnedler-Sørensen
Script: Alfred Kjerulf
Cast: Ella Sprange, Henry Seeman, Frederik Jacobsen,
Anton Salmson, Carl Schenstrøm, Birger von Cotta-
Schønberg

Length: 620 m.

MENNESKEABEN (The Human Ape) (1909)
U.S. title: The Human Ape or Darwin's Triumph
    Production: Nordisk Films Kompagni
    Length: 167 m.

MORMONENS OFFER (The Mormon's Victim) (1911)
U.S. title: A Victim of the Mormons
    Production: Nordisk Films Kompagni
    Direction: August Blom
    Script: Alfred Kjerulf
    Camera: Axel Graatkjær (Sørensen)
    Cast: Valdemar Psilander, Henry Seeman, Clara Wieth,
        Carlo Wieth, Emilie Sannom, Frantz Skondrup, H. C.
        Nielsen, Carl Schenstrøm, Otto Lagoni, F. Jacobsen
    Length: 1,080 m.

MOTORCYKLISTEN (The Motor Cyclist) (1908)
U.S. title: The Non-Stop Motor Bicycle
    Production: Nordisk Films Kompagni
    Direction: Viggo Larsen
    Camera: Axel Sørensen
    Cast: Petrine Stone, Frederik Buch, Knud Lumbye
    Length: 117 m.

NATTEN FØR CHRISTIANS FØDSELSDAG (The Night Before
Christian's Birthday) (1908)
    Production: Nordisk Films Kompagni
    Direction: Viggo Larsen
    Literary source: Hans Christian Andersen
    Camera: Axel Sørensen
    Cast: Agnes Nørlund, Holger-Madsen, Aage Brandt, Gus-
        tav Lund
    Length: 175 m.

NED VED VAABNENE (Down with Weapons) (1914)
U.S. title: Lay Down Your Arms
    Production: Nordisk Films Kompagni
    Direction: Holger-Madsen
    Script: Carl Th. Dreyer
    Literary source: novel by Bertha von Suttner
    Camera: Marius Clausen
    Cast: Philip Bech, Augusta Blad, J. Fritz-Petersen, Alf
        Blütecher, Olaf Fønss, Carl Lauritzen
    Length: 1,509 m.

EN NY HAT TIL MADAMMEN (A New Hat for Madam) (1906)
Production: Nordisk Films Kompagni
Direction: Viggo Larsen
Camera: Axel Sørensen
Cast: Margrethe Jespersen
Length: 120 m.

DEN NYE HUSLAERER (The New Private Tutor) (1910)
Production: Nordisk Films Kompagni
Cast: Victor Fabian, Erik Crone, Ella la Cour, Julie Hen-
    riksen, Kai Voight, Rigmor Jerichau
Length: 114 m.

DEN NAERSYNEDE GUVERNANTE (The Short-Sighted Gover-
ness) (1909)
U.S. title: The Short-Sighted Governess
Production: Nordisk Films Kompagni
Camera: Axel Sørensen
Cast: Petrine Stone
Length: 85 m.

DEN NAADIGE FRØKEN (The Gracious Miss) (1911)
U.S. title: The Thunderbolt
Production: Nordisk Films Kompagni
Direction: August Blom
Script: Harriet Bloch
Cast: Rigomar Jerichau, Frederik Jacobsen, Henny Laurit-
    zen, Else Frölich, Thorkild Roose, Valdemar Psilander
Length: 750 m.

NAAR MANDEN GAAR PAA BØRSEN (When the Husband Goes
to the Stock Exchange) (1913)
Production: Nordisk Films Kompagni
Direction: Eduard Schnedler-Sørensen
Script: Paul Sarauw
Camera: Carl Fischer
Cast: Oscar Stribolt, Johanne Fritz-Petersen, Bertel
    Krause, Lauritz Olsen, Carl Alstrup, Olga Svendsen
Length: 768 m.

PAT CORNER (1909)
U.S. title: The Master Detective or The Attack on the Strong
Room
Production: Nordisk Films Kompagni
Direction: Viggo Larsen

Camera: Axel Sørensen
Length: 250 m.

PAVILLONENS HEMMELIGHED (The Secret of the Pavillion)
(1914)
Production: Nordisk Films Kompagni
Direction: Karl Mantzius
Script: Carl Th. Dreyer
Literary source: Viggo Cavling
Camera: Louis Larsen
Cast: Karl Mantzius, Mita Blichfeldt, Svend Aggerholm
Length: 810 m. (surviving material)

PAX ÆTERNA (Eternal Peace) (1917)
Production: Nordisk Films Kompagni
Direction: Holger-Madsen
Camera: Marius Clausen
Cast: Frederik Jacobsen, Philip Bech, Marius Egeskov,
    Anton de Verdier, Carlo Wieth, Carl Lauritzen
Length: 6 reels

PEDER TORDENSKJOLD (1910)
Production: Continental
Direction: Rasmus Bjerregaard
Script: Ernst Munkeboe
Literary source: Carit Etlar
Camera: Rasmus Bjerregaard
Cast: Vilhelm Stigaard, Kolja Svendsen, Amelie Kirkegaard
Length: 620 m. (surviving material)

PIGEN FRA PALLS (The Girl from Palls) (1917)
Production: Nordisk Films Kompagni
Direction: Eduard Schnedler-Sørensen
Camera: Johan Ankerstjerne
Cast: Karen Caspersen
Length: 4 reels

PJERROT (Pierrot) (1916)
Production: Nordisk Films Kompagni
Direction: Hjalmar Davidsen
Cast: Gunnar Tolnæs, Zanny Petersen, Erik Holberg
Length: 1,549 m.

POTIFARS HUSTRU (Potiphar's Wife) (1911)
U.S. title: The Temptress

Production: Nordisk Films Kompagni
Direction: August Blom
Script: Louis von Kohl
Camera: Axel Graatkjær (Sørensen)
Cast: Adam Poulsen, Emilie Sannom, William Bewer, Karen
    Lund

The story concerns an unemployed young clerk whose
family is near starvation. He gets a job as a private secretary to a wealthy man, partly through the intervention
of the employer's wife who is attracted to the young man.
When she inevitably makes her advances, he repels them.
She gets revenge by convincing her husband that the secretary has tried to force himself on her, and the young
man is fired. In addition, she writes a letter to the man's
wife giving the reason for her husband's dismissal. The
shock of the letter causes the wife's death, which, in turn,
sets the clerk on his own path of revenge. His daughter,
however, stops him from killing the temptress. Instead,
he denounces her within hearing of her husband, who,
seeing the mistake he has made in believing his wife, turns
her out of the house.

PRO PATRIA (1914)
U.S. title: Pro Patria or In Defense of the Nation
    Production: Nordisk Films Kompagni
    Direction: August Blom
    Script: Fritz Magnussen
    Camera: Johan Ankerstjerne
    Cast: Carl Lauritzen, Valdemar Psilander, Alma Hinding,
        Gunnar Sommerfeldt, Aage Hertel, C. Willumsen, A.
        Mattson
    Length: 1,358 m.

The story concerns war between neighboring countries.
Elsa (Alma Hinding) is engaged to Lieutenant Alexis von
Kirkhowen who is a military attaché at the enemy's legation.
They have to part when the war breaks out, Alexis return-
ing home to fight for his country. She gives him a carrier
pigeon to use for sending her a message should something
urgent happen. Elsa's father, General Wimpfen (Carl
Lauritzen) and brother Erich (Valdemar Psilander), a lieu-
tenant, go off to war. Lieutenant Rudolph Swaiz (Aage
Hertel) is a traitor and supplies Alexis's side with information that tells them when to storm battery five. When
Alexis sees the traitor's note, he sends Elsa a carrier

pigeon message informing of Swaiz's plan. The message
asks Elsa to stop a tour of the battery by General Wimpfen
and the king. She gives the message to Erich who in turn
gets through with it just in time to save the battery.
Troops under Erich's command take a position held by
troops under Alexis's command, and Erich tells Elsa he saw
Alexis fall in battle. They go to the field and find Alexis
still alive. One more fort must be taken to achieve a victory, and Erich tells his father of a plan he has. Erich
sneaks into the enemy fort and there comes across Swaiz
who has been told to leave by the enemy because they do
not respect a traitor, even one who has betrayed the other
side. Swaiz asks to be killed, but Erich shows him only
contempt, though Swaiz does get killed in an explosion that
Erich sets off. The explosion acts as a signal to his father's forces, and the fort is taken. The enemy general
offers his sword to General Wimpfen, though he is told to
keep it because he fought so bravely. Erich is decorated
by the king, and, with the war's end and because of his
role in foiling Swaiz's plan, Alexis is allowed to marry Elsa.

ET REVOLUTIONSBRYLLUP (A Revolution Marriage) (1914)
U.S. title: The Heart of Lady Alaine
  Production: Nordisk Films Kompagni
  Direction: August Blom
  Literary source: Sophus Michaëlis
  Camera: Johan Ankerstjerne
  Cast: Betty Nansen, Nicolai Johannsen, Johannes Fritz-
    Petersen, Valdemar Psilander, Philip Bech, Svend Korn-
    bech, Peter Jorgensen
  Length: 1,182 m.

Alaine (Betty Nansen) has been engaged since childhood
to Erneste (Nicolai Johannsen), the leader of a division of
Austrian hussars. They hesitate to marry since France's
political situation is so unsettled, though they finally agree
to do so. Prosper (Peter Jørgensen), a servant in Alaine's
palace, is with the revolution and receives word that a
revolutionary force is near the palace. The rebels capture
the palace and Erneste escapes, though he is soon captured
by Marc Arron (Valdemar Psilander), the rebel leader.
Erneste is condemned to death; however, he is allowed to
have his wedding night before he is to be taken away. To
save Erneste, Alaine offers herself to Marc, who allows
Erneste to escape. Alaine and Marc discover that they

really love each other, and the next day Marc allows himself to be shot claiming he is Erneste.

DEN RØDE KLUB (The Red Club) (1913)
    Production: Kinografen
    Cast: Adolf Tronier Funder, Edith Psilander, Einar Zan-
        genberg, Ellen Rassow, F. Rau, Christian Schwanenflü-
        gel, Peter Kjær
    Length: 1,185 m.

RØVERENS BRUD (The Robber's Bride) (1907)
U.S. title: The Robber's Sweetheart
    Production: Nordisk Films Kompagni
    Direction: Viggo Larsen
    Script: Arnold Richard Nielsen
    Camera: Axel Sørensen
    Cast: Robert Storm Petersen, Clara Neblong
    Length: 230 m.

SHANGHAIED (1912)
U.S. title: Shanghaied
    Production: Nordisk Films Kompagni
    Direction: Eduard Schnedler-Sørensen
    Script: P. Lykke Seest
    Cast: Clara Wieth, Carlo Wieth, Christian Schrøder, Agnete
        Blom, Cajus Bruun, Peter Nielsen
    Length: 718 m.

Willy (Carlo Wieth) has just passed his seaman's exams
and is about to ship out as a second mate. At a party
given by Clausen (Cajus Bruun), a shipowner, Willy's engagement to Clausen's daughter, Lilly (Clara Wieth), is
announced. Herr Bang has consistently tried to get Lilly
but has been met only with rejections. Bang finds out
where Willy's ship is headed and goes there himself to arrange for Willy to be shanghaied. At the foreign port he
makes sure to meet Willy and invites him out on the town.
After the theater they go to a waterfront café where Willy
gets drunk and signs a sailing contract. Mary (Agnete
Blom), the daughter of the café's owner, sees Willy's unconscious body being carried to an upstairs room. Bang
sends an evil captain, who is looking for a crew, to the
café. The captain buys Willy's contract.
    Meanwhile, Clausen receives a telegram that Willy is
missing from his ship. He and Lilly go to find Willy. Mary

goes to Chaplain Brown (Peter Nielsen) to get help in rescuing Willy. Knowing that Willy is missing from his ship,
Brown takes Mary to the ship where they meet Clausen and
Lilly. Mary identifies a picture of Willy, and with the police they go to the café. The café owner (Christian Schrøder), with the help of his black servant, hides Willy in a
hollow piano.
   Failing to find him, Lilly dresses up as a sailor and
goes to the café with Brown. Brown gets angry over the
black servant's brutality and beats him in a fist fight.
(Previously, the film gives indications of Brown's physical
fitness.) Mary takes Lilly and Brown upstairs only to find
Willy gone. He has already been taken aboard the shang-
haiing ship. Mary finds a note which reveals Willy's whereabouts, and Brown, Lilly, and Mary chase after the shang-
haiing ship in Brown's ship. Willy jumps overboard and is
picked up by Brown. At the end Brown proposes to Mary.

SKÆBNENS DOM (Fate's Judgment) (1915)
   Production: Filmfabrikken Skandinavien (formerly Bio-
      rama)
   Direction: Aage Brandt
   Length: 1,100 m.

DEN SORTE DOMINO (The Black Domino) (1910)
   Production: Nordisk Films Kompagni
   Cast: Einar Zangenberg, Agnes Nørlund
   Length: 261 m.

   A man steals money from the safe in his brother's office.
He has also made advances toward his brother's wife. The
good brother catches the bad one attacking the wife and,
in their struggle, the stolen money falls on the floor.
Despite the conflict, the good brother gives the bad one
some money and sends him away. He goes to a secret
organization of which he is the leader. Later, a cab in
which the good brother and his wife are riding accidentally runs down the bad brother. They take him to their
home for first aid, where the bad brother asks for a reconciliation. The good brother agrees, but is soon kidnapped
by the secret organization. Escaping, he returns home
just in time to save his wife who is being threatened at
knife point by the bad brother.

DEN SORTE DRØM (The Black Dream) (1911)
   Production: Fotorama

Direction: Peter Urban Gad
Script: Peter Urban Gad
Camera: Adam Johansen
Cast: Asta Nielsen, Valdemar Psilander, Gunnar Helsen-
    green, Ellen Gottschalk, Peter Fjelstrup, Ellen Feldmann,
    Poul Boastrup
Length: 1,206 m.

DEN STORE FLYVER (The Generous Aviator) (1911)
U.S. title: An Aviator's Generosity
    Production: Nordisk Films Kompagni
    Direction: Peter Urban Gad
    Script: Christian Nobel
    Cast: Poul Reumert, Christel Holck, Einar Zangenberg,
        Ellen Kornbeck, William Bewer
    Length: 780 m.

DEN SORTE KANSLER (The Black Chancellor) (1912)
U.S. title: The Black Chancellor
    Production: Nordisk Films Kompagni
    Direction: August Blom
    Script: Christian Schrøder
    Literary source: William Magnay
    Cast: Poul Reumert, Thorkild Roose, Ebba Thomsen,
        Valdemar Psilander, Robert Dinesen, Jenny Roelsgaard
    Length: 915 m.

DEN STAERKESTE (The Strongest) (1912)
U.S. title: Conquered or The Madcap Countess
    Production: Nordisk Films Kompagni
    Direction: Eduard Schnedler-Sørensen
    Script: Alfred Kjerulf
    Cast: Valdemar Psilander, Robert Dinesen, Else Frölich,
        Anton Salmson, Axel Mattson, Aage Lorentzen, Axel
        Boesen, Alf Nielsen, Miss Valkyrien
    Length: 680 m.

TELEGRAMTYVENE (The Telegram Thieves)
    Production: Filmfabrikken Danmark (formerly, Det
        Skandinavisk-russike Handelshus)
    Cast: Valdemar Møller, Emanuel Gregers, Agnes Rehni
    Length: 904 m.

DE TOSSEDE KVINDFOLK (The Foolish Female) (1916)
    Production: Nordisk Films Kompagni

Direction: Lau Lauritzen
Length: circa 1 reel

TRYLLEKUNSTNEREN (The Conjuror) (1909)
U.S. title: The Conjuror
Production: Nordisk Films Kompagni
Camera: Axel Sørensen
Length: 104 m.

TRYLLESAEKKEN (The Magic Bag) (1907)
U.S. title: The Magic Bag
Production: Nordisk Films Kompagni
Direction: Viggo Larsen
Camera: Axel Sørensen
Length: 75 m.

DEN UDBRUDTE SLAVE (The Escaped Convict) (1911)
U.S. title: The Two Convicts
Production: Nordisk Films Kompagni
Direction: August Blom
Script: Nicolai Brechling
Cast: Thorkild Roose, Dagny Schyberg, Zanny Petersen,
    Frederik Christensen, Karen Lund, Henry Seeman
Length: 625 m.

Black Carl (Nicolai Brechling) and another man have
escaped from prison. While hiding in the bushes they are
passed by two students, Lind (Henry Seeman) and Beck
(Einar Zangenberg), who are on a hike. Black Carl and
his friend separate and Carl gets new clothes from a farmer
friend, Per. Judge Paff (Frederick Christensen) receives
a letter telling him about the escaped prisoners. Carl
writes a note to the judge telling him that the convicts
were seen in his vicinity dressed as hiking students. Paff
sees Beck in his apple tree picking apples and thinks he
has spotted one of the convicts. Bech and Lind meet a
local landowner, Brülle (Thorkild Roose), and he invites
them to sleep at his house that night. Carl shows up that
night and enters the house in order to burglarize it. Lind
catches him and gives him money so he does not have to
steal. The next day Judge Paff shows up and warns
Brülle that the students are really escaped prisoners. Because the wallet of one of Brülle's daughters' suitors was
stolen that night by Carl, Brülle believes Paff's warning.
Brülle confronts them. The next scene shows Beck and

Lind by the sea with Brülle's daughters (Dagny Schyberg
and Zanny Petersen).

A Moving Picture World plot synopsis from the issue of
April 19, 1913, fills in the missing scenes. Early in the
narrative Lind and Beck see Brülle with his two daughters,
Emma and Karen, riding in a carriage. The students immediately fall in love with them. Later, when Beck and
Lind are being accused by Brülle, Black Carl shows up,
returns the money that Lind had let him keep, and confesses the whole truth. This paves the way for a romantic involvement between the two students and Brülle's
daughters.

EN UHELDIG DANSER (An Unsuccessful Dancer) (1917)
    Production: Nordisk Films Kompagni
    Direction: Lau Lauritzen
    Cast: Oscar Stribolt
    Length: circa 1 reel

EN UHELDIG JÆGER (The Unlucky Sportsman) (1910)
U.S. title: A Would-Be Sportsman
    Production: Nordisk Films Kompagni
    Camera: Axel Sørensen
    Cast: Oscar Stribolt, Kai Voigt
    Length: 116 m.

    Jæger is a portly man who dresses in an elaborate shoot-
ing outfit for a day's hunting, taking with him an equally
overdressed page. After being snickered at by passersby,
he begins his shooting. First, he brings down some birds,
but then accidentally shoots a fat man he thought to be an
animal. After paying damages, he decides to try fishing
and swaps his gun for a fishing pole, but is only able to
bring in some dead cats. Finally, he falls into the water
and gives up his day of sport entirely.

UNDER BLINKFYRETS STRAALER (Under the Flashing Light's
Beam) (1913)
    Production: Nordisk Films Kompagni
    Direction: Robert Dinesen
    Script: Alfred Kjerulf
    Camera: Sophus Wangøe
    Cast: Svend Kornbeck, Theodora Wolfgang-Hansen, Nicolai
        Johanssen, Alf Blütecher, Cajus Bruun, Agnet Blom
    Length: 2,061 m.

UNDER SAVKLINGENS TÆNDER (Under the Saw Blade's Teeth)
(1913)
U.S. title: The Usurer's Son
   Production: Nordisk Films Kompagni
   Direction: Holger-Madsen
   Script: Laurids Skands
   Camera: Marius Clausen
   Cast: Holger-Madsen, Svend Rindom, Frederik Jacobsen,
      Alma Hinding, Torben Meyer
   Length: 746 m.

UNGDOMMENS RET (The Right of Youth) (1911)
   Production: Nordisk Films Kompagni
   Direction: August Blom
   Script: Alfred Kjerulf
   Cast: Valdemar Psilander, Zanny Petersen, Robert Dine-
      sen, Else Frölich, Einar Zangenberg, Aage Hertel
   Length: 712 m.

UNGKARL OG ÆGTMAND (Bachelor and Husband) (1914)
   Production: Nordisk Films Kompagni
   Direction: A. W. Sandberg
   Script: Valdemar Andersen
   Camera: A. W. Sandberg
   Cast: Oscar Stribolt, Agnes Lorentzen, Lauritz Olsen
   Length: 380 m.

EN UROLIG VAGT (The Disturbed Sentry) (1912)
U.S. title: The Disturbed Sentry
   Production: Nordisk Films Kompagni
   Direction: Eduard Schnedler-Sørensen
   Script: Eduard Schnedler-Sørensen
   Cast: Frederik Buch
   Length: 110 m.

   Some soldiers are looking out a window at a pretty girl
on a balcony across the way. An officer comes in and
reprimands them, but joins in when he sees the girl. A
higher officer enters and reprimands them all. While he is
doing so, the girl goes inside and her mother comes onto
the balcony to yell at the soldiers. When the higher officer looks out the window to see the girl, he sees her
mother instead. The fragment ends with the girl walking
along the street and waving good-bye to the soldiers.

VED FÆNGSLETS PORT (At the Prison's Gate) (1911)
U.S. title: Temptations of a Great City
    Production: Nordisk Films Kompagni
    Direction: August Blom
    Script: Erling and Ljut Steensgaard
    Camera: Axel Graatkjær (Sørensen)
    Cast: Valdemar Psilander, Augusta Blad, Holger Hofman,
        Clara Wieth, Richard Christensen.
    Length: 820 m.

VERDENSGIFTEN (The World's Poison) (1913)
    Production: A/S Dansk Film
    Script: Maria Garland
    Cast: Litta (?) Lange, Else Mantzius, Holger Holm
    Length: 725 m. (surviving material)

    A young ship's officer and a girl become engaged just
before he receives sailing orders for a long voyage. When
the voyage is over, and prior to sailing for home, a party
is given on board the ship. The officer meets a woman
with an Indian servant and is aroused by her. Before
leaving the ship the woman slips him a note inviting him
to visit her. The next day they meet, and he misses the
sailing of his ship. When he finally leaves, in an attempt
to catch up to his ship in a motor launch, she is angered
and consoles herself by smoking opium. He fails to catch
the ship when the engine of the motor launch overheats
and he is knocked unconscious. He is rescued by another
boat and taken to a hotel. The next day he goes to see
the woman, having decided to give himself up to this new
life. The woman's servant becomes jealous, however. After suffering an accident while on an excursion, the officer
sees an ad put in the foreign paper by his fiancée who
has been trying to find him. He then discovers that the
woman uses opium and in a fight kills the Indian servant.
Leaving, the officer is run down by a train.

VIDUNDERCIGAREN (The Wonderful Cigar) (1909)
U.S. title: The Wonderful Cigar
    Production: Nordisk Films Kompagni
    Direction: Viggo Larsen
    Camera: Axel Sørensen
    Cast: Sofus Wolder, Holger Pedersen, Maggi Zinn, Anton
        Seitzberg, Erik Winther
    Length: 106 m.

VORS TIDS DAME (A Modern Woman) (1912)
    Production: Nordisk Films Kompagni
    Direction: Eduard Schnedler-Sørensen
    Script: Lykke Seest
    Camera: Axel Graatkjaer (Sørensen)
    Cast: Viking Ringheim, Clara Wieth, Valdemar Psilander,
      Lauritz Olsen, Torben Meyer
    Length: 835 m.

APPENDIX B:

ADDITIONAL TITLES AND INFORMATION

CHAPTER ONE

Note 54

Fra Bagdad (U.S. title, From Bagdad)

Djævlespillet i Zoologisk Have (Diabolo Play in Zoological Garden)

Det Nye Bud (The New Errand Boy)

Nyborg Riddere (Nyborg Knights)

Champagneflasken (U.S. title, The Champagne Bottle)

Drengen med den Sjette Sans (The Boy with the Sixth Sense)

Pierrot og Pierette (Pierrot and Pierette)

Hjortens Flugt (The Deer's Escape--based on a well-known Danish romantic poem by Christian Winthers)

Lodsens Datter (The Pilot's Daughter)

Møllen (The Mill)

Vaadeskud (U.S. title, A Chance Shot)

Bien (The Bee)

Feltherrens Hævn (The General's Revenge)

278

Trilby, Fra Puppe til Sommerfugl (U.S. title, The Puppa
    Changes into a Butterfly--despite the title this was a fic-
    tion film)

Æren Tabt--Alt Tabt (U.S. title, Honor Lost-Everything Lost)

Feens Rose (Feen's Rose)

Sømandsliv (Sailor's Life)

To Gentlemen (U.S. title, Two Gentlemen)

Note 59

Militærmanøvrer paa Ski (U.S. title, Winter Manoeuvres of
    the Norwegian Army)

Klipfisk (U.S. title, Codfish--a documentary about codfishing
    that shows the industry from catching to consumption)

Sommer i Norden (U.S. title, Summer in North Europe--scenic)

Hojfjeldbanan Ryddes (U.S. title, Clearing the Mountain Rail-
    road Track--scenic)

Østens Børn (U.S. title, Children of the East--educational)

Note 83

Sport:

Nordiska Spelen (U.S. title, Winter Sports at Stockholm,
    Sweden, 1909)

Boksekamp (U.S. title, Boxing Match or Jim Smith, the Cham-
    pion Boxer)

Floretfægtning (U.S. title, Art of Fencing)

Vandsport (U.S. title, Water Sports)

Islandsk Brydning (U.S. title, Wrestling)

Travel:

Intermezzo fra Zoologisk Have (U.S. title, A Walk Through
   the Zoo)

Søndag i Semmering ved Wien (U.S. title, Summering in the
   Austrian Alps

Stockholms Skærgaard (U.S. title, Winter Landscapes Around
   Stockholm

Livet i Nordsiam (U.S. title, Street Life in North Siam)

Karnevalsløjer i Norden (U.S. title, Carnival Merriment in
   the North)

Københavns Omegn (U.S. title, Surroundings of Copenhagen)

Norrköping (U.S. title, Norrkobing)

Gotakanalen (U.S. title, Gotacanal: Over Norway's Rocky
   Shores)

Livet i Dalarne (U.S. title, Life in Dalerne, Sweden)

Trollhättan (U.S. title, Trollhattan)

Vierwaldstättersøen (U.S. title, Lake of Luzerne)

Vaudeville and Theater:

Siamesisk Skuespil (U.S. title, Siamese Actors and Actresses
   Play a Siamese Drama)

Menneskeaben (U.S. title, The Human Ape or Darwin's Triumph)

Akrobater (U.S. title, Brothers Laurento)

Occupations:

Sildefiskeri (U.S. title, Herring Fishing)

Cowboys i Argentina (U.S. title, Cowboys in Argentina)

Georg Stage (U.S. title, Life on Board a Training Ship)

Personalities:

Dr. Cook, Nordpolens Opdager (U.S. title, Dr. Cook at Copenhagen)

CHAPTER TWO

Pages 128-129

Fabian har Tandpine (U.S. title, Fabian's Hollow Tooth)

Fabian henter Jordemoder (Fabian Fetches a Nurse)

Fabian kører i Skoven (Fabian Goes into the Woods)

Fabian ordner Gardinstang (U.S. title, Fabian Arranging
Curtain Rods)

Fabian renser Kakkelovn (U.S. title, Fabian Cleaning Chimney)

Fabians Skovtur (U.S. title, Fabian Out for a Picnic)

Fabian som Afholdsmand (Fabian as Teetotaller)

Pages 132-133

Boscoe (U.S. title, Saved by Boscoe). A woman, who along
with her dog Bosco, goes to help a rich woman, is robbed
and thrown into a cellar by thieves. She attaches a note
to her dog's collar and he returns with the woman's husband.

Christian Schrøder i Biograf-Teater (U.S. title, Willie Visits
a Moving Picture Show). Willie, a henpecked husband, is
sent shopping by his wife. On the way he encounters a
movie crew and is asked to take part in the film they are
making. He is photographed in a fight scene and talking

to a pretty girl. Sometime later, he goes to a cinema with
his wife, and she sees Willie on the screen. Angered by
what she sees, the wife gives him a beating.

La Femme (U.S. title, Who Is She?). A man forces his wife
   to leave home when he discovers she has been unfaithful
   to him. She goes to America and gets into trouble, ultimately shooting a man who wants to blackmail her son,
   now a lawyer. She refuses to give any evidence in her
   own behalf, in order to protect her son. Much to her
   shock, she discovers that it is her son who has been
   appointed to defend her, though he, of course, does not
   know his mother. At the trial she also sees her husband
   who has come to watch the son conduct the case. The
   son pleads the case so well that she is acquitted. As she
   is dying, the husband relents in his anger against her
   and tells the son who the woman is that he has saved.

Fødselsdagsgaven (U.S. title, The Birthday Present). The
   child of a well-to-do home is taken out by her nursemaid
   and wanders off while the nursemaid gazes into a shop
   window. An old woman finds the child, dresses her as
   a boy, and sends her into the streets to beg. A ruffian
   takes the child's money away, and the old woman throws
   the child out. A boy takes the little girl home to his
   parents. They see an ad offering a reward for the child's
   return and take her home to her parents. The day of the
   return is the mother's birthday so that the child becomes
   the birthday present.

Svendsen holder Systue (U.S. title, Mr. Muggins Has His
   Sewing Done). Finding his clothes in a bad state, Svendsen tries to do his own sewing. After making a bad job
   of it, he puts an ad in the paper for a wife who must be
   able to sew. A great many women show up for the job,
   resulting in numerous complications for Svendsen.

Den Livegne (The Life of a Muzhik). A Russian peasant
   leaves early one morning for his daily work in the fields.
   At lunchtime his wife takes food to him and on the way
   home is waylaid by a local official. The peasant hears
   his wife's cries for help and goes to her rescue, knocking
   down the official. The official has the peasant arrested and
   whipped. Some time later, the official is injured when
   thrown from his horse. The peasant happens by and is

ready to take revenge when his child persuades him to help
the official. This act of kindness changes the official, and
in repentance, he makes the peasant a bailiff.

Zigeunerskens Kærlighed (U.S. title, The Love of a Gypsy
  Girl). A young count falls in love with a gypsy girl but
  marries the daughter of a neighboring aristocrat. Five
  years later, some gypsies beg money from the count, but
  he turns them away angrily. In revenge they kidnap his
  child. The gypsy girl recognizes who the child is by a
  locket that belongs to the count. When the others are
  asleep, she slips away with the child, intent on getting
  her to her parents. The other gypsies pursue them, but
  the girl and the child reach the count's estate. The count
  is filled with repentance when he learns that his old love
  acted so generously despite the wrong he had done her.

Den heldige Bananmand (U.S. title, The Lucky Banana Seller).
  A banana seller wins a lottery and with the money gives
  up his business. He then begins to imitate a gentleman,
  with comic results.

Page 137

Spøgelset i Gravkælderen (U.S. title, The Ghost of the Vaults).
  A girl has two admirers, a blacksmith and one of her cous-
  ins. Her father, a miser, wants her to marry the cousin,
  but she refuses. When the blacksmith tries to visit the
  girl, her father has him locked in a cell. Later, the father
  goes into a vault under his house to look at his treasure
  which he keeps in a large coffin. The nephew follows him
  and, after the old man leaves, climbs into the coffin to
  get a better look at its contents. He is startled to see a
  white apparition appear in the vault. It is the girl who
  walks in her sleep. She accidentally knocks into the rod
  which holds up the lid of the coffin and it falls, trapping
  the cousin inside. The noise wakes the girl and she faints.
  Just then the blacksmith arrives, having found a way out
  of the cell which has led him to the vault. The girl's
  father also arrives, having heard the sound of the coffin
  lid. After denouncing the cousin, he agrees to a marriage
  between his daughter and the blacksmith.

BIBLIOGRAPHY

Aftenposten (Copenhagen). May 30, 1920.

Aktuelt (Copenhagen). December 29, 1969.

Archer, William. "The Royal Danish Theater." Harper's New Monthly Magazine (February 1892).

Anderson, Robert T. Denmark: Success of a Developing Nation. Cambridge, Mass;: Schenkman Publishing Co., 1975.

B.H., Edm. "The Debate in Denmark on the Cinema in Relation to the Theater, 1910-1914." Masken, April 23, 1911.

Balazs, Bela. Theory of the Film. New York: Dover Publications, 1970.

Balshofer, Fred, and Miller, Arthur. One Reel a Week. Berkeley: University of California Press, 1967.

Bardeche, Maurice, and Brasillach, Robert. The History of Motion Pictures. English edition. New York: W. W. Norton and Co., 1938.

Barry, Iris. D. W. Griffith: American Film Master. New York: Museum of Modern Art, 1965.

Bazin, André. What Is Cinema? Vol. I of essays selected and translated by Hugh Gray. Berkeley: University of California Press, 1971.

Berlingske Tidende. (Copenhagen). January 30, 1933, and October 17, 1954.

Bowser, Eileen. Unpublished notes for the 1978 FIAF Congress, Brighton, England.

Brage, Ole. Compiler. Danmarks Radio Præsenterer Elfelt Film. Copenhagen: Danmarks Radio, 1975.

Brusendorff, Ove. Filmen I-II. Copenhagen: Universal-Forlaget, 1939-41.

Bucher, Felix, in collaboration with Gmur, Leonhard H. Germany. Screen Series. London: A. Zwemmer Limited and New York: A. S. Barnes & Co., 1970.

Ceram, C. W. Archaeology of the Cinema. New York: Harcourt, Brace, and World, 1965.

Danstrup, John. A History of Denmark. Second edition. Copenhagen: Wivels Forlag, 1949.

Dreyer, Carl. "New Ideas About the Film." In Dreyer in Double Reflection. Edited by Donald Skoller. New York: E. P. Dutton & Co., 1973.

Eisner, Lotte. The Haunted Screen. Berkeley: University of California Press, 1968.

Ekstrabladet. (Copenhagen). April 7, 1938; October 1, 1942; January 12, 1943.

Engberg, Harold. A. W. Sandberg og hans Film. Copenhagen: Aschehoug Dansk Forlag, 1944.

Engberg, Marguerite. Den Danske Stumfilm. Copenhagen: Det Danske Filmmuseum, 1968.

_____. Dansk Stumfilm. Two volumes. Copenhagen: Rhodos Internationalt Forlag for Videnskab, Kunst og Debat, 1977.

_____. Registrant over danske film, 1896-1914. Three volumes. Copenhagen: Institut for Filmvidenskab, 1977.

Ernst, John. Benjamin Christensen. Copenhagen: Det Danske Filmmuseum, 1967.

Filmen (Copenhagen). IV, no. 3 (November 15, 1915); V,
    no. 6 (January 1, 1917); V, no. 10 (March 1, 1917); V,
    no. 18 (July 1, 1917); V, no. 20 (August 1, 1917).

Fønss, Olaf. "Omkring Atlantis." Filmen (Copenhagen). II,
    no. 1 (October 15, 1913).

Gad, Urban. Filmen: Dens Midler og Maal. Copenhagen and
    Kristiania: Gyldendalske Boghandel, 1919.

Grau, Robert. The Theater of Science. New York: Broad-
    way Publishing Co., 1914.

Hampton, Benjamin B. History of the American Film Industry.
    New York: Dover Publications, 1970.

Hending, Arnold. Herman Bang paa Film. Copenhagen:
    Kandrup & Wunschs Forlag, 1957.

Jacobs, Lewis. The Rise of the American Film. New York:
    Teachers College Press, second printing, 1969.

Johns, Eric. "The Theater in Copenhagen." Theatre World
    (October 1934).

Jones, W. Glynn. Denmark. New York and Washington:
    Praeger Publishers, 1970.

Jyllands Posten. April 4, 1959.

Lauring, Palle. A History of the Kingdom of Denmark.
    Translated by David Hohnen. Second edition. Copen-
    hagen: Host and Son, 1963.

Leprohon, Pierre. The Italian Cinema. Translated by Robert
    Greaves and Oliver Stallybrass. New York: Praeger Pub-
    lishers, 1972.

Leyda, Jay. Kino: A History of the Russian and Soviet
    Film. London: George Allen and Unwin, 1960.

Low, Rachel. The History of the British Film, 1906-1914.
    London: George Allen and Unwin, 1949.

Low, Rachel, and Manvell, Roger. The History of the British

Film, 1896-1906. London: George Allen and Unwin,
1948.

Manvell, Roger, and Frankel, Heinrich.   The German Cinema.   New York: Praeger Publishers, 1971.

Marine Bladet (Copenhagen).   September 1966.

Mitchell, P. M.   A History of Danish Literature.   New York:
The American Scandinavian Foundation, 1958.

Mottram, Ron.   "Influences Between National Cinemas: Denmark and the United States."   Cinema Journal (Winter
1974-75).

Moving Picture World.   New York: 1907-17.

National Tidende (Copenhagen).   January 23, 1921; March
26, 1949.

Neergaard, Ebbe.   The Story of the Danish Film.   Translated
by Elsa Gress.   Copenhagen: Det Danske Selskab, 1963.

Nemeskürty, Istvan.   Word and Image.   Translated by Zsu-
zsanna Horn.   Budapest: Corvina Press, 1968.

The New York Dramatic Mirror.   1907-17.

Nielsen, Asta.   Den Tiende Muse.   Copenhagen: Gyldendal,
1945.

Niver, Kemp.   The First Twenty Years.   Los Angeles: Lo-
care Research Group, 1968.

_____.   Motion Pictures from the Library of Congress Paper
Print Collection.   Berkeley: University of California Press,
1967.

Nordisk Biograf Tidende (Copenhagen).   I, no. 2 (October
1909); I, no. 5 (January 1910).

North, Joseph.   The Early Development of the Motion Picture.
New York: Arno, 1973.   (Originally published Cornell
University, Ph.D., 1949.)

Oakley, Stewart. A Short History of Denmark. New York and
    Washington: Praeger Publishers, 1972.

Olsen, Ole. Filmens Eventyr og Mit Eget. Copenhagen: Jes-
    persen og Pios Forlag, 1940.

Politiken (Copenhagen). April 16, 1911; September 22, 1946;
    January 31, 1954.

Pratt, George. Spellbound in Darkness. Greenwich, Conn.:
    New York Graphic Society, 1973.

Sadoul, Georges. French Film. London: The Falcon Press,
    1953.

Sandfeld, Gunnar. Den Stumme Scene. Copenhagen: Nyt
    Nordisk Forlag, Arnold Busck, 1966.

Skoller, Donald. Editor. Dreyer in Double Reflection. New
    York: E. P. Dutton & Co., 1973.

Slide, Anthony. Early American Cinema. The International
    Film Guide Series. New York: A. S. Barnes & Co.,
    1970.

Starcke, Viggo. Denmark in World History. Translated by
    Commander Frank Noel Stagg and Dr. Ingeborg Nixon.
    Philadelphia: University of Pennsylvania Press, 1962.

Strong, Evan. "War's Black Mark." Moving Picture World,
    September 12, 1914.

Vardac, A. Nicholas. Stage to Screen: Theatrical Method
    from Garrick to Griffith. Cambridge, Mass.: Harvard
    University Press, 1949.

Young, Filson. Editor. Trial of Hawley Harvey Crippen.
    Notable British Trials Series. London: William Hodge &
    Co., 1920.

INDEX OF FILM TITLES

Since most of the film titles listed are in Danish, it has been necessary to incorporate three letters that are not part of the English alphabet: Æ, Ø, and Å (or AA in the older Danish alphabet). These letters follow Z and are used in the order listed. Following each Danish title there is either a literal translation into English or, when known, the title under which the film was distributed in the United States.

NAME INDEX

Aggerholm, Ellen 168
Aggerholm, Svend 187
Alberini, Filoteo 70
Alberti, Peter Adler 30, 74
All-Star Feature Film Company 97
Alstrup, Carl 41, 42, 80, 101, 175, 176, 178
Ambrosio, Arturo 73
American Biograph Company 15, 22, 23, 73, 94, 138
American Film Manufacturing Company 148
American Vitagraph Company 15, 73, 78, 94, 110, 117, 208, 227
Andersen, Hans Christian 4, 28, 29, 35
Andersen, P. 231
Ankerstjerne, Johan 213, 222, 227
Apollo Theater (Budapest) 2
A/S Dansk Film 124, 125
A/S Hermansen, Thomas S. 14
Astra Films 213
Augustinus, William 192, 212

Balasz, Bela 81
Bang, Herman 103
Barrymore, Lionel 111
Bazin, André 140, 154
Bech, Lili 121, 122
Beck, Philip 184, 218
Belasco, David 98
Bendixen, Aage 191
Benzon, Otto 5
Bergman, Ingmar 161, 185
Bernhardt, Sarah 154
Betzonich, Victor 12
Biograph see American Biograph Company
Biograf Teatret (Copenhagen) 16, 38
Biorama (Filmfabrikken Skandinavien) 42, 80, 99, 101, 102, 135,
    232, 234 see also Filmfabrikken Skandinavien
Bison 78
Bisson, Alexander 202
Bitzer, Billy 11
Bjerregaard, Rasmus 17